bouncers

Julian Davies & Terry Currie

milo books

First published in November 2003 by Milo Books

ISBN   1 903854 21 0

Typeset by e-type, Liverpool

Printed and bound in Great Britain by
Cox & Wyman Ltd, Reading, Berkshire

MILO BOOKS LTD
The Old Weighbridge
Station Road
Wrea Green
Lancs PR4 2PH
info@milobooks.com

contents

DEDICATIONS

To everyone who has shared their stories and helped me write this book. Thanks – *Julian Davies*

To the greatest man I have ever known, my father Terry Currie Snr – *Terry Currie*

foreword

'EVENING FOLKS.' AH, the familiar sound and calling card of the club/pub bouncer. A complicated man who has myriad emotions stirring underneath his calm façade, the bouncer is indeed a strange breed of individual, loved by few, hated by many but respected by all. These individuals encounter the very worst that humanity has to offer: alcoholism, drug abuse, sexual promiscuity, anger, theft and, of course, violence. So much nastiness that one of the most common phrases spoken by patrons is, 'I don't know how you guys do it night in and night out.'

Well, the bouncers keep their vigilant watch and wait for the moment for someone to step out of line. And when they step out of reality, they step right into the world of the bouncer. It can be the most thankless job on the planet and yet the most rewarding at the same time. Often chastised for being 'dumb lugs', the backgrounds and personalities of bouncers are as varied as the nightclubs and bars they work in. Never underestimate the bouncer and his abilities. He is there for a reason, after all.

'You're a bouncer huh?'

'No, I am in the *people management business*.'

The bouncing world offers some of the most entertaining stories to be found. We couldn't even make this stuff up if we tried. Truth is stranger than fiction and the bouncer is the eyewitness to it all. Julian Davies and Terry Currie finally bring the stories together of the men who put their necks on the line every night for the safety of others. They have collected tales from around the UK and even further afield to finally shed light on the inner thoughts of this misunderstood profession. The respect I have for my fellow 'brothers' runs deep. For everyone else, enjoy the trials and tribulations, laughter and sadness of the toughest job around.

Ari Bolden, bouncer and author of *The Doorman's Credo*

the first night

A BAD DOOR man is like a weak link in a chain: when the pressure increases, it will snap. This is why doormen are usually recommended by a friend or by someone who knows they can handle themselves. Managers and workmates don't look favourably on you if you get your mate a job just because he needs the money. You have to earn the respect of the customers and the guys you work with by standing your ground or by pitching in when things turn nasty. The worst night for a doorman is the first one; they can never be fully prepared for what's about to happen. To become a good doorman takes years of experience and when the first shift starts, that's when the learning begins.

Mickey Jones, London

I became a doorman not long after my mother died and my father started to find the answer to his questions at the bottom of the glass. I had no choice but to go out and find extra work; it was the only way I could keep the roof over our heads. I had got friendly with the landlady of the local pub and she suggested that as a Saturday night was becoming very hectic, I might like to keep my eye on the door for her. Not coming from a family of fighters or having many fights under my belt, I reluctantly accepted her offer. Saturday night came and I was very tense. I didn't know where to stand, what to do or where to put my hands. My first night and no fights. Eventually I settled down and started to relax, my hands fell into place and I decided that this was what I wanted to do. When working in my local I became pally with a bloke who is well known in the town as a right nutter, he'd slit your throat if you looked at him the wrong way. He taught me everything I know. I spent three years looking after the pub and eventually I got offered a job at a London nightclub. It was only then I realised how hard door work could be.

Anthony Thomas, Merthyr Tydfil

I started bouncing after a boy from my boxing gym asked me to cover for someone who had a night off. I jumped at the chance of extra cash as I didn't have a job in the daytime. The first night I was very nervous and kept drinking all through the night. I soon stopped that, as I had spent most of my wages. I was working with this boy named Cleaver who was a kickboxing black belt and he showed me a lot in that first year.

Things have changed so much in the last few years. Back then only a few pubs had doormen but these days nearly every pub has them. The money's always been shit for the work that you are doing unless you can get a bit of a reputation and end up with a head doorman's job. You'll always have the rival firms scouting for business and trying to undercut you, that's why the money always stays down when it should be getting better. Throughout the years I've worked with all sorts of doormen, some good, some bad, but I wouldn't knock none of them because at least they have had a go at it. I don't think I've ever been frightened of anything on the door. I've had all sorts come at me, I've been stabbed, bottled and glassed but when adrenalin kicks in and there's no time to think about things, you just get on with whatever is happening.

I've always found the best doormen are the ones who can talk to people. I'm not very good at it and I often have to use other methods to get people out. Only the other day this boy was playing up in this nightclub. Instead of making a scene I went over and told him his taxi was there. I then walked out behind him to the front doors. He turns to go back in and says, 'But there's nothing there.' I said, 'I know,' and closed the door in his face. It saved a scene and I wish all incidents could be handled that way.

Dave Harper, Reading

My first night, the head doorman asked if I'd worked the door before. I said, 'No,' but he said that I was big enough and had the right attitude to do the job. I must have been about twenty. The guys on the door at this nightclub were mostly ex-convicts, which didn't bother me as I knew them all well. All the ex-convicts had to go away for at least a couple of hours to do a private job on someone now and again. The head doorman was my friend and was beaten up by six guys once but was still able enough to put three of them in hospital, being a martial arts expert. He knew where they lived so he gathered up guys and paid them a visit. When I was in the club I saw these guys dressed up in army gear going out the back exit into a van. They looked the business. When they came back they looked pretty pleased with themselves but I wasn't at all worried who I was mixing with. While they were away there was a bit of trouble at the club, which I dissolved quite quickly. I didn't really think about it, I just got straight in between these two guys and broke up the fight and escorted them out. The owner of the club was impressed and told my friend the head doorman that he wanted me to stay on, and that's when I started the many years of being a doorman.

Michael Vaughan, Newcastle

Out drinking in a club one night I notice two bouncers struggling with this big rugby player. They can't get him out and he breaks away from their hold on him and chins one of them, who drops to his knees clutching his face. The other one shits himself and informs the guy that he's just doing his job. I walk over because I'm a right nosey bastard and the rugby guy sees me as a threat and turns on me. 'You want some as well then tough guy?' he screams. 'I've spent ten years on the rugby field beating pricks like you up.' I step in close then smash him in the ribs with all my strength. Down he falls, clutching his broken ribs. 'Have you now?' I say. 'I've spent ten years in the boxing ring beating up bullies like you.' With that the two doormen drag him out and stamp all over him. The manager came on to me at the end of the night and after a few free drinks he persuaded me to become head doorman with all the free drink and fanny I could handle. Well, I'm not the biggest drinker in the world but fanny...

Mark Thomas, South Wales

I became a doorman in 1990 to earn some extra money. My initial feelings were excitement and apprehension. I didn't have any training on the door but ended up a couple of years later attending a course run by the police. Throughout the years, I have seen lots of changes to both the music and the way people dress and act. Many of the pubs and clubs originally employed doormen independently, not through any firms, whereas now almost all of the pubs in our town are covered by one or two firms. I think doomen are now more carefully vetted. I never trained in any martial art or I never carried a weapon. One thing I picked up from other doormen was how to spot trouble before it started and never show any fear. Some of the best doormen I've worked with were the ones who could defuse a situation just by talking to people. I was working in this nightclub on a Sunday night and there had been a bit of trouble. A large group of men had turned up, hard men, and we were seriously outnumbered. The situation was luckily defused by one of the doormen who knew them all and started talking to them.

Cass Pennant, South East London

I remember two starts roughly same period, late Seventies. I used to go around with a right handful that met up in the Swan in Stratford and the George in Wanstead. Both firms used to frequent the Spooky Lady, a nightclub. It would invariably kick off before the end of the night either with rival lads, the bouncers and even amongst themselves. The characters within that group were too powerful to restore any order to – four even have 'hardman' autobiographies out today. Club management had a decision to make. Clubs back then were few and far between so there was no actual loss of punters but there was a problem of finding any more security prepared to work the Spooky door. Well, the heads within our group were offered this option: either the club closes or we took over the door, so that was my apprenticeship in the east.

© Don Barrett Photographer

Former West Ham hooligan Cass Pennant and his team worked
some of the roughest doors in East and South London

In the south I remember being handpicked to work with Big
Nick Netley at a new club opened in Deptford, which was part of
the chain of Strawberry Bars. This was interesting from the first
night as it wasn't the punters we were worried about – there weren't
any. The place was about to be hit by a local mobster who operated
the protection rackets. Nervous, excited, calm was all part of the
buzz of going on a door. The term bouncer was a badge to wear back
then. Today it's a dinosaur word the security world won't ever use.
As far as training goes, don't make me laugh. As Elton John said,
'Saturday night's all right for fighting', and you don't apply to join
a door, you are chosen by people that have seen you in action.

The difficulty then of getting licence hour extensions meant
Friday and Saturday nights only; on Sundays the clubs would shut
one hour after the pub closing time of 10.30 P.M. The film *Night
Fever* kicked off this country's first-ever clubland scene. We now had
discos with DJs set up like the out-of-date chaps you hire to do

wedding receptions. Carpet replaced wooden floors and everyone went big on mirrors and hanging giant silver balls, no jeans and quite a few membership clubs where punters had to sign the book to get in. The hot summer of '77 destroyed the no-jeans rule until disco fever brought white flared trousers in. Music changes obviously but the clubs stayed pretty much the same until the rave scene of the late Eighties into the Nineties changed security and clubland forever.

London was too big to have any one top door security firm. You could run an area though but it wouldn't be a known, legit security firm, they were pretty anonymous in the Seventies and early Eighties. All the serious doormen were individual groups of mates. Someone with big enough respect would get offered a door and pull a few handy mates in with him to do it. There certainly wasn't a *Yellow Pages* of hired muscle. It was whom you knew and could have a word with.

I took the horses-for-courses approach to which men you picked to work which doors. Violence-wise, the worst scenario was always the tools. So you always made sure you had the better armour. If they wanted to play with blades you showed them the axe. Don't get me wrong, you did your searches but you had no CCTV or metal detectors and every place seemed to have a car park. The set-to would often take place there rather than the dance floor. You never worried about the use of guns as you would today. Back then they were part of a very different trade.

Shaun Kelly, Ebbw Vale

I was out one night in a club with friends having a good time. There was a big fight so my mate and I had joined in to help the doormen. From then on I decided I wanted to become one. It wasn't about the money – the money was shit – it was just that I enjoyed working on the door. The first night on duty I had a lot of different emotions running through my mind.

The clubs have become a lot more violent. When I worked a few years ago you'd get trouble every now and then but these days I'm up against bottles and gangs of boys most weekends. The music hasn't changed much, it's still the pumping beat that winds a lot of these people up. Whenever there's been a situation on the door I've always gone for the one with the name for violence or the one giving it out to others. You take care of him and the rest usually bottle it. I move in very quickly from the side and put the person straight into a headlock and then start talking to him, making sure I'm in control at all times. I then remove him from the club still in the headlock.

I have found that the most dangerous people are the ones that use the weapons, the people who would glass you as good as look at you. You've got to take them out as quickly as possible. Only the other day I had a bottle put over my head. It had been a good night and everyone had been enjoying themselves but a fight had broken out over by the bar and myself and the other doorman, Taskers, had gone running in. Now these boys who were fighting were big blokes who dwarfed me and my partner. We got stuck in and tried breaking it up. We both ended up getting bottled but still came out on top.

I have always worked very well with the police as well. One night I had to help a WPC who had come under attack from some drunk that they were stopping fighting. It's amazing how many of the regulars hated me for helping her; she's a woman for God's sake. They wanted to see the WPC have a good beating.

Andrew Moffat, Edinburgh

I must have been about twenty-four years old and argued with this lump of a guy down the gym. I can't remember what the argument was about but he pulled his hand back to take a shot and I beat him to it. I knocked him to the ground and stamped all over his head until the ex-pro heavyweight pulled me off him. I was going to lay into him as well but two things stopped me. Firstly he was only trying to stop the fight and didn't have anything against me; secondly he would have punched fuck into my head if I had tried it on with him. A few days later I get a knock on my door, which I open to one of the tallest men I have every seen. He must have been about six foot eight and about twenty stone, if not more. 'Are you the lad who put my head doorman out of action,' he enquired. 'Yes, but it wasn't my fault,' I replied. Next thing I know he was offering me a job and before I could think it over we had shaken hands and I was thrust into the world of bouncing, and I've been here ever since.

Lee Morris, South Wales

I started bouncing in this nightclub in Caerphilly named Pulsars. I was pretty young compared to the other boys I was working with. The first night I was very nervous and didn't know what to expect but I was working with a good team of boys who taught me a lot. There would be big gang fights most nights and we'd be fighting nearly every night. The money was all right; I suppose it's much better these days though. I also started boxing to get fitter and learn how to punch tidy.

I have seen some sights working on the door, people overdosing and stuff. I once saw this fight outside this club, we had just chucked these boys out for fighting and they were all going for it outside. This one boy has got this boy's ear in his mouth and bit it clean off, greedy bastard. We stayed inside as it was nothing to do with us; outside the club is work for the police.

I can still remember the first time I ever knocked someone out. I was working in this pub in town where there'd be trouble nearly every night. It had a lane by the side of it where we would always end up fighting. We had refused this boy entry and he was offering to fight me outside up the lane. In the end I went up the lane with him and just smashed him in the face. He was lying on the floor unconscious in a pool of blood. I shit myself and left the building. I then went to see one of my mates Carl who was working on another door and I told him, 'I think I've killed someone.' He started laughing at me and told me, 'Don't be stupid and go back down there.' I went back and I could see people putting him in an ambulance. The police had turned up and the other bouncer told them he'd been fighting with some boys who'd run up the alleyway.

Carlton Leach, East London

When I started on the door I was a known football hooligan with a reputation for a row and everyone in East London knew me. My mate was doorman at a club called Mooro's. What happened was, one of their doormen got knocked out on a Friday night and my pal Ralph rang me and asked if I would cover. That was about twenty-two years ago. I had never thought about being a bouncer before, it all started as a favour.

The first night and the job in general was no problem for me as

I was working with all my mates. We had grown up together and been in loads of rucks along the way, so it was like home from home. The only strange thing was that I had spent years fighting bouncers and now I was one. The first night it all went off and I fought my bollocks off. The only training I had for this kind of work was kicking fuck out of people on the football terraces; no courses and shit like that. Bouncers then were chosen on how they could handle themselves in violent situations. It was all down to reputation.

These were the days of disco music and girls in high heels dancing around handbags. All the doormen were smart in bow ties, not like now with bomber jackets. There was great camaraderie between us; we were all mates. Everything closed at 2 A.M. and we would all go for a curry and laugh. They were great days really. Now it's completely different, it's another world. Then most of the troublemakers would be pissed up and you can handle that no problem. Now with drugs it's a different thing altogether. You don't know what to expect or what the fuck's going to happen next. It's a lot wilder and a lot more dangerous than it used to be.

Lyn Morgan, South Wales

The first night I got offered work, a mate of mine had moved on to a different club so he asked would I help out. It was an under-eighteens night and the place would be packed out. I was working with this other doorman named Lee. He'd been doing it for years and he showed me the ropes for the first couple of weeks. The first night I had mixed feelings as I didn't really know how to handle kids. I couldn't have been there an hour and we had two girls fighting. We finally managed to separate them; they had clumps of each other's hair and there was blood everywhere. I got told it would be an easy shift but we didn't stop putting people out all night. There were two of us working up against 200 kids and most of them looking for trouble. We ended up getting another doorman because there were fights going off every ten minutes. The place ended up closing down after one week because there was a big gang fight with about fifty people fighting. We managed to get most of them onto the street and the rest followed. So much for an easy shift.

Darryl Taskers, South Wales

I started on the doors a couple of years ago after a good friend asked if I wanted some work. I'd always wanted to work the doors so I told him that I'd give it a go. I didn't know what to expect as I turned up at this pub to work. I then received a phone call instructing me to go down to this other pub because the boy who was working there was by himself and was expecting trouble. I was now really nervous and I wasn't too sure what to do because I'd had no training as a bouncer whatsoever. I was on my way down to this other pub with another doorman not really knowing what to expect.

Minutes after arriving there it has kicked off. There were now three of us against about fifteen of them. Now the two doormen with me were man mountains, both well over six foot, and thankfully they could do the business. I went straight at this one troublemaker and smashed him in the face, knocking him down. I then start stamping and kicking him until this other one ran at me. He's got to have it now so I start beating on him as well. After throwing a few out the door we made our way back into the club, picking up and throwing out everyone involved in the fighting. I had on a new white T-shirt for my first night; this was now drenched in blood and gore. Straight from my first shift I had to drive to the airport to pick a few friends up with no time to go home and change. I had some strange looks at the airport as I turned up looking like a car crash victim.

One of the worst nights to look out for as a doorman is just a few days before Christmas when all the factories break up. We call it Black Friday as there are always murders in the town and it seems like the whole world is fighting. As any good doorman will tell you, on that night you'll have your work cut out for you, because every fucker is pissed up.

Ian Hews, Essex

My boxing trainer approached me and asked if I wanted a job on the door of a local nightclub. I said, 'Yeah, no problem.' Mind you, at eighteen years old and just eleven stone I wasn't your normal-sized doorman but it was good money and, although I was still a kid, I fancied giving it a go. I told my mum that myself and two mates were singing in the local nightclub. She soon sussed that out and sent my older sister up to see what I was up to. My dad went mental but I still kept the job.

One night I got up the club early. When I walked in there was this big lump causing trouble, he looked like a prop forward for a rugby club. I thought *shit, why did I have to walk into this?* Now I hate bullies and this slag was an out and out bully. Soon as he seen me walk in, his eyes light up. He'd been giving it to the bar staff, then he looks around at me and as loud as he could shout out he bellows, 'Who's this, the fucking bouncer? My little boy could do him,' pointing directly at me. I knew I had to face up to him and couldn't be branded a coward; after all, nobody else was going to help me, I was on my own and the barmen had already been bullied by him so they were no help. He was about nineteen stone and I was eleven stone with only the strength of an eighteen-year-old lad, but one thing I had going for me was my fast hands, so I wanted him outside where I could move around him and not get grappled to the floor. I quickly walk back to the front doors, telling this prick to come outside where we could settle it in the car park. He must have thought that I was going to leg it but when he comes through the doors I've gone at him with everything. Before he had realised it I had hit him with twenty of the hardest punches I could throw and down he went. I couldn't believe it and neither could the bar staff. I had done him good and proper and everyone had seen it. It was a good feeling; I felt like King Kong. Mind you, that was short lived.

The next night I'm in the club but luckily I'm in the kitchen eating and not on the front door. I hear a lot of screaming and a shotgun blast shakes the room. Apparently the guy I had done was a well-known villain and two of his mates had come up there looking for me. The doorman told them I had been sacked but just to make sure everyone knew they let rip with the shotgun into the ceiling. The owner was terrified of them and I weren't too happy neither, so he gave me four weeks money and told me to piss of. So they got me the sack!

Almost five years later and I had formed a security company and was looking after various pubs, clubs, and massage parlours, making sure no one got any trouble. One night I walk into a club with my partner, a very well-known professional fighter, and the regular doormen are filling their pants; there was two well-known criminals upstairs demanding money from the club to protect it from local villains. I was fuming so I ran upstairs with my partner to sort it out and when I got up there I realised it was the same two slags that came after me with a shotgun when I was eighteen. We just tore straight into them, two against two. One of them ended up in a coma; I didn't give a fuck. They both went to hospital, it was payback time and they lost good and proper. Two years later they got arrested for two gangland murders. They got two life sentences and are still in prison now. They won't be getting out for a long time yet.

John Scrivens, South Wales

One day I was in the car with my missus going shopping and my phone rang. It was a good mate of mine and he asked me if I would be interested in doing some door work. A guy phoned him but he didn't want to do it, but told him that I may be interested. I was a bit unsure at first because I liked spending all my free time with my missus. But the money seemed good, so I told him okay.

On my first night I worked in this hotel and it was a wedding reception. I can't say I was nervous, I wasn't really bothered, I didn't really have any feelings about working the door, I just done it. When I got there, I told the guy I was working with that I've never done door work before and I just basically asked him what was expected of me. I was told that night that the work was there for me regularly if I wanted it. I had a phone call the next day off the head doorman and he told me he wouldn't be in the following night and that he had to have a few days off due to sickness. He said if I knew anyone that wanted to work up there with me, to give them a shout. Two weeks went by and he wouldn't answer my phone calls and when I did get through his missus told me that he wouldn't be working there any more. I felt a bit shit-on first of all. Then I thought *what the hell, the head doorman gets extra money and it's the same work*. I was then head doorman up there after a few weeks. It all became very clear why the last doorman left; I was bored shitless. There were never regulars up there, so you couldn't really socialise with the guests. There was no trouble.

I arranged with a group of boys that I had working for me who should take over as head doorman and there were plenty of boys for cover, so I left and moved down into this nightclub in the town. I had been going drinking in this club for a while and always used to help the doormen out when they were having trouble. This one night a couple of boys had gone into the club looking for trouble. There were only two doormen on and it's gone up. I've jumped in and helped the doormen get these idiots out of the club. Now, outside there's about ten of them calling the doormen out. The one doorman has enough and leaps the wall and runs straight at them on his own. I thought *fuck it, I'll give him a hand.* The next thing you could see was the ten of them turn around and run like fuck away. Both the doorman and myself walked back to the club laughing as he thanked me. The following week they asked me did I want a job in the club.

Marty Dee Donovan, South London

My first night on the door was as scary as hell. I was seventeen years old and working on the door of a reggae party in Brixton. As a young boy, learning the ropes those days were my biggest eye-opening. I saw fights with machetes and I saw people have petrol thrown in their faces and set light to. The Rastas back then were vicious when they fought and I knew I had my work cut out. I made many good friends in those early days and lost a few as well.

In my early days I was known as a slugger, a big puncher with no fear. When I was on the door, people knew it and respected it. These days I'm much the same but with more wisdom, patience and humour. I have grown from an unapproachable thug to the most approachable doorman you'll ever meet. I like to think that I have grown up and matured in my mind and body. Nowadays, the door job has courses that teach us that it's more than just hitting people. This is progression and a big step forward, a welcome step forward.

Douglas Gentles, Cardiff

I wanted to work the doors from a very young age. I can remember watching *World of Sport* one Saturday and for some reason they had this piece about the fastest doorman in the world. It was a competition set in the USA, where doormen ran round this bar, crashing through a door at the end. On this piece was Mr T [later BA in *The A-Team*], he won the competition in a time of about nine seconds and I remember thinking, *yeah, I would like to do that.* Getting work was not that easy as I was young, inexperienced and didn't know anyone. Then I started working with the council and met a guy who knew some doormen and he put me in touch with one of them.

I went down and saw the manager of this club called Luigi's. He was a character, small tough ex-boxer who would punch you in the ribs just for fun and to make sure you were on guard. I told him I was looking for work and he took my number and told me he would phone me. Not expecting to hear from him again, I was shocked to have a call from him a few days later offering me a couple of nights work that very week. Waiting for that first Friday was a nightmare. Would I survive? Would I get hurt? Would I make a fool of myself?

I went along at nine o'clock to meet the other doormen. All of them were much older than me and all were very experienced. The head doorman was a guy called Peter, forty years old, hard as nails – and gay. Well of course the others were all telling me to watch myself, don't bend over, he likes them young. In fact he was the nicest guy you could wish to meet and to this day the best head doorman I have met. There was no training: I was told where the exits were and that was it. Thankfully that night there was only one fight, I was first in and with the help of the head doorman I threw my first customer out the door and in the process knocked the arm of the head doorman into a wall, smashing his new watch. Thankfully he told me not to worry about it; as he put it, 'These things happen when you work the door.' He said that I was a bit too keen getting in there so fast but that I would learn with time. I overheard him telling the manager at the end of the night that I was keen and he thought that I would be good at the job. Saying that about me on my first night working with such an experienced group of doormen, there was no greater compliment that anyone could have given me, especially after breaking his watch.

People out in a club have very little understanding of a doorman. To them, a doorman is just someone that stops a fight, is a bully or a thug working the door because it's the only job they can get. They don't understand that we are family men. After working the door in the evenings, often as a second job, just to earn that bit extra for our families, we have mortgages and debts to pay, we have kids to feed.

They don't understand that they have enjoyed a trouble-free night inside the club because we the doormen have kept the shit out, we have taken the crap on the front door to ensure the trouble-makers, who we have to get to know to make sure that we stop them, don't enter the club, so that they, the ungrateful customers, have a good night. They often don't see the trouble inside a club because our experience enables us to deal with it quickly, even stop it before it starts – often just by walking the troublemakers out of the club.

As the customer enters the club, we welcome them. As they leave, we wish them good night and a safe trip home. Many, and I do mean many, don't even look at you as you speak. They walk past as if you're not there. These customers need to remember that manners cost nothing. We are doing a job, a job that I would love to see some of these people try, especially when a fight breaks out or someone suffers a heart attack and you have to save someone from attack or even dying.

Dave Courtney, South London

I became a doorman in my early twenties. I was training one day at the world famous Thomas a' Beckett gym, Old Kent Road, when a guy named Gary Davidson asked me to come and work downstairs. At the time it was owned by a lady called Beryl and that's when I started on the door. Some of the lads I was working with were David, the son of the famous unlicensed fighter Columbo, and Fred the Head. On my first night it went off big time. At this time the Beckett was notorious for aggravation and the whole place went up. I wasn't worried or impressed, as I am a fighting bloke anyway. It looked like me and the door lads had sorted all the trouble out ourselves but actually a lot of the club steamed in and helped us out – but my first night was action packed.

It was during the rave scene it really took off for me. Doormen really came into their own and security firms were starting up every-where. Everyone had their own little firm. Normally the person who put the rave on liked to pick their own doormen so whoever was in charge of selling the drugs was familiar to them. They had to be friendly to certain dealers and throw others out, so they picked their own doormen. Since I was putting on all the raves at the time, I had the biggest security company there was.

Wayne Price, Mountain Ash

I would never let my kids work the door when they grow up. It's a thankless job; you're regarded as a bully if you beat someone or weak if you just talk tidy to them. You can't win. I told my boys right from the start that if ever I caught them working a door the hardest fight they will have would be with me, because I'm not having it. You see, I had to work the door. I was just a young lad with a wife and a little baby in the house. Back then I was only earning £14.50 a week with my day job and could earn a £5 a night on the doors. I couldn't refuse to do the doors; we were desperate for the money. I was maybe eighteen and was fit and could fight the world if need be. Looking back now and knowing the score, I realise that I was too young. A man would have had more experience and would have known what to expect. I had no idea and didn't know how dangerous it would become over the years. Door work hasn't bought me any luxuries but at least it has helped with the bills. Standing around watching everyone get drunk just waiting for trouble to start is not fun, I can tell you.

Jamie O'Keefe, London

I never set out to be a doorman; I never felt tough enough or tall enough. My mate Mo Hussein had the same thing. We were a pair of short-arses so had to direct our thoughts into being something else. Mo became British Commonwealth boxing champion and I become known for reality fighting arts within my world. We both followed different paths but still ended up as doormen. Unfortunately Mo had an incident on the door one night which evolved into him being jumped by a few lads, but in the process of defending himself one of his attackers received an injury which cost him his life. Mo received four years in prison so our working relationship came to an end. Anyone that has truly worked the door for a period of time in real challenging venues will tell you how easy it is to have your whole life turned round over an incident that lasts for minutes or even seconds.

So no, I never wanted to be a doorman. I did it through needing to provide food, shelter and creature comforts for my family. I actually started off this career by fighting with doormen when I was a skinny teenager. In the late Seventies, after the punk rock explosion, we had the second generation Mod movement developing. We were a group of seventeen-year-olds who needed some direction and guidance in life. This came in the form of Paul Weller who started up a band called The Jam. We were a group of angry young men following Mod bands all over the country and part of that was that we pissed off a lot of people who were not impressed with a gang of flash Cockneys walking all over their manor. So it kicked off everywhere we went. We became known for violence and went under the banner of the Glory Boys. Our reputation would arrive at venues before we did. It ended up with gangs of lads setting themselves up to kick off with us wherever the gigs were, with the support of their bouncers.

We would get into venues by guest lists, fire exits, windows, and even set ourselves up as a thirty-piece band just to get in. We really took the piss. There were never enough bouncers to be able to handle us. It's okay when you have six bouncers dealing with a couple of lads kicking off but it's a bit different when six bouncers have to deal with fifty jack-the-lad Cockney bastards. If the bouncers left us alone we gave them respect but if they started that bullying shit we gave it to them big time. That's how I got into looking after people, by looking after mod bands like The Jam, Secret Affair and the Purple Hearts. This then progressed into doing the door at music venues. I spent a few years working at the famous rock venue The Borderline in London so worked alongside Hells Angels, Outcasts, rappers, grungers, et cetera. Many a time I've felt vulnerable and out of my league but you just do what you have to do.

I know that many 'tough guys' lay claim that they fear nothing and never get that sickly feeling but they are liars. It's a biological reaction that we have no control over. What I would say though is that even at times when I've been shitting myself, I would disguise it as best as possible. A bit like a duck on water which on the surface appears to be all calm when danger approaches but underneath its little webbed feet are going like mad in a panic to get away from the danger. Fight or flight appears in all walks of life.

I can count the good doormen I've known and worked with on two hands and the rest have been pretty bad doormen in my opinion, but not always through their own fault. You cannot gain any experience from doing a few days of training on a door supervisors' course and there are no real training sessions on the positive outcomes of doorwork. It's a real hands-on learning curve and if you're with another doorman who knows fuck all, how are you supposed to learn? You end up with bad habits, bad attitude and bravado until you learn the way things work.

Working as a team is essential in a confrontation: one bluffer or coward can weaken an entire door squad.

Jamie O Neil, Wales

I first became a doorman back in 1992. I was twenty-one and pretty full of myself. I had been bodybuilding seriously for about three years and was a big lump for my age. I then got offered work by someone from the gym who asked would I work in this club called Stryker's with these other two lads named Ross and Lee. As far as trouble was concerned, well it was a doddle – there wasn't any. Most of the people coming in were over forty and just out to pull the women. Nearly everyone was polite and respectful. I had wound myself up for the first night, not knowing what to expect, but we were treated like royalty. The drink was free but I soon decided to pack drinking in whilst working. I ended up there for the best part of a year.

Ross then got us a job in the biggest nightclub in the town and that's when things changed. It was totally different to what I'd been doing. This was a town centre club where trouble went on every night. I was partnered for a while with big Ross and was glad of that. I knew I could count on him and vice versa. The first major incident came when I was working with my mate Blaine and it went off on the dance floor. Blaine has grabbed the one, I have grabbed the other guy and I started leading him to the back stairs. The guy was pleading with me to leave him walk out. Being a fair guy, I've left him go. He immediately spins round and catches me right in the ear. I have then gone into one. I caught him with a half-decent punch but too high on the head to do much damage. As soon as I'm just getting to grips with him I can feel myself getting lifted up. Suddenly I'm being held by my arms and legs by all these guys in suits all around me.

As I'm by the top of the stairs, they have launched me into the air. I've landed halfway down the steps and rolled down the rest. I look up: the boy I had been holding is charging down the steps towards me. I try to get up but my knee's fucked. As I'm nearly up, he jumps on me, knocking me back down. His mates are now trying to kick my head in. I'm using the guy as a shield, holding him tight to me to take most of the blows. I can hear the air gushing out of his mouth so they kick him instead of me. I kept thinking to myself, *where the fuck are the other doormen?* The whole incident was just over a minute but felt like hours. We finally got them all out and then found out they were a rugby team on a drinking session. I ended up with a bruised knee and bad ear but luckily they seemed to get in each other's way and hurt their own mate more than me.

Eric Jones, Edinburgh

I started as a favour which was supposed to last for six weeks. Three and a half years later, I must have had one whole weekend off the doors. I started off working at Edinburgh's first ever sports bar, owned by three Scottish international rugby players. I played rugby for the same team as one of them and so did the head doorman. Seems the head doorman had broken his leg and they were desperate for someone to stand in for him. I thought I'd give it a go for a while. I wasn't really sure what to expect, as of course I was new to the job. I met the guy that I would be working with and his name was Derek. I thought, *great, Derek and Eric working the door*, we sounded like a bloody comedy act. The place was known as the Grassmarket, known for stag weekends and basically an area for big drinking men. There were a lot of pubs in a small area, so we all got to know each other. Our names got to be a standing joke throughout all the pubs.

Not long after I had been introduced to Derek, in fact about five minutes after, there was shouting and glasses being smashed. We both ran up the stairs to find five or six fighting. Straight away I throw one up against the wall and roll one down the stairs. I now grab hold of the one against the wall, only to realise it was one of the owners. *Great start to work*, I thought. We get the three troublemakers out; the other two were bar staff that had been started on. The ones we threw out had a few cuts and bruises on them and one left his teeth by the front door. Welcome to the first night of door work!

Neil Lewis, Treharris, South Wales

I started working on the doors when one of my mates I used to play rugby with was finishing on the door. He had been involved in a massive scrap the week before and ended up with glass in his eye. His family were giving him a lot of hassle to finish. A good friend of mine, Big Shirley (called Shirley because as a child he had pretty Shirley Temple ringlets; believe me he's not so pretty these days), who I was boxing with at the time, asked if I wanted any work. I jumped at the opportunity and the extra cash and the following week I started.

We were working in this rugby club down the Valleys, a right shit-hole of a place.

I was eighteen and didn't know what to expect but my first night was a night to remember. Shirley took me under his wing. He was the one to look up to and learn from, he'd been bouncing years and was well respected in the game. He told me to keep with him because the other boys we were working with were a bit wild with their fists. Throughout the night it nearly kicked off a couple of times but nothing came of it. I was hoping something was going to happen just to get it out of the way but the night went quite smoothly. Then on the way out, this six foot five rugby player opens his mouth and starts having a go at Shirley. Shirley replied with the biggest, loudest right hook I have ever seen; it was like a big tree falling over which echoed around the room. There were people rushing around, girls screaming. I thought, *he's killed him.* The boy wasn't moving at all and this girl checks him for a pulse. She then starts screaming, 'I can't find a pulse, I can't find a pulse.' Shirley by now is pacing the hall looking very worried. The boy eventually came round, which eased the tension a bit.

Big Shirley was my mentor if you like. All he showed me that night was to smash someone up if they start having a go. Looking back, I'd say that was actually the best advice I could have got. It helped me over the years a good few times.

Steve Wraith, Newcastle

My first shift was a Thursday night, which anyone will tell you is as busy as a weekend in other areas. I was dressed in a white shirt, black pants, Doc Martens with a bomber jacket and I felt and looked the business. I wasn't nervous, as Gary introduced me to the lads who would be watching my back and vice versa. There was Gary first and foremost, then Irish, Buzz, Dave and John Lillico, who remains one of my closest friends to this day. What a night! There were two key positions – front door and back door – with buzzers and flashing lights to let you know where a fight had broken out. Six fights in just over four hours, and this was a quiet night, according to the lads. I've got to admit that I loved every minute of it.

The festive season was crazy. Once-a-year drinkers swoop on city centres up and down the country and drink too much, eat too much, score with the opposite sex, empty the contents of their bowels and stomach on any available footpath or shop doorway and generally do things that they wouldn't normally do. Up until that Christmas I would have been doing exactly the same thing and it was only then that I realised that there was more to life than spending my hard-earned cash on booze. Xmas never changes, it seems to take ages to come around and then it's all over in a flash, and you wonder what all the panic was about. January on the door is one of the quietest months of the year, as people are often in debt and have to stop in to sort their finances out.

As I had been the last in, I was first out when shifts had to be cut amongst the door staff, and I lost my Thursday to Sunday shifts. I was gutted, and missed the adrenaline rush that I got when those lights and buzzers came to life. I also missed the lads who I had become part of a team with. I left it for a while, and it was not until I was asked by an old friend, George Poulter, who ran the Filament and Firkin and Scruffy Murphys, if I would be interested in sharing the head doorman's job with a lad called Paul Tinnion, that I decided to give it another go.

By now Newcastle City Council had decided that all door supervisors should be licensed. This entailed four days' training covering all aspects of the job, including fire regulations, health and safety, drug awareness, licensing laws, and of course first aid. The final day saw each potential doorman sit a multi-choice test on what he had learned. I passed with flying colours and was given a weekend shift as joint head doorman on George's bars at the Haymarket end of Newcastle. So Paul Tinnion and I started work together. Paul is the kind of doorman you would want in the trenches with you, always on the ball and not someone to mess with. Over the months we handled every situation that came our way. The bars weren't as hectic as Masters had been at Christmas but nevertheless we had our fair share of bother. The football matches always bring trouble and more often than not rival fans would clash with Newcastle fans before and after each game. I came in for stick as well as I was the fanzine editor, but I had broad shoulders and was never unduly bothered by the verbal threats from some of the narrow-minded yobs that call themselves supporters.

Doormen in general have a bad reputation. They are looked at by the public as paid thugs who chat up women and give any man who looks at him the wrong way a good hiding, hence the name bouncer. The council, in association with the police, wanted to change the image and rid the bars and clubs of the criminally minded doormen, hence the licensing. What publicans wanted now was a customer-friendly doorman, someone who talked to the customers and ejected them if they misbehaved but with reasonable force. I learned very quickly that doing the door was as much about front as physical size. Never back down when you have made a decision because it shows weakness. Always maintain eye contact with a customer who you have a problem with and be aware of who that person is with. Most importantly, make sure someone is watching your back.

Kris Cermele, Tampa, Florida

As a kid my father taught me to box before he lost his eyesight. I found a straight right hand puts a stop to any would-be trouble-maker. He told me put my hands up and gesture that I don't want any trouble and when they think you're not going to fight then you plant your feet and aim for their chin. My father did some doorman work in the Sixties, so when I decided to do the same when I was twenty-six his advice came in handy.

I asked him once, 'What if I get trouble off a boxer, how do I land a punch on someone who knows how to move and ride a blow?'

'Get close and kick him straight in the balls, don't mess with them, don't hold back. You can always knock them out when they fall to their knees,' he answered.

I started on the club doors in 1984, working with an old wrestler called Sean Mason. There were a few others with us at the time but he was the head doorman. He showed me how to hold someone, choke them out and how to search for blades, guns, drugs and anything else that wasn't to come in the club. I was nervous all night and everyone looked like a potential attacker. Every time I searched someone I kept thinking they would take offence and take a shot at me. I'll be honest, I really wished I hadn't taken the job; it looked easy when you are sitting down watching the doormen chat to some chick.

The first confrontation I had was with a drunk who wanted a job behind the bar. I told him I was new and didn't know the score. Before long I was in a full-blown argument that seemed to last for ever. Sean was watching from a distance as I had to grapple with the drunk and drag him screaming to the exit. Later Sean explained that he left me alone to watch how I handled the situation. He thought that I handled it well but should have ended it faster and not let it drag on so much.

That same night two guys were trading blows outside the front entrance. I rushed out, split them up and laid the biggest out cold when he went to throw a punch. Sean pulled me to one side and told me that I handled myself well but that I must never get involved in anything outside the club unless I had to. As soon as he left me on my own I vomited into a plastic palm tree by the main door. It was not the worst first night a doorman could have but any man who tells you he's not scared the first night is lying.

Stellakis 'Stilks' Stylianou, Crayford, Kent

A friend called Don asked me if I fancied going out one night over to watch Sid Vicious at the Music Machine. I agreed and got picked up and taken to the venue. I thought it was great just being at the Music Machine, never mind getting to watch Sid Vicious as well. Don introduced me to the doormen, then said to me, 'Stilks, just stand on the edge of the stage and if anyone tries to get up on it, tread on their fingers.' I got to watch the show and tread on a few fingers. Don asked me if I enjoyed the night. I said, 'Yes, I had a good night thank you very much.' On the way home he gave me £15.

'What's that for?' I asked.

Don replied, 'Well, that's for helping out.'

'You mean to say I get to watch the show and get paid for it?' I enquired.

'Not only that,' Don said, 'but can you come tomorrow because Toyah Wilcox is on?'

I stayed there working for six months after that. Don later went on to become the mayor of Greenwich! He asked my eldest daughter Emma if she would become mayoress and she agreed and became the youngest mayoress in Europe.

Don finished at the Music Machine and this meant I lost my lift there. I couldn't drive at this time and it made it difficult to get to work. Full of confidence, I went into a pub called the Station Hotel and informed the owner, 'If you get any trouble, I'm standing over there, just give me a call and I'll help you out.' At the end of the night the governor asks me if I wanted to work there regular. I accepted and ended up there six nights a week for over thirteen years. My reputation grew and I had other places under my supervision and about fifteen doormen working for me while I stayed at the Station.

Ari Bolden, Victoria, Canada

It was a warm September evening when I started in the nightclub business. I was visiting a good friend of mine who tended bar at a local watering hole. I had at that time been working in radio for some years and I had just completed my university degree in philosophy. I had worked in security and pubs during that time but never a nightclub. I was just out for the night with no particular plans in mind. I believe it was around 12.30 A.M.

The nightclub was rough around the edges. Not that it was an unattractive establishment but the clientele usually could be expected to fight on any given night. And it was one of those nights. A fight broke out only a couple of feet away from me. I grabbed the aggressor (which, I now know, was one of the stupidest things I could have done) and the bouncer grabbed the other guy. I wrestled with this yahoo, finally putting him in a joint lock. Then I tossed him out the door. The next day, my phone rang. It was my bartender friend, and he told me his boss wanted to see me about a job. This really surprised me, because I had never, ever, thought myself capable of being a doorman for a nightclub. I failed to meet the minimum size requirements for the job. Didn't you have to be over 200 pounds and have a neck the size of a bull ape?

I started working once a week and filling in when needed. My position was what we call in the nightclub business the 'starter'. That is a stationary place for new recruits, whose job it is to watch for glassware leaving the club and to greet customers. I wasn't given a lot of 'heads up' or training. I muddled my way through for a while, watching the other door staff for clues. I soon discovered that they didn't have a whole lot of training either. I decided I had to acquire the necessary skills on my own. I took it upon myself to learn how to become an effective doorman. And like anything I do, I wanted to be the best.

During the years that followed, I read every piece of literature I could get my hands on about nightclubs, bouncing, security operations and conflict resolution. I then furthered my educational background by becoming certified as a private investigator, learning more about investigation, law, and human psychology. I continued to enrol and take conflict resolution seminars when I could. I have now been in more confrontations than I can recall. But there is one thing all doormen have in common. When it goes down, we're there to bail your ass out of trouble and prevent it from being fed to you. We are the guys who are willing to jump in without a second thought and help out a complete stranger. We aren't animals. Hell, we have more humanity than most.

Richard Horsley, Hartlepool

In 1988 I was training at the boxing gym and the coach used to work the doors. He asked me if I'd like to give it a go. I agreed as the extra money would come in handy. I felt nervous doing my first weekend shift, even though I knew I could handle most situations. Every bouncer I have spoken to admits the first time you're on the door you feel the old butterflies in the stomach. There were four of us on the door and I learned how to control a crowd and keep the queue sorted by watching the other bouncers work. The place had a bar with two pool tables downstairs and bar and disco upstairs. Both areas would be packed to the rafters every Friday and Saturday night. Every time I hear the Womack and Womack song called 'Footsteps' I'm reminded of the place.

Denim Thomas and Mick Sorby were top dogs on the door scene. Denim was always fighting, he was a good fighter who worked all the roughest clubs, a nice bloke when you got to know him. Later he became a publican for a short time and asked for me personally to look after the door of his pub. Mick Sorby was also a well-known fighter. He would let his fists and boots fly then ask questions later. He was a never-say-die type of fighter who wouldn't give in no matter what. Once I got to know Mick he quickly became my best mate, a gentleman who would give you the shirt off his back. The police didn't like me or Mike Sorby as the outpatients was getting full on the weekends from our escapades. They just wanted us banged up. We came out of a pub at about seven o'clock one Saturday night, making our way to the club to start work. Police were waiting for us and we got strip-searched by the pricks. Needless to say they found fuck all. I don't know what their informants were telling them but it was obviously shit.

In those days there was no bouncer licence and most of the guys on the doors could handle themselves. Nowadays there's too many just there to make the numbers up. When it goes off you need someone who's going to be there for you, who you know can back you up in what sometimes can be a life threatening job. I look at some guys on the door these days and think to myself, *I'm glad he's not watching my back*. I always dealt with the trouble with my fists and never used a weapon. I'd let people know that I took no shit and if they wanted to fuck around they'd have to face the consequences. There was a doorman called Gary around here in the Nineties who couldn't fight for toffee but what a patter merchant. An expert with the charm, there was almost no situation he couldn't defuse with his gift of the gab.

Mick once told me about a guy who worked the same club door with him back in the early Eighties. The guy was a coward who, when you'd meet him, would make out he was a right animal. Mick was the head doorman at the club (which was later closed down because there was too many murders) when it all went up, with loads going at it. Guys were laid out covered in blood all around. When they got the place under control and everyone was calming down and getting their breath back, Mick noticed the shitty arsed doorman sneaking out of the toilets. He stooped down to dip his hands in a pool of blood on the floor and wipe them over his shirt and face. Mick watched him in disbelief, having never seen anything like it. The guy went around the club telling everyone how many he had just done and how he was in the thick of it. Well the prick got sacked and chinned for good measure.

Another guy I worked with is known as Vulture. He was a good kickboxer who I witnessed putting many guys to sleep with just his elbow. In fact some called him 'The Elbow' behind his back, in good fun of course.

Rodri Cartwright, South Wales

I first got to work on the doors when I was seventeen. I was a big boy for my age and got asked would I cover for this bloke in a bowling alley. The money was good for four hours' work and I jumped at the chance. I felt confident, as I had been training on the weights since I was thirteen and was now six foot two and fourteen stone. Friday came and I get a phone call off the boss asking can I work in the town instead of the bowling alley in the night. I thought about it and rung him straight back for details on where I was working. I settled into the job with ease and didn't get much trouble for the first few weeks.

Three weeks later I was working with this girl in this venue which held a few hundred people. The place was full of pissed arseholes from rival rugby teams and the local town idiots. With only ten minutes left of my Saturday shift, a guy with eyes like piss-holes in the snow approached me. He wanted to know if I had seen his jacket. I said I hadn't seen it and asked him where he had left it. He drunkenly mentions something about another venue from the previous night. I politely tell him, 'Unfortunately sir, I have not seen your jacket, leave your name behind the bar and if it turns up they will call you.'

With that he screamed, 'You've got it,' and leapt at me. I gripped hold of the mental's shirt and flung him over a table, breaking glass has he came down with an almighty crash that made everyone stop what they were doing. His mate jumps on my back and the fat lard-arse takes me down to the floor. I was fuming and as I shot back up I dropkicked Lardy in the balls, leaving him for my mate to take out. I grabbed the first guy in a chokehold and charged him to the door. By the time we got there I'd choked him out. His head smashed into the bolted door and along with his fat friend he got thrown into the street.

About 30 minutes later we were all having a drink after work when the two guys turn up at the front door with three others. I recognised two of the guys as being two of the hardest men in the town. I opened the door to see what they all wanted. One of the hardest guys spoke to me. 'We've just phoned a few guys from your gym. They told us you're a straight guy and not a bully. My brother here has been an arsehole, in fact if he gets in any more trouble he's going to prison. Therefore he wants to apologise to you.' We all exchanged handshakes and the fact that I opened the door to the five of them on my own got me respect from the customers and my workmates.

Terry Turbo, North London

I used to box and do martial arts and all of my friends tended to be the same sorts of people: doormen, thugs, football hooligans, gangsters, scammers, streetfighters – what I call real people. There is a sort of code between you all and you stick together and look out for each other. One day, a couple of my mates saw me knock out some bloke in a pub who had come over to me running off his mouth and they said, 'You should be on the door.' This was the beginning of me working on the door and to be honest it was a fun few years. A good doorman can earn £1,000 per week if he's working for the right people. Is it worth it? In a word, no! Not if you think you could quite easily lose your life or you could be crippled, but if you are a good fighter and you've got a family to support and you can't earn that sort of dough any other way, then do it.

I didn't feel anything when I worked except the adrenalin rush when it all kicked off. From working the doors I've gone on to run One Nation, Garage Nation, Rave Nation, RnB Nation and Dreamscape over the last ten years and become the biggest club promoter in England, having been crowned the best promoter three years in a row at various industry award ceremonies. I ran my own security firm, which I sold in March 2003 to become a full-time actor, having appeared in several high-profile TV documentaries, TV series and feature films.

Cliff Fields, Dunstable

In 1970 I boxed Richard Dunn in an eliminator to fight Muhammad Ali. I was on the verge of making big money. Turns out Dunn's a southpaw and I hate southpaws. I was hitting him up the guts in the fourth round when he threw a hook that split me open. The ref stepped in and stopped the fight. I still get gutted when I think about it but that's showbiz. Anyway Bobby Neill, my then manager, sorted it with Mickey Duff for me and [British light-heavyweight champion] Johnny Frankham to fly to Milan and Rome to do two exhibitions with Ali. We never got to speak with Ali a lot but he did seem a nice man.

After Rome I decided to come out of the ring and give up the pro game. What was the worth of it? The slightest bit of blood and the fight would get stopped. I started on the doors and once worked for [notorious gang boss] Eddie Richardson on his pub. I got known as a handy sort of guy so I got into minding the likes of Oliver Reed. I started to work for Joey Seagram minding a club in London. Outside one night there must have been about 200 coloured lads all pissed up wanting to fight us on the door. I smash up two with a big right hand each when this bloke comes up waving this knife at me. I threw all my weight behind my punch and as it struck him his face disintegrated. He fell to the floor with his face smashed to a pulp. We manage to get back into the club before the situation got worse.

The next day I'm arrested, charged with GBH and end up in court. They showed photos of the guy's face in court and I was nearly sick, I just couldn't believe what I had done to him. They gave me eighteen months in Wormwood Scrubs. My dad came to visit me and told me how lucky I was, as the guy nearly died. It was 1978 and I was banged up in a prison cell day and bloody night. I asked an officer if there was anything I could do to get out of the cell, I felt like I was going mad in there. The only job available was cleaning up the shit that the prisoners dropped from their cell windows. I didn't give a fuck what I had to do, I just wanted out of the cell. That job was the best job there at the time, next to looking after the pigs. I came out in 1979 and before I left I had a look around at the prison and thought to myself, *I'm never coming back here again.*

I ended up fighting my last fight against some gypsy whose name

I can't remember. It was 1984 and I was working in a place called Caesar's Palace, near Luton. I had an argument with one of the bargirls who was Irish. I was in a right temper with her and I barged past these bunch of gypsies, telling them to get out of my fucking way. One stood up and hit me with a beer glass in the eye. I got taken straight to the hospital and when I come around from the operation they told me I had lost my eye. I was gutted and hit the bottle and ended up on the dole. I couldn't box or work the doors any more so the only work I could get was working for the scrapyard.

all in a night's work

THERE ARE NOT many jobs that can change dramatically from one night to the next, but that's how it is on the door. The doorman gets paid to adapt to any situation, constantly aware of what goes on around him, waiting for something to occur that has to be dealt with. If someone works in a factory and the boss asks them to pick up rubbish in the car park, then that's something that they have to do, no matter how they feel about it. When a doorman has to disarm someone with a knife or throw out some Aids-infected junkie, then that's what he has to do; it's his job. A doorman's night's work isn't like a nine-to-five job, it constantly changes, nothing is predictable and a fun night can turn to terror in a second. Whatever occurs, the doorman is expected to sort it. What job would you prefer: dull but safe or unpredictable and dangerous?

Terry Turbo, North London

I have never had a good experience with the police. I just think they like to be a pain in the arse. I mean, we never, ever got heavy-handed with anyone unless they really deserved it, and these muppets always go to the police and say, 'I don't know what happened, the bouncers just kicked the fuck out of me for no reason at all.' The funny thing is the police go on about reasonable force; if there's some guy throwing drinks over people in the club for a laugh, what's reasonable about that? The cunt could cause a riot and how are we supposed to deal with that? 'Sorry sir you can't do that in here, we are going to have to ask you to leave.' I don't think so. If I was in a club and some arsehole threw a drink over me for a laugh,

I'd want to hospitalise them. Wouldn't you? And if you fuck the police around when they nick you and you're in the van or in the station, they are more than happy to spray CS gas in your face or give you a good kicking in the cells, but that's all right because they are the police. When we have to bash someone or really restrain them, we've gone too far. All the police seem to do is sweep up the mess afterwards and if they can nick someone for doing their job in the interests of public safety and order that's OK, they may get a nice promotion or a pay rise. It's one-sided bollocks!!

Jamie O'Neil, Wales

There had been a bit of a scuffle at the club and I had missed it. I'd gone to the toilet and by the time I got back it was over and the people had been chucked out. Well, the rest of the weekend went by and I went to work to my day job on the following Monday morning. My missus then phoned me and told me that a mate of mine in the CID had been to the house and that they wanted to see me. My wife asked me what it was all about but I couldn't give her an answer.

I went down the station and the police start interviewing me and coming on pretty strong. Turns out the boy who had been chucked out was in a bad way and the police wanted names. I thought to myself, some fucking mate this guy is. I told them the truth; I hadn't seen anything. They then pull out this diagram showing where the entire doormen were working and their names. He then states, 'You must have seen something as he was put out of the exit door next to you.' I told them the truth again that I'd gone to the toilet but you could see he didn't believe a word I said.

They ended up letting me go with no charge. My three mates were not so lucky; after a few weeks on remand they went on to get three months in prison and two of them never even threw him out, they were just in the wrong place at the wrong time. I was lucky I needed to use the toilet.

Jason Dicks, Bristol

A big fight breaks out, so we all run in and start pulling these men apart. There's glass smashing everywhere and people are screaming, which doesn't help the situation. I pull this one guy off the top of

Technique and teamwork comes with experience and cannot be
learned on a college course

another and he starts yelling, 'It's OK, I'm a policeman.' The bloke
underneath has a gash above his eye, I've never seen a cut like it,
deep as fuck and blood soon covers this guy and it's all over me as
well. I usually don't give a fuck about them if they've been fighting
but this guy was losing a lot of blood. I get him off to the toilets and
the copper fucks off before I can have a word with him. I get wads
of toilet paper over the cut and get him to the main doors, where we
wait for an ambulance to come for him. The fight inside has been
dealt with and the police turn up and start asking questions.

'Did you do that to him?' this cheeky little ginger prick of a
copper asks.

'No mate, a copper did it,' I answer. After a few more questions
he realises that I'm serious. The guy who was cut open didn't know
the guy who did it was a copper, and after saying he didn't want to
press charges he goes off in the ambulance.

'Would you recognise him again?' he asks.

'Yes mate, I would, he had the biggest nose I have ever seen in my life, I'd know him anywhere,' I answer.

The copper said he knew him and would be back to interview me soon. Of course he never came back; he didn't want to be the one who arrested a workmate, did he? A few weeks later I saw the copper with the nose. He just put his head down and pretended he didn't see me.

Bryan Fisher, Asheville, North Carolina, USA

This was St Patrick's Day, 2003. St Pat's Day is a really big drinking night here in the States; all sorts of people out partying and carrying on. The whole day had a holiday atmosphere, with tons of booze and everyone in search of their own level of stupidity. Everyone who came into our little bar that night seemed drunk, there was no weeding out the good from the bad, it was just check ID and let them in so they could drink more beer. There were only two of us working the door. Two is about all you need with a bar our size and we seemed pretty in control of the loud, pissed-up mob.

Around midnight one of the cocktail waitresses came over and told me there was a guy at the bar so drunk he could hardly stand, and to top it off this lout was grabbing every female ass that he could get his hooks on. I informed the drunk that he was out of line and he was going to have to leave. After an eternity of watching this guy try to sign his credit card slip he finally managed to stumble out the door and he only grabbed two more girls on his way out. The drunken lech was, I came to find out, roommates with a rather large and somewhat sleazy regular by the name of Jerry. Jerry was always chatting up the girls and they all hated him for his overly creepy approach and shifty mannerisms. Jerry was easily six foot six and had a fair amount of meat on him. I told Jerry that his mate was outside and was probably not going to make it ten feet down the sidewalk, much less all the way home in his state. Jerry assured me he was going to finish his drink and take his buddy home.

I had all but forgotten the incident when the butt-grabber returned. For some reason two cops were following him and trying to figure out where he lived; the drunken jerk must have fallen because his forehead was scraped, the guy was a mess. The cops just wanted to be sure he wasn't going to drive. I told someone to call him a cab, so the cops and I stood out front with the drunken ass-grabber waiting for a taxi.

A few annoying minutes later the guy wants to come back in. He started carrying on about needing to get his credit card slip and slurring and just making a nuisance of himself. I had already told the cops about throwing him out earlier so they knew I wasn't going to let him back in. This was in March and it was rainy and cold. There were a million other places I'd rather be than standing in the drizzle with this slob begging me to come inside. The cops were also growing bored with it and they sort of wandered a few metres down the sidewalk and were talking between themselves. I decided that I'd had enough, so I told the drunk, 'Look, there is no way I am going to let you back inside after you sexually assaulted those women.'

I should have seen it coming, but I didn't. This guy didn't seem like the physical type and my hands were behind my back and my mind was a thousand miles away. So when he threw a big lazy right at me, I barely had time to turn and didn't get my hands up to block. The idiot hit me right in the side of the neck. It hurt and I knew it was going to be sore but it didn't put me down. I stepped right into him and locked his arms up. Meanwhile the other doorman and the cops had both seen him hit me and were on him in an instant. My co-worker made it there first and got the guy by the throat; a split-second later the cops were on him, so we backed off and let them put him in handcuffs. I'm not really sure the guy even knew what he had just done or that it was the police kneeling on his face, but they arrested him and carted him off to jail, leaving me with a sore neck and in a bad mood. I figured it was a good lesson and it would make me more alert in the future.

The evening wasn't over; St Patrick's night had a bit more in store for me yet. About thirty minutes after the ass-grabber was hauled off to the clink, his tall, creepy roommate walks up to me. 'Why did you have my friend arrested?' he asks me, in a belligerent tone. Jerry was obviously drunk, and by the look in his eyes maybe had a bit of something white and powdery in him as well.

I told him, 'Look your buddy hit me and was lucky the cops got him instead of me.' I was still annoyed at getting punched, but was trying to be professional.

Jerry got angrier: 'You can't press charges on him.' So now he's giving me orders. Wonderful. I was suddenly fed up with the whole night and I told Jerry, 'Look if I hit you, I know you'd press charges against me.'

He took the bait, giving me a contemptuous look and scoffed, 'No way. Punch me.'

'Look get out of here.' I was getting tired of him. 'Just leave the bar, you're fucked up.'

'No way man, hit me.'

Oh I wanted to slug him, but there was a ton of punters watching. 'OK,' I told him, 'I'm tired of this, get out. I fucking mean it.' I motioned to the door. My partner gave me a quizzical look. I'm pretty sure he would have slugged the idiot by now but that's me, always a soft touch.

'Look, fight me. If you win, you can press charges. If I win you won't press charges. OK?' At that point I could see where this is heading, and I was more than ready for it. I was still trying to be professional, but I was looking forward to seeing Jerry unconscious.

'Right, you're fucking nuts, get out of here.' At this point one of our regulars who had been standing nearby shoved Jerry out the door and into the foyer. I hadn't expected that but it worked. Jerry grabbed the door and slammed it open. I was amazed it didn't break since it's glass. I guess trying to break the door was enough and I stepped into the foyer and gave him a boot in the gut.

Now, I am a bit small for a bouncer, I'm only five foot ten and right at 185 pounds, and as I've said, Jerry was well over six foot. I was really concerned about his reach; I think he could have hit me before I was in punching range, so I decided to give him a Doc Marten in his breadbasket. It seemed to stun him a little and he staggered back. Then he ran right at me. I have no idea what he was trying to do but it didn't work, I let him come, then slipped in and got him in a tight front chokehold, his head behind me and him bent over almost double. Meanwhile my partner grabbed his arms because he was swinging them wildly. I wasn't sure if I had him tight enough so I kept applying pressure. After a bit of this I figured we should get him to the door, so we started moving him that way and when we got to the door we kind of heaved him out.

Jerry fell to his hands and knees gasping for air. I figured he would fuck off now that he could breathe again, but I was wrong. He got up and came right back at me through the door. He took a punch at me; I slipped under it, got behind him and almost had to jump up to grab him in a rear naked chokehold. I arched my back and kneed him in the back of the legs, to bring him down to my level where I could manage him better. The rear naked choke is a great way to control big unruly assholes that don't seem to want to behave, and it is my favourite move when I am at work. I kept applying pressure, thinking maybe I had missed or didn't have the hold applied properly, but a second later I was rewarded by a gasping gurgle sound coming from Jerry. I ease up a little, thinking maybe he's had enough, and he starts trying to grab my face. His arms were long enough that he could get to me even when I was behind him. I tucked my head into his back to protect my face from his huge hands and my partner grabbed Jerry's' arms to control his thrashing.

At this point people are yelling at him to stop, girls are crying, people who know him are telling him he's is going to die, half the bar was watching and the entire street was gathered around. I can remember one of the bartenders, who sort of knew him, saying, 'Jerry, see you can't breathe and you're turning purple, that means you're going to die. Quit fighting!' At this I decided surely he was done, so I sort of laid him down and I went back in the door, breathing hard, hoping the crazy prick would go away. Nope. He got up and started yelling, and I got ready for round three. Jerry came to one of the doors; there were five glass doors so it was hard to pick a spot to defend. He came in one of the doors, looked me right in the eye and started cussing. Then he kicked the regular who had shoved him right in the balls. Tricky bastard. The regular sort of fell away, and Jerry charged me again.

Again I'm not really sure what he was trying to do, but I grabbed his head and pushed it towards the floor so that he was bent over. I was getting tired of choking this guy, it obviously wasn't scaring him and I didn't feel like having him unconscious at the front door, so I decided to start throwing a few punches. Since he was bent over this was pretty easy and I nailed him with three uppercuts and my partner gave him a few chops in the back as well. His nose started to bleed and he kind of pushed me into the wall. I remember throwing a kick to his mid section and then I tripped and fell.

I recovered from the fall and saw the regular who had been helping had him in a chokehold (again). I told him to be careful not to kill the guy. Finally another regular grabbed Jerry by the leg and unceremoniously dragged him out the open door onto the wet pavement outside. Jerry recovered, stood up and started pointing and screaming at the guy who had probably just saved him from being choked to death. He was yelling at the poor guy asking him if he worked there, over and over.

We went outside and saw the cops were coming up the street, so we stepped back inside because we didn't want them to think we had been fighting in the street. At about the time the cops got there, Jerry hit the regular who had dragged him outside. The cops jumped on Jerry pretty good. I remember he was laying in the flooded gutter, half under a parked car, nose bloody, eyes glazed and a really big cop kneeling on his shoulder blades trying to put handcuffs on him.

My partner and I were a bit hyped up still but we both put on our professional faces; an expression like, *yeah, this is our job, same old stuff*. When we stepped back inside the bar people were looking at us sort of funny, everyone was chattering excitedly about the to-do and some of the regulars who had helped were slapping us on the back. My partner hardly seemed fazed. He had been cool as an ice cube through the whole thing, helping where I needed it and watching my back the entire time; he was efficient, professional and calm, a great guy to work with. We just grinned at each other as if to say that's what they pay us for. Can you believe it?

Jamie O'Neil, Wales

It was a pretty normal Friday night at the club. I was partnered with my mate Ray downstairs. It was quiet so I went upstairs for a walk. As I get to the top of the stairs, I can see a few guys going for it on the dance floor. I sprint over and grab one of them. Blaine the other bouncer and the door girl Nerys also have hold of one each. I've pulled mine to the top of the stairs when I suddenly notice the other bouncers are being swamped by this group. I let mine go and run back in to help them. Blaine hits one to the floor. This woman in a red dress then starts smashing him over the head with her shoe. By now Nerys was really getting stuck in as well but it was starting to look a bit dim for us.

The DJ had called for help on the microphone. We managed to get them to the top of the stairs with a struggle. At the forefront of the group were two brothers who were drugged up and flying their tits off and were right up for it. One caught me and I stepped backwards, tripping over somebody. As I fell to the ground I could hear another doorman shouting at me to get back up. I got to my feet and we managed to get some control again. We started to eject the troublemakers a few at a time and return upstairs to get more. Trouble was there was no one left on the front door, so half the people that were getting put out were walking back in.

A line of police officers was now standing opposite just watching us struggle and they really looked like they were enjoying it. Just when I thought it was coming to an end, one of the brothers from earlier ran back in. He was up on his toes bouncing around. 'Come on then,' he shouted. We both punched each other at the same time. His punch struck me on the right shoulder and followed through, hitting the manageress in the face. I caught him a peach on the side of his left eye. I then dragged him to this area at the side of the club where two of the other doormen were teaching some of the others a lesson. I had a firm grip on my one's hair and was beating his head into the wood flooring. It was at this point that the other two doormen stopped me. I know the fucker deserved it but I'd gone over the top a bit. I think because all the doormen were all such good friends that we managed to keep it together, work as a team and get the better of them all.

A couple of weeks later my second child was born, so I decided to call it a day. I have to say I really enjoyed my time on the door. I had more good times than bad and I made many friends and very few enemies. I'll always hold those days as special.

Cass Pennant, South East London

The guys I worked with didn't do the doors to supplement their incomes. Most were self-employed or in business. We worked for each other and ourselves. The money was handy and always top dollar. Some of the bouncers I'd seen at some places were taken for mugs by club management because of the real risk they put themselves up for the small amount of money they were earning. They would be better off working behind the bar for the same amount of money and a lot less risk.

Daniel Seery, Birmingham

It was a cold night and Joe and I were shivering our bollocks off checking to see who had paid. Suddenly we hear a high-pitched scream followed by a crashing sound. Joe shot off like a dart, I followed behind him. All we saw was a young girl who must have been eighteen or nineteen crying on the floor with blood leaking out of her head – a lot. We tended to the girl then phoned the ambulance. I kept asking her who did it but she wouldn't tell us. It was so weird; everyone else was acting like nothing had happened. Why wouldn't she tell us who did it? This bloke still had to be inside the club because we got there as soon as we heard anything, yet we never saw anyone. We was still attending to the girl, telling her everything's all right. Then Joe announced he knew who it was.

I said, 'How the fuck do you know?'

He turned around and said, 'Trust me, I know who it is.' He then pointed to a real big chap sitting down with a few other birds. Joe started walking over to him. 'You have to leave the club,' he said in that always-calm voice that he has.

'I aren't leaving, I haven't fucking done anything,' the big guy growled.

'You just hit that girl over there,' Joe said.

The big guy was just getting a little too big for his boots and replied, 'So fucking what? The bitch deserved it.'

Joe lost his temper. 'You fucking asshole,' he shouted. The bloke was about to reply when Joe hit him, knocking him off his chair. He was sprawled across the floor but got back up and charged at Joe. Joe nutted the bastard, then followed up with two quick successive punches into his face which dropped him to the floor, not daring to move. We threw him out and carried the night on.

The club had closed and we were waiting for everyone to get out when we heard, 'Oi, there's the wankers, let's get them.' Three guys had just turned up and fuck me, were they big: the smallest one was probably sixteen stone. Joe didn't say a word, he just went over to the one he had battered earlier and smashed him in the face, full power. The bloke spun round and slumped on the floor unconscious. The other two turned on Joe forgetting about me. I went up to the biggest one from behind, kicked him in the bollocks, threw him back by his throat and kicked him in the face while he was falling. He started to get back up so I booted him again straight into his jaw. Again he tried to get up. I got a metal pole that was lying on the floor and bashed him until he was out cold. Then I turned to Joe. The big bloke was pushing him to the floor and was about to give him a good kicking. I whacked him over the back of the head with the pole and he dropped to the floor. Joe stood up and stamped on him until he went out cold.

This was just another night working the door.

David White, Caerphilly

There's never really a right way of getting people out. Even if you just walk someone out with minimum force you still get called every name under the sun. Use a bit of force and you get the law called on you and everyone calls you a bully. If a local hard nut wants to fight you and you talk him out of it then you're called a coward. If you take him on and beat him, word would go around that it only happened because he was drunk and any day now he would be returning to sort you out. You're dammed if you do and dammed if you don't.

I always hated having to ask customers to drink up at the end of the night. Some were all right about it but others would just ignore you completely. You could be fighting all night, cut, bruised, worn out and to end it all some twat won't drink up. It's enough to make you crazy. In fact one night that's just what happened. I had been around the club three times asking politely if customers would finish their drinks and most left the club but some just wanted to act like knobheads. I approach two lads by the bar and drag the pair of them out; they were kicking and screaming but out they went. In the corner of the club a few guys sat by their table chatting and ignoring me. I walked up, turned the table over and started to slap them around for making me look a prick. They left the club and I had to explain myself to my boss. The only way I could explain it was that I had been fighting earlier and had a gut-full of it all. I'm a reasonable guy and I do this job to get my family the luxuries that just working in the factory can't always bring them.

It can get so frustrating having people look down their noses at you while it's your job to protect them if it comes on top. I bet the police get a similar problem: when you're not needed you're treated like dirt but when there's a problem you're their best friend in the world.

One guy came in the club and as soon as he walked in he said he didn't have to pay and looked at me with contempt. I could tell by his body language that he fancied his chances but before I could say anything the manager said, 'It's all right David, he hasn't got to pay.' I saw him snigger as he and his hangers-on made straight for the bar and started knocking them back like there was no tomorrow. I had seen this guy a few times and didn't like him at all, he had that sort of 'I'm better than you' aura about him. He was a big guy in his early forties but was out of shape and hadn't been in a real fight in his life. It was getting late and I just knew we would end up getting it on, I just knew it. I watched him by the bar making rude remarks to the women who passed by and in general being a twat. His friends gathered around listening to all his jokes and he loved being the centre of attention.

End of the night and I'm walking around the club asking everyone to drink up and as I ask him and his posse of twats, he turns his back on me. His friends laugh and I feel my blood start to boil. I tap him on the shoulder and ask him to drink up. He laughs and without turning around says, 'Ask me nicely and I'll think about it.' I'm thinking of smashing his face up but I speak to him in a soft, polite voice, 'Could you please drink up sir or I'm afraid I'm going to take the drink off you, beat the fuck into your fat face and kick you from one end of the club to the other.' I don't think anyone had ever spoken to him that way before ever.

He froze for a second and slowly turned around. He put his glass on the bar and went to punch me, thinking he'd get a cheap shot in. My reactions were a lot faster – I threw a right hand that I sunk deep into his fat belly. I stepped back as his legs started to buckle and threw a few sharp punches to his nose, which I felt crunch on my knuckles. I knew it was broken before I even had a good look at it. He fell backwards onto the club floor, arms and legs spread out like a giant fat starfish. I'm not the type to just leave a guy alone if I've knocked him out or if he admits defeat in a fight. If I was knocked out (and don't think I haven't been) I'd get kicked to fuck so that's what I do to him. First I stamp on his balls to make sure the fight is all out of him when he awakens. Then I lean over and punch fuck into his ribs because it takes weeks for the pain to subside and every morning when he rolls out of bed in pain he'll regret trying his luck with me. I tell his stunned friends to drag the fat fuck out in the next few minutes or I'm going to repeat what I just did.

After they dragged him out one of them came back and said, 'Tell you the truth David, he's had that coming for a few years now. He was a bully when we were small and he's still a fucking bully. Well done!' At the end of the day the guy didn't have any real friends, just guys who were scared to get on the wrong side of him. I'd rather have friends who like me for who I am, not what violence I'm capable of doing. I know most of you are thinking why did I carry on hitting him once he was out. The reason is that you have to hurt them just enough so they don't come back. Also after word got around about what I did, everyone drunk up on time for a good few months after.

Anthony Thomas, Merthyr Tydfil

I was working in this pub one night and we'd a few scuffles but nothing major. This lesbian turns up and informs us that she's finished with her girlfriend and that her ex had just started on her in another pub. After a while her ex turns up and the other doorman puts her straight that we don't want any trouble in the pub. The end of the night comes and the other doorman says to me, 'You just watch her go at her ex-girlfriend when she gets outside.' As we are clearing everyone out of the pub I noticed a scuffle outside. It turns

Anthony Thomas and Wayne Price: 'Never let your kids work the door when they grow up. You're regarded as a bully if you beat someone or weak if you just talk to them.'

out the one lesbian had turned back to men and she was with her new boyfriend, the ex is going bonkers and is trying to punch the girl's face in. A couple of people start screaming at me to break them up because I was the doorman.

By now the other doorman who was with me was collecting the money from the back of the pub. I thought, *I'm not missing this*, so I rang him on his mobile phone. He was only twenty yards away and I knew he liked to watch a good scrap. He came running through the pub laughing. Now this lesbian was one of those hard little fuckers, she had done a bit of bouncing in the past for this other firm. The new boyfriend starts shouting abuse at her, winding her right up. She has then broken free and smashed him in the face. He pushes her away, not wanting to hit a woman, she goes at him a few times and in the end he hits her with a right hook, knocking her back. She shakes her head and runs at him again. They both end up on the floor. He's on top of her punching her face in; it was now time to go in. I know they think they are men but at the end of the day she was still a woman.

I put him in a headlock and pull him off. By now this other bloke had seen this and turned on him, so I just went back on the door and watched them all go for it. The lesbian's gone at him again but this time he's caught her with a right hook and split her ear open. By now these other lesbians have joined in and it's gone up again. A couple of her girlfriends tried bringing the lesbian back into the pub but they had more chance of growing cocks than getting let back in. She was pissing with blood and the police started arriving. We locked the door to the pub, leaving them all fighting and arguing outside as we made our way to the car to go home as if nothing had happened.

Duncan Ferguson, Torbay, South Devon

I worked a lot of bad nights but 'Bloody Tuesday', as I like to call it, was definitely the worst. It all started with the police and council coming in to do a licence check. It seemed weird that they wanted to do it on a Tuesday and right at the beginning of the night. The normal trick is to do it on Saturday night and hope to catch us over capacity. There were two of us on that night. As we were opening and waiting for the council, one of the other doormen came in and was in uniform. When asked what he was doing here he said he got called in as they were expecting a busy night. This should have sent alarm bells ringing, but we didn't have a clue.

When they arrived, we all got called into the manager's office one by one and asked the same questions they always asked. Last to go in was 'Rocky', for want of a better alias. Now Rocky did six nights a week and was 'the man' of this place. He wasn't the head doorman but he was the one we called when we needed some muscle. It turns out that Rocky shouldn't have been working the doors as the local council and police had taken his licence away some years previous. This whole thing was a cover-up for taking his licence away again. Obviously Rocky was very pissed off but being a good friend of mine I convinced him to stay the night and have a few bevies. The reason his name was brought into the limelight was that we had a guy pull a knife on us about a week before and had to give police statements. They saw Rocky's name and realised he shouldn't be working the door anymore.

Next door to our pub is another pub and Rocky was good friends with the manager of it. He went in there after I calmed him down for a drink to get himself together again. Well guess who walked in – the guy who pulled the knife on us. Rocky grabbed him and, picking him up by his trouser belt, dragged him into the 'blind spot' at the pub, which was just in from the door. He pleaded with Rocky not to harm him, as he would get in more trouble with the law, but Rocky rammed his head into a wall and knocked the guy out. Lucky for the guy, as Rocky was a pro boxer and could have given the guy permanent damage. Rocky then went into our pub for a drink.

The other doorman, who we called 'Sex Machine', and I wanted to wait till the guy became conscious and then throw him out. The thing is we have a radio link-up system with the CCTV operators and the police; our manager, who will be known as what he is, 'Dick', radioed to the police when Rocky brought the guy in. The police came about ten minutes later, just as the guy came round. We got Rocky out the fire exit and he went into another pub till the police went. We made up a story that the guy came at us threatening that he had a knife again, so we grabbed him and restrained him. Luckily the guy is known to the police, so they believed us. Rocky came back a few minutes after the police went.

About twenty minutes later, a known troublemaker who was banned for life and had a particular disliking towards me, decided to come in and try his luck. At the door he saw me and instantly began the routine of kicking off on me, which was getting old now. He began telling people about how he made me his bitch in prison and how after he knocked me out he'd give me one up the arse for old time's sake. 'You should stop trying to live out your fantasies, it will get you hurt,' I replied back. This just fired him up even more. He made a grab at me and I whacked him just under his eye and cut it open. He walked off but gave it the old 'I'll be back for you' and 'I'm in court on Monday so I can't fight you anyway' routine, which really meant 'Ow, my fucking eye is sore and I underestimated you.'

Ten minutes later I get a radio call to come upstairs. I go up and a group of three guys and two girls had smuggled some cans of lager and a bottle of vodka into the place. We told them they had to leave and they all started to move except one, a big girl who could have been a double for Joe Brand. She sat on the floor and said, 'If you want me out you'll have to move me.' *Great*, I thought, *I didn't do weights today and need a good workout*. 'OK then,' I replied. I grabbed her under the arms – deodorant and a razor could have been helpful – and Sex Machine grabbed her legs. The look on her face was priceless; I bet she had used that trick and lesser men would refuse to touch her sandpaper-soft skin or speak back to her foul-smelling, tombstone-toothed mouth. But we did.

We got her to the door and she gave a bit of verbal and strolled off when her mates disowned her. I was commenting to Sex Machine about how eventful the night had been and that it was still early. Man, I wish I hadn't said that. About an hour went past and I got a radio call. I went to the location and it was an old guy who was very pissed and had to leave. I took this one upon myself and talked to him as he left. I sat him down on a step near to the pub and just as I was telling him to get a taxi I got another radio call. This time I went in and found Sex Machine holding a bloke round the back of the neck and by his trouser belt, from behind. He torpedoed the guy towards me and told me he would get another. I grab the guy in mid-flight and wrestled him to the front door. I let him go and he immediately turned and tried fighting me, I pushed him very hard backwards and he stayed on his arse for a few minutes.

Just after the push I heard shouting from up the stairs and saw a guy laying down holding his nose and Sex Machine running down to him. He was struggling so much Sex Machine threw him into a wall and the guy then fell down the stairs. I grabbed him by his legs and T-shirt, took two steps and his T-shirt got ripped off and he whacked his head. I then simply used his legs and forward-rolled him out of the door. I didn't mean to hurt him as I didn't know what they did inside and I know that Sex Machine has an over-active temper (and sex drive). His mate had regained himself and ripped off his shirt and was threatening us. Now these two looked like they had gone on the Gandhi diet and didn't even impress the pigeons on our roof with their chest muscles. Anyway, a quick radio call to the police and they came and took it from there. It was nearly the end of an action-packed night. The last incident topped the night off.

A doorman who works the weekends for us came in to see Rocky and console him. They both got rather drunk but weren't acting up. I was now the one inside and was keeping an eye on a very drunk individual. I went up to him and asked him to be careful as he kept bumping into people as he was walking about. 'Whatever,' he replied. *Fair enough*, I thought. Five more minutes of him bumping people and spilling his drink everywhere I went up again and asked him to calm down a bit and refrain from dancing, as he was throwing all his drink about as he was doing it. 'Stop picking on me,' he said and then one of his mates came over and said he'd keep an eye on him as it was his twenty-first and he didn't want him thrown out. I told him to just keep him calm. About a minute later the guy was dancing and knocked over a gentleman and then said, 'Fuck off,' when the guy got up and asked him to be careful. Three strikes, I thought, so I went up to him and told him he had to leave. 'Fuck off, twat' was the response I got.

I grabbed his pint from his hand and put in on a nearby table. As I did this he began swinging punches at me that were so bad it was as if they were in slow motion. I grabbed his arm and locked it up. As I was escorting him out, someone tripped me up from behind. We both fell on the floor and began to grapple. I quickly gained the upper hand. He was laid out on his back and I had him in a strong chokehold. All of a sudden someone stamped on my leg. I looked around and saw the weekend doorman who was very drunk.

'Don't worry mate, I got him,' he slurred.

'That's my fucking leg' was my reply.

As this was happening, the stamp on my leg took my mind off the guy I was trying to get out and he bit into my bicep very hard. After yelling, 'Get the fuck off my fucking arm!' I put the thumb of my other hand into his eye and pushed it in till he stopped biting, which wasn't very long, believe me. Weekender and myself then dragged him out of the fire exit after I tried radioing and my radio didn't work. Well, Weekender is a big guy, six foot four and nineteen stone, and was stood over the guy giving him the beating of his life. I was quite annoyed because the fire exit is so small, I couldn't get past Weekender to give the guy some payback of my own. When Weekender stopped, the guy wasn't in a good way.

'Aren't you going to hit him to get him back for your arm?' he asked.

I prodded the guy and he just let out a gargling sound. 'Nah, he's in a bad way,' I concluded.

'Yeah, let's get back inside,' Weekender said.

When I went back into the pub it was drinking-up time and needless to say people drank up very quick that night. Could have been the fact that I was covered in blood, and looked very pissed off about my arm. I went to A & E at the local hospital and got my jabs and went home. I had a purple arm for about a week, then a greeny-yellow one, and now just a scar. I know this is a normal Saturday night in most clubs, but this was a Tuesday night and we had managed to throw out almost as many people as had come in. Remember doormen are there to stop trouble, not be eaten.

Kevin Trottman, Liverpool

Stag nights can get right out of hand, as everyone thinks they're a comedian and want to make a name for themselves, either fighting or doing something so completely stupid that they will be the talk of the workplace for days. There must have been ten guys on a stag night who turn up at the front door asking to come into the club this one Saturday night. They seemed all right but I hate letting large groups of men in because if they start up in the club you have to fight them all, not just one of them. Thing was, they met the dress code and the one I spoke to promised us that there would be no trouble and in fact they had a kiss-a-gram coming to the club soon. The thought of seeing some strippers' tits swung it for them and we let them all in.

A few hours later and loads of drinks and we have a few of them up on the tables dancing. I can never work out why they do this, there's a perfectly good dance floor but they'd rather make dorks of themselves up on the tables. Also they always seem to do the same thing: start dancing and as soon as their friends notice them they start doing some sort of striptease act. I walk over to the two who were on the tables and tell them to get down or they're out of the club. They get down and the one I spoke to on the door apologises. I decline his offer of buying all us doormen a drink.

Things have calmed down for a while when the stripper turns up with her protector. We let them in and I tell them that if they are in the club for more than twenty minutes they will have to pay. I leave the other doorman to watch the kiss-a-gram do her thing and return to watch the front door. From what I gather while I was on the front door a few of the stag party tried touching the kiss-a-gram up halfway through her act. I'm called to the dance floor to find the other doormen trying to calm things down after the girl's protector had laid a few punches into two of the group. We let him get away with this as he was only protecting the girl and wasn't out to cause trouble.

After throwing a few punches and grabbing a couple of the group, we manage to get them outside where we left them to argue amongst themselves. The kiss-a-gram came up to me and thanked me for helping and I explained that next time anything like this happened her minder should stay closer and call the doormen over to sort matters out. She seemed to agree with me but the guy who was looking after her came marching out of the main hall straight at me. 'Call yourselves bouncers, you're fucking crap the lot of you. I could run this club on my own, you bunch of wankers,' he growled in my face. Before I could explain that I was on the front door and he should have left things to the other doormen, he threw a punch which struck me between the eyes and launched me across the main foyer. When I regained my senses I threw a few more punches back at him and we traded blows for a while before we both ended up on the floor. I manage to get on top of him and after a few digs in the face he shouted out that I had beaten him and he didn't want to fight anymore. I let him up off the floor and two of the other bouncers escorted him and the kiss-a-gram out of the club.

Later on I was in the foyer of the club waiting for my taxi to turn up, while the other doormen checked the toilets and the exits. I'm wiping the blood off my fat swollen lip when I notice in the corner of the entrance where I'd been fighting lay a wallet which was stuffed with cash. It had fallen out of the pocket of the guy I had been fighting with so took it into the toilets and after putting the money in my own pocket I flushed it down the toilet. I went home in the taxi with a swollen lip and a few hundred quid. Turned out to be a good night after all.

Brendan Driscoll, South Wales

One Saturday night I was teamed up with another doorman when these two pig-ugly twin brothers walked past us. They looked us up and down and one started laughing at us whilst his brother walked on. About ten minutes later they came back and stood next to us, trying to wind us up. The other doorman then says to me, 'I know what's coming next, I'm going to nip this in the bud.' We approached the brothers and asked them what their problem was. They said to us, 'There's no problem,' so we left it at that. Shortly a pal of us came over and informed us that the ugly twins were letting everyone know what they were going to do to us. Without any hesitation, I and the other doorman went straight over to sort it out. The other doorman approached the first brother and noticed he had a bottle in his hand; the other brother also had a bottle. Before he had time to raise his hand with the bottle in it, he was staring at the ceiling after getting caught with a peach of a right hook. I was now pulling the other doorman off him and we seemed to have had the situation well in hand.

His brother thought twice about getting involved until he saw the mess on his brother's face; that's when the sneaky bastard tried sticking a bottle in us. There was no holding back now and he got everything he deserved. We dragged the two brothers out of the club and there were about fifteen steps we had to get them down. You had to be there to believe it, two unconscious twin brothers being dragged down steps by two bouncers. Halfway down the stairs the ugly twin that I was dragging started to come round. I grabbed him by the ankles and ran him down the stairs as fast as I could, then the other doorman started shouting at me to stop because his head was hitting every step and he was out cold once more. We left them outside the club in a right mess and went back inside. A couple of minutes later and they are outside giving us the usual abuse about comebacks. All of a sudden this local prick that had been banned from the club started fighting with them. It only lasted about ten seconds as the police turned up and arrested them. We later found out that because of the state of the brother's face, that the prick they were fighting with was charged with GBH and had been sent down for eighteen months.

Dave Harper, Reading

This white guy walked in with his very attractive black girlfriend. They went straight up to the bar. For some unknown reason I felt trouble was on the cards; working the door you sometimes get that feeling and it usually proves to be right. Must have been an hour later when these three black guys started to cause trouble towards this guy and his girlfriend. It was obvious that they didn't like what they saw, a white guy with an attractive black girl. They started to push this white guy around a bit, so I rush downstairs to stop the fight. I grabbed two of the guys while the other door staff grabbed the other one and threw them out. The white guy thanked me for basically saving his life – well that's what he tells people today. We have kept in touch since then and have become good friends.

Douglas Gentles, Cardiff

While at Luigi's we had problems most weekends with the gypsies from the big site over at Roverway in Cardiff. They were friendly enough with the doormen but there was always a group of guys that would not take kindly to them being in the club and before you knew it all hell would break out. Nine times out of ten the gypsies would win the fight. I can only recall one time when we had to fight with them, again started off by some guys picking a fight with them. The gypsies didn't take kindly to us the doormen throwing them out when it was the other group of guys that had started the fighting. Overall the gypsies were a dangerous group of people; they fought hard and always looked after their own, something I respect. They also never let someone take a liberty with them, again something I respect. Something I have noticed with gypsies over the years working the doors is that people still hate them being in their pub or club. Whenever gypsies came into Berlins while I was working there, there was normally a fight involving them. There is something about gypsies – they always seem to attract trouble.

Brendan Driscoll, South Wales

It was still quite early and we hadn't had any trouble so far. I was standing in front of the DJ box with this other bouncer. There were two dance cages right by us next to the bottom of the dance floor. I could see this boy was starting to get a bit rowdy; he was clearly out of his head on pills. He then got up in one of the cages and starts dancing like a lunatic. All of a sudden he jumped straight out of one of these cages onto the dance floor about ten feet below. Luckily he didn't land on anyone but quite a few people were upset by him, so I went over to have a word. Before I could say anything he comes running at me throwing punches. He was a big guy and looked right off it. The other bouncer got in between the two of us and things start to calm down, but you could see he wasn't going to leave without a fight. He fancied his chances with me, so I told the other bouncer, 'OK then, just leave him go.' The boy then comes flying straight at me.

I hit him once to the temple and flattened him. For such a big guy I thought he would have put up more of a fight. As he came around we took him to the top of the stairs and he started getting aggressive but this time to the other bouncer. I grabbed him by his belt and rammed his head into the side of the staircase. He still put up a fight so I threw him down about twelve stairs. When he hit the bottom there was a sickening thud and the head doorman comes running over to see if he's still alive. He picked the boy up and when the boy tried to get to his feet he couldn't stand, as his legs were fucked. The tough guy then starts yelling for the police, so the head doorman let him drop to the floor.

The police turned up and asked what had happened. I explained that the guy had jumped out of a ten-foot cage out of his head on drugs and he must have done the injury then. I told the policeman there was a whole dance floor full of people who seen the guy jump, so I was in the clear if it went to court. Anyway, he wouldn't have had a leg to stand on.

Shaun Kelly, Ebbw Vale

One of the most frightening situations I've been involved in was when there had been a fight in this pub. We ran over and grabbed hold of these three boys and chucked them out as quick as we could through the doors. We turned back around to go into the pub and there were loads of people running at us. Both myself and the other doorman thought that we were 'brown bread'. Next thing you know they are running straight past us. It turned out they were coming out to help us. We were very lucky as we wouldn't have had a chance against all these people. It turns out the boys we chucked out weren't much liked in the town. You can always tell if you've doing a good job on the door by the respect the regulars give you.

John Scriven, South Wales

We had a couple of famous DJs in who thought they were something. One of the DJs had taken some Es and was staring at some boys and losing it. I went over and told him to calm down or we'd chuck him out. I don't know if he thought himself royalty or he thought we wouldn't throw him out of the club. The other bouncer Lee went and had a word with him and the DJ starts getting in his face saying, 'You can't chuck me out, I'm the DJ.' Lee grabbed him by the face and chucked him over this table. A couple of his mates came running in. I started screaming at them and it turns out that all his mates were the DJs. By now we didn't give a fuck and threw most of them out. We ended up with one or two DJs left. Lucky they didn't get involved as well or there would have been no night left.

Duncan Ferguson, Torbay, South Devon

I had been working the doors for about four months in a nice, quiet and posh type of pub. It was £3.50 for the cheapest beer, so trouble from the types of people that can afford a round of Red Bull and vodkas (£5 for one) was a rarity. The owner of the pub had four other pubs and a nightclub and explained to me that he was not a middleman. He went for the very top and the very bottom. I was asked to move to his nightclub and I agreed.

The nightclub was a real spit-and-sawdust affair. When I was being shown round by the head doorman all I kept seeing were streaks of dried blood on the walls and on the backs of doors. This was obviously what he referred to as the very bottom. The first night was Halloween and boy did the monsters come out. When I refer to the monsters, I mean the women more than the men; some of them I just couldn't tell what sex they were. The night began with a tour of the place, then I was put on the door with another doorman who I'd met before. They all had quite a rep. The people that were coming through the doors were the type of people I'd cross the road from when walking down the street: they'd wear hooded tops with the hood over their head, eyes bloodshot and bulging out with a grimace that could scare the Grim Reaper.

Once the place got busier I was moved from on the door to a location in the club at the top of the stairs. Then it began. I had heard stories of this place and fooled myself into believing that it was all hype but I was wrong. Within ten minutes of being upstairs the first radio shout was made. Now, to say the radios were crap is an understatement; two cups with string between them would have done a better job. All I could get was a muffled crackling. I looked up to see the other doorman running. I scanned to where they were running to and saw a fight between five blokes. When I got to it, one doorman was on top of one of the blokes and had him under control. Another one legged it to the dance floor and so I jumped into what was left, a rugby scrum of two doormen and three blokes fighting. Luckily for us the fight was by the fire escape, so after taking a few and giving a few we managed to push them out through it.

Outside two of the blokes ran off and one was on the floor not moving. That didn't concern me at the time as I was more worried about my colleague in the club with the bloke on the floor. I ran in and we both picked the guy up. A female bystander said that he was the one who got picked on. I said to the bloke, 'Are you all right now?' to which he replied, 'What the fuck's it got to do with you?' I was shocked and before I could blurt out a quick-witted reply, which I had lined up obviously, he swung for the other doorman. We quickly grabbed him by his arms and the other doorman smacked him one once we were outside. We then pushed him down the steel steps.

On congratulating me on a job well done – after all, this was the first time he had really met me – the other doorman noticed the man who was still on the floor by the fire exit with a rather large pool of blood under his head. We called up our first aid guy and got an ambulance to him. I was quite worried as this was the first time I had seen so much claret. It turns out he only lost three-quarters of a pint of blood. It shocked me a bit, like when you spill that much milk on the floor and it spreads out widely and looks a lot more – especially when it's round someone's head.

I went back to my post and thought to myself how great it was and how *this is why I started this job*. In my admiration of self, I was switched off and didn't realise something kicking off under my nose. I looked down at the bottom of the stairs and saw a doorman holding two people apart. I legged it down the stairs and he said it was the guy on his left, who could have been an extra in *Night of the Living Dead*, who had to go. We both grabbed him and started the trudge through what looked like a cemetery. After taking three steps with this guy, the bloke he was initially kicking off with started to punch him in the back of the head. I let go of the *Living Dead* extra and grabbed the other guy. After a brief struggle we got them both out of different exits. I went back to my post yet again.

After twenty minutes the head doorman came over to see how I was doing. As we were talking we saw a woman throwing up all over the bar. We carefully escorted her out but I got two nights' worth of dinner down my leg. We were holding her from behind yet she still managed to tilt her head back and dribble it down her shoulder and onto my leg. I had a few more to throw out over the course of the night for being too drunk, but nothing too hard. It was at the end of the night when things got bad.

The last song of the night was 'Operation Blade' by Public Domain. How fitting that the scenes to come looked like the club scene in the film *Blade*. I saw a scuffle between two blokes. I ran over and began to split them up with another doorman. Six or eight blokes started to whack me and the other doorman. What erupted after that was a bar brawl. There were five other doormen and myself and those guys, all being circled by the punters on the dance floor. What made the fight even better was that the punters were throwing drinks and ashtrays at us as we were fighting. We managed to knock a few over and buy time to chuck a couple out.

After about a minute of fighting, which felt like an hour, I stayed by the fire exit and was chucking out anyone on the outside of the brawl – people who were involved, of course. We got them all outside and thankfully the police were out the front so they took it from there. It turns out it was a rugby team and the two blokes knew each other and were fighting over a disagreement that happened on the pitch the day before. The end of the night came and not a minute too soon. We cleared up and kicked out and sat back and reflected on the night. I was shocked at just how rough this place was, but somehow it felt good working there, so when the head doorman offered me a permanent place, I accepted. I went home to my girlfriend and she asked how my night went and if it was different to my posh pub. I looked down at myself: blood splatters and patches on my shirt, sick down my leg, a sore, swollen head and totally fatigued. 'Not that much,' I replied.

Bernard Driscoll, South Wales

Once on the door in Birmingham years ago, I had gone in to break up this fight. I bent down to grab this one boy off the other and felt a pain in my back. I thought nothing of it and took the boy out. Five minutes later one of the doormen says to me, 'Look at your shirt.' I found the whole back of my shirt was red. I had been bottled in the back and hardly felt it as I was so worked up in getting those boys out.

Kirk Johnson, Stoke on Trent

It was a routine night on the door: me in charge, my Welsh mate Taffy and my girlfriend Nicky on reception/main door. The regular crowd started to enter, as it usually does on a strip club door – you get more regulars than passers-by, though God knows why; who doesn't want to see naked women dancing for them with no strings attached? The night is going really well until the local non-league football team decide to show up on the door. I have running through my mind, *not bloody likely, not tonight, we are under-staffed and I feel like shit with the flu.* So I said to the team, 'Not tonight lads, it's a private party.' As they are about to walk off, out comes the owner of the club and states, 'It's OK lads if you want to come in at the usual price.' I already have thoughts running through my mind about the carnage that is to follow, after me first jumping up and down on the fat shit's head for letting them in. All thirty-two of the team are let in (it's the A team and the B team plus subs and coaches – oh joy). Our door team are on full alert and waiting for it to start.

No longer than an hour had passed when it started to happen. At first it was just a minor argument amongst themselves which was easily sorted with a bit of tact. Fifteen minutes later it started to go tits up again. This time one of the dancers complained of one of the team trying to touch her up, which was the last straw. The culprit was removed from the venue with minimum fuss but this left thirty-one of his friends inside and only three door staff. The odds looked good – for them. Thankfully these guys had had a lot to drink by this time and it took them a while to notice that their friend was missing. This gave myself and my team the time needed to come up with a game plan, which basically was to knock out as many as possible without getting killed. At the time it sounded like a good idea until the boss came out again asking if we could throw them out all in one go. This was my reply, 'Fuck you, fat boy, you let them in when I never wanted to. You want me to run the door how I want to, then you undermine me. Now when the shit hits the fan you want me to bail you out. Well fuck you. Sort it out yourself.'

Unfortunately I only got to the 'bail you' bit when a body came flying past me at Mach 1, followed by another at about the same speed. Taffy had had enough and the anti-social twat had started without me (just bad manners that). I turn to see a player going for Taffy with a bottle, so on reflex I get a headlock on the player and hurled him outside. By this time Nicky had disposed of a couple more from the side exit. They were now at the front door. Still with the headlock on the player, I felt a faint blow to the side of my head. One of the cheeky twats had come through the main reception area straight past the boss and slapped a sucker punch up the side of my head. When the realisation hit me I had just been punched, I heard, 'Come on, let's twat the doorman.' I am thinking to myself, *doorman singular, oh shit! I am on my own here*. That's when it happened: I saw this mop-headed youth come running headlong for me waving a bottle.

Little beknown to mop-head boy, I have been training in martial arts on and off for ten years. As he's running at me shouting he's giving me the warning to look up that I need and the valuable time required to gather my thoughts enough to front-kick him straight under the chin, which sent him straight to the floor, crying like a little bitch. Thankfully at this time Taffy has come flying through the main doors into everyone like a little Welsh Scud missile and Nicky is following, throwing punches at anything that moved, which gave the management enough time to actually do something useful and drag us back in by the scruffs of our necks like little schoolchildren.

After fifteen minutes of them trying to punch and kick the door down, they got bored and went for a curry, I think. Taffy ended up with a split lip, a black eye and a bad jaw. I ended up with a black eye and a bump on the side of my head and Nicky ended up with bruised knuckles from punching people. On seeing the devastation done to his club, the boss says, 'If they come back again don't let them in, they are barred.' My reply was, 'No shit Sherlock, if I'd had my way in the first place this wouldn't have happened. You fucking fat cunt, now fucking fuck off before I batter you as well.' And that's how three door staff managed against thirty-two people. It wasn't pretty and was scary as hell. After the night we sat around talking about how lucky we were that not all the team wanted to fight and that most of them just walked – and for that I thank God.

Brendan Driscoll, South Wales
A mate of mine had taken the night off from the door and was out with his wife drinking. This one drunken prick comes up behind her and starts grabbing her arse. Now, as any man would have done, he's smashed the prick straight in the mouth. I ran over with this other bouncer to break it up. Everyone had stopped in their tracks to watch what was happening. I then noticed that the prick he was fighting with was with about fifteen guys from an amateur boxing club from the Valleys. Before you know it, it's gone right up and there's this huge fight, which goes on for about five minutes. We managed to get them all out in the end. Now those guys weren't your average pissheads on a Saturday night, they knew how to fight. The fight ended up spilling onto the street and I accidentally got booted in the balls by one of our own doormen.

There were bodies lying everywhere unconscious and blood all over the pavement. When the police came, they moved the boxers on and we had all the threats of comebacks. They were all shouting, 'You're fucked next week because we are bringing up our mate who's going to kill you all.' We started pissing ourselves laughing. You could see the confused look on all of their faces. The thing was the guy they were on about who was going to kill us was actually a doorman who had worked for us for years. When we told him about the incident, he wasn't very happy they had been throwing his name about, so he went to see the boxers and they ended up having another beating, off him this time.

Steve Wraith, Newcastle

The stars were arriving thick and fast at Sea nightclub. I had looked after a few people in London so was designated to look after any VIPs that came in. Looking after the stars is the easy bit, it's keeping the public at bay that tests your patience.

With Robbie Williams, we weren't sure whether he would be turning up at all, so we kept the whole club open. Then out of the blue he arrived with about thirty people in tow. We had to ask ordinary punters to leave their seats and make room for him. Needless to say there were a lot of people with their noses out of joint: 'Why should we move for him, has he paid to get in? Will he be here next week?' I agreed with their arguments but I was just doing what I was told.

Once the area was cleared, Robbie appeared and the drinks started to flow. Bottle after bottle of the finest champagne was downed as more and more people flocked upstairs to get a view of their idol. He was a lot smaller than I imagined and was jumping all over the place. If he had been anybody else he would have been chucked out. A lot of girls were trying to get past me to get to Robbie, some even offering their services if I would just let them past. Not a chance. Even some people who should have known better started to say that they would report me to the owner if I didn't let them in. I couldn't understand why someone would want to embarrass themselves like that.

Just as we had things under control, Robbie jumps up again and starts singing his number one hit 'Angels'. Well the place went mental as his fans sang back to him. I wasn't impressed. I was just glad I wasn't his personal security because they really had their work cut out. The paper next day reported that Robbie had bought everyone in the club a drink. Well we didn't get one and there was talk of an alleged £3,000 bar bill outstanding. That's rock and roll.

Pop band Steps caused the same kind of mayhem. They didn't have as many followers as Mr Williams but their security asked us to make sure that no one took any photos of them. Talk about mission impossible. The usual faces tried to gatecrash the VIP section but with no success. The owner had taken to switching his phone off when a VIP arrived so it was no use those wankers phoning him either. As the flashes went off, their security started to argue with punters and some arguments became quite heated. One couple just wanted a photo for their kids and the band had said yes but the security said no. The couple started to hurl abuse at the minders, who expected me to throw them out, but they caused it so they could deal with it.

I was waiting for them to burst into song just to round my night off but thankfully it never happened. One star I wouldn't have minded singing was Marti Pellow, former lead singer with Wet Wet Wet. I always enjoyed their stuff but when he visited us he was very low key, no minders, no entourage, just himself, a very nice feller indeed.

Wayne Power, Swansea

It was near the end of the night and I was about to order my food when trouble flared up in the club. Peter, the other doorman with me, and myself ran into the club. We dragged a few out and things then calmed down. Off I go and order my food in the Chinese fish shop nearby. One lad who had just been thrown out of the club was now outside the fish shop, challenging anyone to fight him. I walk around him and make my way to the shop and I notice the lad approach two guys and ask them if they wanted trouble. Suddenly one of them steps forward and sprays him in the eyes with CS gas. They then turn to walk away. As they pass by me one of them looks over and winks at me. I ignore the lad screaming on the floor and enter the fish shop and try to place an order with the lady behind the

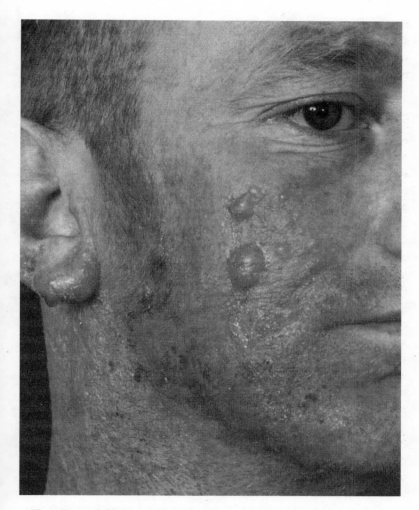

The effects of CS gas on the face: 'If ever a copper threatens you with CS gas or pepper spray, back down, because it's a nightmare.'

counter. I'm still laughing about what happened even as I was being served. My own eyes now start to burn like they were on fire and I had to leave my grub on the counter and make my way back to the club. Seems even though I was quite a distance away from the club the wind had carried some of the CS gas in my direction. I let Peter know what happened and he leaves the club to take the piss out of the lad who is still on the floor screaming his head off. I'll tell you now, if ever a copper threatens you with CS gas, pepper spray or whatever they call it, back down, because it's a nightmare.

Mickey Jones, London

Most of the time in clubs you knew all the scum. They would be the ones who came in every night, knew you by name and always would try to talk themselves out of a situation. I remember going into work and standing talking to the boys when this man came on to us, wanting to know which one of us was the hardest, as he was the so-called hard man in the area. He had a gun and a posse of followers and the attitude of a complete twat. One of the bouncers with us steps forward and says, 'That will be me then.' He was only messing around but this bald bloke steps forward and gives him a left hook to the jaw. The bouncer falls to the floor like a sack of shit.

I decided enough was enough and stepped forward and said to them all, 'Look boys, stop looking for it or you will find it and believe me you won't be the ones walking away.' With that, this bloke looked at me and started walking back and fore, winding up the boys he was with. By now I was really wound and knew there was only one way this could go. I threw a good right at the twat and caught him on the side of his face. He stood and took it and I thought to myself, *this is going to take some doing*. He then proceeded to wind me up some more, each time turning back to the boys and rallying them up. As he turned back to face me, I swung at him and caught him square on the chin.

We all ended up in the middle of the street fighting, fifteen doormen and a passing dog against what seemed like thirty boys. It was after that night I realised that I enjoyed the thrill of working on the doors. I've made a lot of friends and a hell of a lot of enemies. The bald guy came back once more after that and apologised to me for starting the trouble. He didn't realise that I don't take apologies from guys like him and I never forget a face.

Dave Harper, Reading

It was just a normal night at a club where I was head doorman with four guys working for me. Two of them were ex-convicts, the other two had reputations for handling themselves and I knew them from years ago, so I could trust them. I was known as 'the Cooler': I would cool a situation while the other guys were talking with their fists. I always use my mother's quote, 'If you don't listen, you'll feel.'

The night went smoothly until I was outside with the owner chatting away when this girl came out and said, 'There's a man keeps pestering my friends.' I casually walked in and saw these two guys fighting. The other doormen were nowhere to be seen. I grabbed one of them who was causing trouble and threw him out with his friend. I didn't think of the danger I was in. Once I got them outside I told them not to come back. One of them decided to take his chances and try to take me on. He insulted my family by saying, 'You black bastard, you come here and take our jobs and our women.' I was seething inside. I asked the receptionist to look after my watch and bracelet. I went up to him and asked him politely not to be so rude (I had a smile on my face). He started to walk towards me. I thought for the moment this guy was brave or stupid and straight away gave him eight punches to the head. He fell to the ground. When I was hitting him his face was swelling and he looked like an alien.

I then looked at his mate and suggested to him to go home to his mum. I looked at my fists and I didn't have a mark on but I had blood all over my shirt. The other doormen came out and wanted to know who did that to the guy's face. The receptionist said, 'Dave did.' They were quite shocked, as they know me as the Cooler. The police were called and I quickly changed my blood-stained shirt (as you never know what may happen, always be prepared for the worst). The police wanted to speak to me. I told them these two guys were fighting and I stopped it. They said, 'How did his face turn out like that?' I told them that I didn't know. The guy turned up two weeks later to collect his belongings and when he saw me he was shaking like a leaf.

Peter Edwards, Chepstow

I have always managed to stay on the right side of the police. Like us, they are just doing their job. You can get some bad ones but most are on your side. I once worked a club by myself and the first function I did was a police party, 150 coppers all getting pissed and making fools of themselves. Some of the bigger rugby players amongst them were weighing me up all night watching me and after every pint they had they felt braver. A few tried to bump shoulders with me as they passed but I told them that, police or no police, if they did it again they were getting clumped. I couldn't believe the attitude on them all. They were acting like infants.

At the end of the night there were only about twenty left. One big fucker was up on the table, dancing like a fool; why they always have to climb on a table I never know. As I walk over to have a word with him, this big lump puts his hand on my shoulder and pulls me back, saying, 'Leave him alone mate, it's my boss, he's only having fun.'

'Well mate,' I tell him, 'I'm all for having fun but if he doesn't get off that table soon I'm going to get him down myself. Oh, and by the way, if you ever put your hand on my shoulder and pull me like that again, I'm going to snap it along with your neck.' He steps back as if to throw a punch but thinks twice about it and walks over to help his boss off the table. The rest of the night went well but what would I have done if the big fucker had thrown a punch? Bet you a pound to a bucket of crap the twenty coppers would have said I started it had we come to blows.

About a year ago some women were fighting outside the club and a pretty young policewoman went up to them and read the riot act. From out of nowhere, one of the girls' boyfriends pushed the police-woman and had his hand clasped around her face. She just stood there in shock; from ticking off the girls she was now in a dangerous situation – something she couldn't handle. I ran from the door of the club and grappled the guy to the floor and the policewoman kept the guy's girlfriend off me until the police wagon came to take them all away. I was expecting the copper to thank me but she just got in the wagon and disappeared with the rest of them. About an hour later someone started to knock loudly on the main door to the club. It was the copper from the party I bounced before. This time he was all in uniform and looked in a temper.

'Who's the bouncer who helped one of our girls out tonight?' he asked.

'I did.'

He shook my hand and told me the officer was a little shaken up and forgot to thank me. 'Thank god there's good bouncers like you on the door mate,' he said, before he left. Don't think he recognized me or maybe he did and just didn't want to say anything.

Ari Bolden, Victoria, Canada

It was a quiet night and for some reason Tony and I were the only ones on. Tony had worked with the company before and came back to work as a bouncer a couple of nights a week. He was Hungarian and had this thick accent. We called him Arnold because he looked and sounded like Schwarzenegger. I had heard stories from my boss about Tony:

'Tony was crazy,' he used to tell me.

I was called inside by one of the bartenders. I looked in and saw one of our former bouncers, Doug, in a verbal argument with a troublemaker named Sid. Now, this guy Sid was a known asshole, bully and had a bad nose-candy habit. He had been barred from every nightclub in town except ours. I looked down to see Doug and Sid face-to-face, yelling at one another. Now, Doug was an old-school bouncer who loved the violence but he was a brother nonetheless.

As I approached, I saw Sid's cousin, Miguel, lift a beer bottle and hit Doug over the head with it. My trigger had gone off. As anyone knows who is in this business, bouncers have a brotherhood between them and the moment you touch a doorman, all bets are off. I ran up and knocked the bottle from Miguel's hand. I spun him around and slapped on a chokehold. I dropped him in about five seconds, right in front of the bar. I noticed that Doug was pushing Sid out the side door.

The next thing I saw was Tony. His eyes seemed to be bursting from his head and he was heading towards me like a freight train. He was a pit bull with a nasty disposition. His face said it all. I yelled, 'Tony, Tony, he's out, he's out.' Tony grabbed the unconscious Miguel by his ponytail and began to drag him out of the club by it. He turned to me and said, 'I'll show you fucking out!' Tony dragged Miguel out the front door by his hair. In the process, Miguel's pants got pulled down to his shoes. Tony grabbed his head and smashed it against the rock wall. He kept saying, 'You want to use a bottle? You want to use a bottle?'

At this point, Sid came around the corner and Miguel was coming to – to a whole lot of pain, I might add. I just stood there, watching Tony do his work. Tony spun around and open-hand-slapped Sid so hard that it sent him crashing to the ground. Miguel stood up, only to get punched out by Tony. Sid stood up, holding his face. He was wide-eyed and scared. Now, Sid is the type of scumbag that picks fights with anyone and tries to be a tough guy. He plays the *I am crazy so don't mess with me* attitude. Tony one-punched him in the head, sending him down for a second time. It was like watching a tennis match. Bing. Bong. Bing. Bong. My boss and I finally pulled Tony away. Both Sid and Miguel grabbed onto each other and limped away.

Tony was a trained fighter in jiu-jitsu and shootfighting. But on top of that, he was *crazy* and *mean*. He was celebrating his fortieth birthday that night as well. I went inside to check on Doug, who had been cut open by the bottle. He was fine but his white dress shirt was ruined from all the blood. He thanked us for doing our jobs and left. The night ended without a hitch and I kept thinking about what I saw earlier that night. Tony sure impressed the hell out of me and you couldn't pay me a million bucks to pick a fight with that man. You see, bouncers fall into two categories: the doorman and the hardman. Tony was the real deal and as hard as they come.

I was standing in the parking lot at about 2:20 A.M. when a Ford Explorer came racing down and stopped in front of the club. Out jumps none other than Sid and his idiot cousin Miguel. They both were holding clubs. Actually, Sid had a shovel handle and Miguel had a four-foot piece of ABS pipe. I ran inside and yelled to Tony, who was walking around the dance floor looking for cash.

'TONY!'

He looked up at me and went into that mode yet again. We ran outside. I saw Sid and Miguel looking for us. They were drunk and enraged. I headed towards Miguel while Tony moved on Sid. As I neared Miguel, I could see the fear in his eyes. Fear because he hadn't counted on us coming after them with weapons in their hands. Fear because he knew he was in over his head. Fear because he was looking at Sid and what Tony had just done to him. I glanced over my shoulder to see Tony walking towards Miguel and me with the club in his hand. Sid was unconscious on the wet pavement.

Tony tossed my boss the club and in his best *Terminator* accent said, 'Hold this.' Apparently, Tony had struck Sid with such force that the club went flying from his hands and Tony grabbed the club in mid-air as Sid fell over. Miguel stood there frozen. I moved to the side and grabbed the pipe. I smashed Miguel's knee with my boot and he crumpled to the ground. Tony and I got on top of him. I put one of Miguel's hands in an arm lock. Tony had the pipe with both hands at this point with his knee in Miguel's chest. Miguel was shitting green. Tony shouted, 'You want to use this on me? You think you are tough with your club?' Miguel was screaming that he was sorry and done fighting for the night. However, that switch had gone off in Tony's head and we couldn't turn it off. He started to push the pipe towards Miguel's eye. *Holy shit, he's going to take out Miguel's eye*, I thought to myself. I grabbed the top of the pipe with the help of my bartender. We kept moving it from left to right, so that Tony didn't make a shish kebab out of Miguel's eye.

It's very rare to see a grown man cry but Miguel was sure good at it. Tony finally got off, not before bitch-slapping Miguel silly. I told Mr Cry Baby it was over and it was time to get the fuck out of our property. I let Miguel up and he was so rattled and scared that he actually shook our hands after and thanked us. Can you believe it? He thanked us after we kicked the crap out of him. He went running off to the truck. Sid had already gotten up and run for the hills, leaving his cousin to fend for himself. So much for family and watching one's back.

We all went back inside, Tony was being treated like a superhero by all the staff. I retired to the back bar with him and said, 'Shit Tony, you were going to put that guy's eye out with that pipe.' He looked at me and smiled slightly. 'I remember putting a guy's eye out at McDonald's one night. The thing just burst, real messy like. I guess I'm just an eye kind of guy.' He went off chuckling to himself, while we all stood there, stunned.

The moral of the story: While it is good to have these guys on your side, you can't control them. You decide which is the lesser of the two evils.

Mickey Jones, London

When I worked as a doorman in London, things were a lot different in the old days. If you gave someone a clout you would have little or no comeback on it. These days you get a lot worse. I've been a doorman for 25 years on and off and have had my fair share of scrapes. I remember one time when I was working in this nightclub and the manager decided that he'd had enough of the scum that would come in to take advantage of the kids in the clubs. The boys I worked with were also in on it; they would let the dealers in for a price (mostly coke) and turn a blind eye to their dealings. I was working with this boy that was new to the trade and was still a little wet behind the ears. I had told him that he should be careful who he chooses as his friends in the club, as I had been tipped off that the police were watching a lot of the boys and he was a nice kid and I didn't want to see him get hurt. A month later and he had settled in well, he had started training and had bulked up quite a bit. Fuck knows what he was taking. We were standing outside waiting for the club to fill up when this bloke walks straight up to me and asks me to take a walk with him. Now I'm not a shit-arse but in London you don't go up alleyways with strangers, not even if they have got a big bag of sweets.

I told him, 'I'm not going anywhere mate.'

'Fine then,' he said. 'I'll ring you in ten minutes on your mobile.'

I didn't know this bloke from Adam, so I thought he was full of it. Ten minutes later my phone starts ringing and a voice comes down the line telling me that he has photos that can prove every doorman in the club is involved in a big drug deal that was going down tonight and that if I didn't want to get involved I was to stay on the front with the big lad. Turned out they had been watching the club for months; they even had Old Bill working the door with us. Ten o'clock came and the place was filling up lovely when all of a sudden a little man starts shouting, 'Go! Go! Go!' and all hell broke out all around me. I ended up on the floor with some bastard's boot on my neck and the other boy ended up with a dog on his. The police took statements from us and let us go; the others weren't so lucky though and got charged.

I worked the clubs for a few years after that but each time the rave music did my head in and I packed it in. I was like the Littlest

Hobo with no club of my own. I've met a few good people on the door and some not so good. The people you meet working on the door are the people who thrive in the thick of it. Doormen are the unofficial weekend police and once you're a doorman, you will be for the rest of your life.

Martin Bayfield, Rhyl

I was working in this pub once and a few well-known hard men came in. I hadn't been bouncing long. Now the one of them, Martin, is right out of it on drink and drugs. The landlord asks us to get him out. I knew Martin a little and asked him to leave but he ignored me completely and carried on. The other three with him start fucking about as well. I'm starting to look a right stupid prick. The boy with me starts getting a bit nasty and threatens Martin, who then decides that now I'm his mate and comes over to chat with me. He's only a small fucker but won't think twice about sticking a knife in your ribs. 'I don't like your mate's attitude so first chance I get I'm going to cut him up with this,' he informs me and puts his hand in his pocket. I knew he must have smuggled a knife into the pub, God knows how because we search everyone, so before he can pull it out I hit him as hard as I can in his mouth. Both his lips split wide open as he slumps to the floor.

Everyone in the pub saw what happened so I knew his mates, who were feared men around here, would be up for it. I walk over to them and point at the biggest and baddest of them all. 'I want you to pick up that twat and get him and yourselves out of here in the next few seconds or I'm coming down on you like a ton of bricks. I've had a gut-full of pricks like you and if I have to put an end to it tonight, then so be it,' I shout at him while screwing my face up to look harder than I am. I expect he could beat me in a fair fight; with his mates behind him he could probably put me and the other bouncer in hospital for a while. The one thing that he wasn't banking on was someone confronting him face-on. Everyone backs down to him and his mates so this was something that they didn't expect. 'Fair enough mate, we were just off anyway,' he very politely tells me.

They walk out with the one with the cut-to-fuck mouth and never bothered us again. Made me a local hero for a while and after word got around we seldom had any trouble off anyone. I can't say that confronting your enemy square on is the best method but in some situations it can be. Oh, and the one who I laid out, Martin, got slashed across the face a while later by someone who had a bigger knife than he had. He's now known as Zorro because he has a perfect Z cut into his cheek.

Mark Thomas, South Wales

I was working in this nightclub and I was on the stairs leading people upstairs into the club. I notice this one boy has a bottle in his hand, so I shout and tell him that he can't take a bottle upstairs into the club. The line of customers starts to go down and this boy is still there with his bottle in his hand. Once more I shout down and tell him again. The line starts moving again and the boy now tries to walk past me still with the bottle in his hand. I thought to myself, *he's taking the piss*, so I grab him and shout, 'Are you fucking deaf or what?' I then grab him and chuck him down the stairs and out through the main doors. As I walk back in, another doorman comes on to me and asks what happened. I inform him and he shakes his head and starts laughing. Turns out the boy was as deaf as a post and was wearing a hearing aid. You can't imagine the shit I had that night off the other doormen.

A couple of years later I was working with this other doorman when the same boy shows up. The doorman then starts telling me that he had knocked this deaf boy out with a slap a few months earlier. It turns out although he was deaf he was a right idiot who was always looking for trouble. After all those years, I now didn't feel so bad.

Michael Jones, London

I've worked the door for a long time and people come and go. There are a lot of good boys out there and sometimes you do get thanks, but a lot of the time you just get shit. Like this one night, I had helped this bloke out. He had gone onto this huge lump of a bloke who had grabbed his missus by the tit. He had given him a few clouts, then dragged him to his feet screaming at him, 'You don't know who I am do you? You don't know who I am.' I grab hold of him and pull him off the bloke. The other bloke then turns round and has a go at me for interfering. By now I was really pissed off and ended up giving the two of them a good fucking clump. Worst thing was, I ended up in the local nick for the night and they went home their separate ways.

beyond the call of duty

SOME THINGS ARE in the job description for a doorman: opening doors, searching customers, stopping trouble and keeping the arse-holes out, to name just a few. The average customer can see them doing those things and the job looks pretty straightforward. The things they don't get to see are doormen picking up hypodermic needles, fighting off gangs on the main door, the attacks on their own homes, defending themselves against knife or gun attacks or the number of times they have to wait for hours in the local hospital to get some wound stitched up.

Beyond the pleasantries and bow ties, there is a constant element of danger. A sixth sense for potential trouble and raw instinct for survival are the invisible tools doormen rely on. A doorman can never remember all the punters that cause trouble but they can remember the doormen and where to find them. Bouncers lose count of the amount of times they hear the words, 'I will be back to shoot you.' Most are drunken Friday-night gangsters, but in the backs of their minds bouncers are well aware it only takes one, just one, lunatic to mean it. So, next time you think to yourself, *I can do that job easy*, think again. There's more to it than you know.

Richard Williams, Aberdare, South Wales
I was just collecting a few glasses early on in the night when, as I walked upstairs, I noticed this thick trail of blood on the floor. I followed it, expecting the worst because of the sheer amount of

blood. The trail led to the men's toilets and this guy stopped me from entering, explaining that his girlfriend was ill inside. I went back downstairs and got Sarah, our female member of the door staff. As we got back to the toilets, the girl was coming out. The long skirt she was wearing was drenched in blood and she looked a right state. As they took her down stairs, I went and checked on the toilets. There was blood everywhere; the cubicle walls had blooded handprints all over. I looked down the toilet and realised the girl had miscarried. I went to check on the girl and found her outside sitting by a wall. Her boyfriend said he was taking her home. We phoned an ambulance and got her off to hospital. Being a farmer, I was the one who had to clean up the toilets; not the best job I've ever done, I can tell you.

Terry Turbo, North London

The most frightening situation I have ever been in was when I was at the Rex in Stratford [East London]. These three guys refused to be searched and were refused entry. It was only 11.30 P.M. and there was quite a large queue outside. These guys kept saying, 'We're going to end your night, we're going to finish your dance.' People started walking away from the queue because they felt intimidated by these guys. I lost it and ran over to them and said, 'Get away from the door or I'll end your fucking night with a trip to intensive care!' They then backed away and started shouting things like, 'You pusshole.'

I walked around the side of the club and one of them shouted, 'Do you fucking want it?' I was like, *yes please*, and as I walked towards this cunt I saw him pull something out of his pocket which I thought was a knife, so I got my cosh out and carried on walking towards him. He kept saying, 'Don't make me do it, don't make me do it.' I thought, what the fuck is this guy on about, and then I heard the words, 'Terry, he's got a gun.' I froze in my tracks and I really did see my life flash before me. I then backed off and the guy ran away. He was willing to do all that, which incidentally was all recorded on CCTV, and he's now serving a long term in prison. How the fuck can you work out how to deal with these people? I blame the parents!

Craig Patterson, Abbey, Essex

The local Safeway store was holding its annual party and one of the clubs I work at was hosting it. The night was going well, no trouble, no unwanted guests, nothing. I even had time to enjoy some of the buffet that was on offer and managed to squeeze in a dance with one or two of the girls (not very professional, I know, but things were going so well). The end of the night came and almost everyone has gone home except myself and the other doorman, the bar staff and the head of the committee at Safeway. We're all enjoying a nice drink and saying what an easy night it had been when WHACK! The committee leader collapsed in a heap on the floor. We go round to take a look and he's lying there, face down, with a pool of blooding coming from his head. Ignoring just about every first aid rule there is, I lift him up and prop him against the bar to see where the blood's coming from. There was a nasty gash just above his eye and the bloke was sparko. We get some tissue but it's bleeding quite heavily so I ask for an ambulance to be called, as he may need stitches. In the meantime he's still out cold and my drink is getting warm.

The ambulance crew turn up and take over. The guy comes round and refuses to go to hospital, saying that he wants to go home. After much deliberation, the ambulancemen state they can't force him to go to the hospital if he doesn't want to. I ask him how he's going to get home, as he can't even walk. He gives me a blank look so I offer to give him a lift, as long as he doesn't bleed or be sick in my car, which I had just cleaned inside that day. I haul him into the passenger seat and he directs me to his house, I lift him over the road and plonk him on the doorstep. I bang on the door a few times in an attempt to wake up his missus – no answer. He gives me a set of keys and I manage to let myself in, leaving him leaned up against the wall in the hallway.

I stamp up the stairs and manage to wake up his missus, who was a little shocked to see the bouncer from the club on her upstairs landing (although she was also probably quite excited). I explain what had happened to her hubby so she's aware if he passes out again, and that the cut on his eye was caused by the floor and not the door staff. She says okay, probably still a little shocked by it all, so I leave him there bleeding over his wife's nightie. If that's not customer service I don't know what is.

Darryl Taskers, South Wales

At the pub I have been working in for the past year you can guarantee there will be trouble every weekend. It's earned the nickname Roadhouse after the film. You'd throw troublemakers out and just close these two reinforced glass doors behind you. They can take amazing amounts of pressure and the stuff that's smashed against them hasn't even scratched them yet. It's only a small pub but when it kicks off, it kicks off big time. It's like everyone's waiting to join in. We try to control how many come in but then the owner ends up giving the manageress shit about why his takings are down. It's not like the bloke's short as he's a millionaire and he won't even buy the pub some police radios for security.

There was this wanker in the pub, one of the town's so-called hard men, and he was waving this Stanley knife about. When he left we couldn't pass the message on to other pubs and clubs as we didn't have the radios. We then found out the next day he went over to the local nightclub and was offering all the doormen out to fight him until the police came. The doormen didn't even know he was tooled up because of our boss being too tight to buy the radios.

Jamie O'Keefe, London

When I worked with my mobile security team, we would get called to go into a club and smash and bash the problem guys, drag them out and then be on our way. This left the in-house doormen out of the situation. These were the most violent times because it was real. Over that five-year period I was stabbed and cut twice, shot at close range and was also on the receiving end of a stomp or two to the head. It amazes me to think of some of the situations I've been involved in and all just for a night's money.

Lyn Morgan, South Wales

I've had some scary times on the door, like when one bloke had a mild heart attack, but the worst I seen was this bloke who had a major haemorrhage. I'd gone to the toilet and this bloke is sitting on the toilet and the floor's like a sea of blood. I've asked him who hit him and he just looks at me, mumbling. I used three rolls of toilet paper trying to stop it. I phoned the ambulance and kept talking to him. Someone came into the toilets and told him to hold his nose back; he then starts choking, so I've put his head forward. The ambulancemen came and thanked me. We had to close the toilets for the night as it was a bloodbath. The bloke came back a few weeks later and thanked me. Turns out he'd had a major blood vessel break in his nose. He would have died if he'd been there much longer on his own; it took them three days to stop the bleeding.

Daniel Seery, Birmingham

After I had finished work, I was walking down the road when I heard some screaming. I went round to have a look and I saw this girl being beaten by a man. I recognised this girl as she sometimes came to our club. She was a tall, fit, pretty girl but a prostitute. You sometimes wondered why she became one. I spoke to her occasionally and she was in fact a really nice character. I stood there wondering why anyone would want to do anything like that to her. Then I realised it was her pimp beating her because she had not made enough money. I went round to him, grabbed him by the collar and said, 'Oi! You leave her alone.' The fool replied and spat in my face. I brought my head back, butted him right on the bridge of the nose and followed it up with a five-punch combo into his head and a kick to his groin to finish it. I left it at that and walked away.

The next week the prostitute came to the club again like she normally would, only this time she looked worried. She came up to me and thanked me for what I did, and of course offered me free sex. Then she told me that her pimp was coming to pay me a visit and get revenge for what I did to him. I waited all night for him to come but nothing. The night went by and we locked up the club. I then made my way home. On the way, I went down the same street as the day before. Halfway down the road, I noticed the pimp in the car waiting. I thought to myself that there was no way I could back off now, so I bravely carried on down the road.

He jumped out of his car and struck a fist straight into my teeth. To this I replied with a well-placed kick into his bollocks and then a knee to his head. He dropped to the floor, got back up rapidly and knocked me down. I tugged him down with me and we both started to scramble, getting each other into locks, punching, kicking and biting at each other. Then all of a sudden my new 'best friend', the prostitute, put on a knuckleduster and started smacking the pimp all over his face. She was in a proper frenzy. She did that till he was out cold, then I stopped her and escorted her home. I'm still to this day wondering if she had been watching us fight from the beginning, because I certainly never saw her come to us.

Lee Callaghan, South Wales

I was about one week out from entering the Mr Universe body-building contest. The money I made on the door helped towards my training, food and the fare I needed to get to Newcastle, where the show was held. I didn't feel like working as I was tired and the dieting was making me grumpy and short-tempered but had to go in and try my best. I didn't want no hassle and wanted a quiet night. We were short-staffed so we split up and took different areas of the club.

I was standing not far from the ladies' toilets. The barman called me over and explained that a woman had just been punched; seemed I missed it. Looking around I noticed that amongst everyone dancing on the dance floor was a young woman sprawled out on the floor, clutching her bleeding nose. I asked the barman who had done it and he pointed to this big rugby player who had his back to me. I can handle most situations in a nightclub with a calm head but one thing that gets to me is when some bastard lays into a woman. I could feel my blood start to boil and as he turned around I threw a right hook that dropped him out cold. His friend put his hand on my shoulder and explained that though he was with his friend, he didn't want any trouble.

Leaving the other doormen to get the guy I knocked out up off the floor, I went off to the foyer to try and cool down some. There I was confronted by the guy's mate once again, but this time he fancied his chances and waved his arms around shouting abuse at me. I was trying to keep calm but couldn't control my temper, as the weeks of contest preparation had made me so very short-fused. 'Listen,' I said, 'I want a word in your ear.' As he leant towards me

Bodybuilder Lee Callaghan: like many doormen, the job
cost him his marriage.

to hear what I had to say, I bit his ear off. He bent over clutching his
head with blood pouring through his fingers. I kicked him out
through the doors of the club and left him outside with his still
dazed friend.

Not the best way to deal with an unruly customer, I know, but
that's what can sometimes happen. On the spur of the moment

you're capable of going to any extreme. Sometimes other things happening in your life can reflect on the way you deal with someone while you're working the doors. I've seen guys come to work and they have just split with their wives, only to lose it completely when some dickhead starts to wind them up. One thing I couldn't understand about the guy whose ear I bit off was that he never went to the police. I was on edge for weeks waiting for them to knock on my door but thankfully they never came.

It was getting to the end of the shift and I was feeling a little light-headed. Seeing as I had brought my food with me, I decided to get something down my neck. A few of the lads I was working with were having a drink, just unwinding as the shift was more or less over. I got my protein drink out of my bag and started to shake it, as it was in a container that is designed so that when you shake it the protein mixes better than if you stirred it with a spoon. With that the lid comes up and about half a pint of white gooey protein drink spills down my leg. I wipe off most of it but the rest stains my trousers. I didn't think much of this and finished my shift and got off home. Stripped off for bed and left my trousers on the floor for the wife to wash, as you do.

I got up in the morning and thought I was lucky that the police hadn't come about the ear incident. Looking for clothes to wear, I find that my wife has packed all my bags and was chucking me out. 'What's going on?' I ask. 'You know what's going on, I saw what's all over your trousers and I know what you've been up to,' she yells at me. I picked the trousers and proceeded to lick the area where the protein was. Didn't work. Ten months later and I'm still out on my arse. The thing that kills me the most is that the mess was about half a pint's worth; if I could do that I'd be in the record books.

Terry Turbo, North London

We have had five incidents in the last two years where we have had people actually pull guns out on us. Luckily they never used them. That was what got me out of door work and running clubs; fuck the money when it starts getting hot with these silly little kids who are in their early twenties and have seen *New Jack City* and think that if they carry guns and shoot people they will earn stripes and be respected. They either don't think or don't care of the consequences and to me it's too unpredictable. My life is too valuable for me to risk it for some chump change. That's one of the main reasons for my career change at 30 from club promoter/security company owner to actor. The people are nice, it's a great environment to work in, everyone respects each other and you don't have to wear a bulletproof vest to work and having to keep looking over your shoulder.

John Scriven, South Wales

The worst accident I've ever seen in a nightclub happened this one Saturday night. This girl had been messing round with a couple of her mates downstairs in the pub. She had fallen through this door down into the beer cellar. I was first on the scene. There was blood coming out of her ears, mouth and head. She was in a hell of a mess; it looked like she had bitten her tongue off. The other doorman, Paul, took over as he knew a bit more than me at first aid and put her in the recovery position. I actually thought she was going to die. We moved all the beer barrels and made the entrance easier for the ambulancemen and we moved her boyfriend and friends who were in shock out of the way. This hit me hard for a couple of days as I knew the girl really well. I went to visit her in hospital a couple of weeks later and took her flowers and a card. She still couldn't open her one eye and she was now talking with a lisp. I actually think if there weren't doormen there that night she would have died.

Robin Barratt, Manchester

I was working on the front door of a bar/nightclub on Deansgate Locks, Manchester. The Locks had been redeveloped into a row of trendy bars, restaurants, cafes and clubs, all situated under old railway arches and along a wooden causeway overlooking the canal. The venue opened at midday seven days a week, closing at midnight during the week and at 3 A.M. Thursday, Friday and Saturday, when the nightclub was open. Most of us started at around 8 P.M. The only other time they needed doormen was on match days. On this particular day Arsenal were playing at Man City and we expected trouble. A team of four of us were due to start at noon; it was going to be a long day, as we were to stay until it closed. However it was going to be a good earner, and we could take advantage of the free food offered to us.

The day passed relatively peacefully. We had a few football knobheads trying to get in before the match started but they were generally in small groups of two and three and were turned away without much trouble. There was also a heavy police presence on the roads, with regular sounds of sirens rushing by, probably to other clubs and pubs, but thankfully not to ours. The match had finished and four of us were standing outside the closed doors of the venue. We were to vet customers carefully and then, once we were sure they were okay, one of us would open the doors and let them pass us and into the unit. Admittedly is was quite an aggressive way of running the door but that day we couldn't take any chances. Both Arsenal and Man City fans were known to be aggressive and both the police and us expected a lot of problems.

As we were standing chatting we suddenly heard a rumble, quiet at first but quickly growing louder and louder as a horde of Arsenal fans quickly and thunderously made their way towards our unit. It seemed to happen so fast and, before we could get inside and close the doors, we had our backs to the glass and were surrounded by what must have been over 100 screaming, ugly, shaven-haired football yobs. There was nothing we could do; we were all expecting to be slaughtered. They were spitting and flicking cigarette ends at us and, with their fists clenched, were ready to have a go. They were just waiting for someone to make the first move. Once the first punch had been thrown we knew the rest of the pack would quickly move in and we would have been murdered. As I wiped their spit off my face I admit I have never been so scared. I knew I could take two or three down with me but we all would have been beaten and kicked beyond recognition. We were going to die.

At the very moment one of the yobs stepped in to throw the first punch, the screaming sirens of the police surrounded us and riot-clad officers, with batons at the ready, spewed from the back of their wagons, causing the yobs to disperse in every direction. Without a second thought or a moment's hesitation, the four of us scrambled over ourselves to get into the unit and to the safety of being behind closed and locked doors. We must have been the luckiest doormen in Manchester that day.

Douglas Gentles, Cardiff

I have seen customers walk out of a club where I've been working and walk straight into the path of an oncoming car/taxi and go flying through the air. One minute they're dancing and having fun, the next laying on the road dying. What a way to end a night.

A few years ago at a club in Cardiff called Scott's, a young guy was out with friends and family at a party, acting the clown. He started messing about on the railing going around the upper balcony and before any of the boys working could tell him to stop, he slipped and fell down twenty-five or thirty feet to the ground, smashing his skull open on impact. The guy was just history. As the ambulance crew picked him up off the ground, parts of his brain were left all over the floor – one hell of a sight. Scott's closed after this and the owner never reopened the venue.

One Saturday night on St Mary's Street in Cardiff a young girl came out of a club, ran across the road and was caught under the wheels of a big lorry. Needless to say she was dead but the sight of all the blood was bad; the lorry had run over her leg before coming to a stop, the leg just popped and blood and bones were all over the place.

Peter Edwards, Chepstow

I remember one night we were working in this club and we had a team of about eight boys. I was on the door with these two boys and a couple of pricks have just kicked the door in, so we've gone outside. The one boy who is with me we called 'the Bear'; he was about six foot three and twenty-two stone, a walking man-mountain who could pick people up with one hand. He has laid into the pricks and he's giving them a right hiding. One backs off with a bust-up nose and the other few join him across the road in shouting insults at us. The police turn up and they inform them that we assaulted them. After talking to the police and showing them the front door they had kicked in, the police, wanting a quiet night, just moved them on.

During the course of the night I was returning to the main door every half hour to make sure they didn't return to kick it in now we have managed to fix it. There's still quite a line of customers waiting to get in the club, as we have been slow because of the door thing. I notice two of the pricks from earlier sneaking up the other side of the street carrying two huge rocks, which I presume they were going to use to smash down the door. I close the door and tell The Bear that there's a chance we can catch the two pricks as they sneak up. Waiting our chance, we peep through the door and as they creep up we jump out. The pricks were just about to throw the rocks but now suddenly drop them and make a run for it. I thought, there's no way I'm chasing them, but The Bear starts chasing them. He's running down the road like fucking Forrest Gump, and as big as he was he almost catches them, before they all disappear out of sight.

About half an hour later he returns and informs us, 'I had to chase them as they could have hurt someone with those stones.' The stupid fucker must have chased them for about two miles before catching one of them and slapping him around a little. We had to leave The Bear lie down in the manager's office for an hour, as he was well and truly fucking knackered. One of the bar staff had to bring him a nice cup of tea when he felt better.

Clark, South Coast

The owner of the club where I work asked me if I wanted a bit of 'private work' for a couple of weekends. Now private work can take all shapes and sizes, so I asked him, 'Where is it? What needs doing and how much is the pay?' The job was for an Asian friend of my boss who had recently bought a pub in Midhurst [West Sussex] called the Crown. He had put a new manageress in there and wanted someone to watch over her in case anyone stepped out of line and she had to tell them off. He said that Midhurst was a quiet country town and it was a small pub and it would be £100 a night. Not bad, I thought, £100 a night for pub hours and it was only a half hour drive away. The only catch was that he only wanted one person as he didn't want to make a point of having doormen in the place. He also wanted someone who wasn't doorman looking, like a big bodybuilder. As I was about thirteen stone at the time and only five foot eleven, I suited the bill.

The first night came and I thought I'd just wear jeans and a blue shirt and I also took a little something inside my jacket for going to and from my car. When I arrived in Midhurst, my initial impression was that it was a lovely Olde English village, with real old houses, about five pubs and no clubs. I thought, *this shouldn't be too difficult as there can't be any real scumbags up here.* I went in the pub, which had just opened, introduced myself to the manageress and the staff and told them that the owner had asked me to help out in any way I could. I even got a rundown of how to use the glass washer and the till. I asked the manageress if there were any specific problems that I needed to know about. She said that she just wanted some moral support really but there were a couple of idiots to watch out for. I said I was also there to deter anyone from causing trouble in the future and asked just how violent did she want me to be if it did kick off. She looked a bit surprised and said that she would leave that up to me if anything did happen, but everyone was usually very friendly in the village.

It took a while for the pub to get many customers in and I thought I was in for a boring night. However in the space of about an hour, between roughly 8.30 and 9.30, the place really started to get busy. Of course in a small village like this everyone seems to know one another and I was sticking out like a sore thumb, standing at the end of the bar chewing gum, sipping water, minding my own business. A few locals asked me who I was and what I was up to in a friendly manner and I just said I was helping out and stuff. They asked if I was a bouncer and I smiled and asked rhetorically if the place needed one. I had a good chat with a few of them and everything was fine until these two gorillas walked in. Two blokes looked out of place themselves. Both were thirty-five to forty years old, big built, around the sixteen stone mark, builder types with tattoos. One had them all up his neck and they were very cocky. They walked in as if they owned the place. Everyone got out of their way and one of them snogged an unwilling girl on his way to the bar. They clocked me straight away and had a little chat, probably saying, 'Who's the bald twat in the corner then?' They ordered a couple of pints and teased the manageress with the money before paying for them. I was thinking, *shit, I hope those two pricks don't start anything, they look like a right handful.*

Everyone in the pub knew these two and it didn't take a brain surgeon to work out that they were the village bullies. From the moment they walked in, the atmosphere had changed. They seemed very interested in me as they kept chatting and staring over. I just kept chatting but kept them in my peripheral vision. Interestingly, they finished their pints and left. *Thank God for that I thought*, and the pub returned to its original jovial self. A couple of the younger customers told me that the two big guys were Steve and Steve and that they were the local heavies and it wouldn't be a good idea to mess with them, as they were very nasty. They told me a few stories about youngsters who'd crossed them and paid the price. One got thrown through a shop window and the other had his head smashed through a car window. 'Good for them,' I said. 'They sound like real tough guys.'

Half an hour later and the two bullyboys are back looking full of courage. This time they came straight over and while one of them stole someone else's pint, the other one asked, 'Who are you then?' Now I am renowned for being polite, even to idiots, but I could see that these two were not going to be interested in making conversation. 'Who wants to know?' I answered, looking him right in the eyes. At that moment the person whose pint had been stolen returned and, realising what had happened, actually offered to buy the culprit another.

'Well, I am Steve and this is Steve and we run this fucking town, so who are you?'

'I'm just helping out, you know bar work and stuff.'

'You're a fucking bouncer, look at you.'

'No I'm not, I'm not even dressed like a bouncer, but if there's any trouble I'll help out.'

Both of them were staring hard at me by now and I was doing my best not to show the adrenalin rush that was working its way through my body. I was trying to look relaxed and made a point of chewing my gum slowly and using an *I really don't give a shit* type facial expression. At one point Steve number one knocked my pint over by accident and I managed to catch the glass before any spilt. He said I should have been quicker but he looked a bit fazed by it. I don't know how I did it, just lucky I suppose, but it didn't half look good.

'You want watch it mate,' said Steve number one. 'You can't come into someone else's town pushing your weight around. If there's any shit, me and Steve sort it out, and you are going get your comeuppance.'

'Possibly,' I replied.

The other Steve hadn't really said much but was looking very agitated and kept clenching and unclenching his fists. This wind-up must have lasted almost an hour and they were both getting closer and closer to doing something. A space had been made around us and the manageress came over and asked them to stop winding me up and call it a night. I was trying to think what certain doormen I knew would do in this situation. I had come to the conclusion that violence was the only way round this and I was going to have to get very nasty because they were big blokes and I was on my own.

'Right, Steve wants it,' said Steve number one.

'Wants what?' I said.

'You know fucking what. You're going get your comeuppance now.'

Steve number two was pacing about like a caged animal, looking like he was going into frenzy. Then he went off to the toilet.

'Well,' said Steve number one. 'Are you going outside with Steve or not?'

'Look, I've already explained that I'm not here for trouble and I don't want a fight. Just call it a night, eh.'

Steve number two returned looking like he'd just snorted his weight in something. 'Come on then,' he scowled, 'Outside, you and me.' Fists clenched, teeth showing. The pub had gone quiet by now and I realised that this was shit or bust time. Both Steves kept pushing the issue, telling me that I was going to have to go outside or it was going to happen right there and then.

'I'll tell you what then,' I said, trying to sound as confident as I could, 'I'll go outside with Steve and I'll be back in to get you in a minute.'

The manageress was saying something behind me about dropping it, it wasn't worth it and stuff, but my gaze was not leaving the two Steves for one second.

'No,' said Steve number one, 'I'm coming outside too.'

'I see, it takes two of you to beat one of me does it?'

'No, I want to make sure it's a fair fight.'

What was he on about, a fair fight? It was now death or glory time.

'Come on then. You go first.' I pointed Steve number two towards the door, and to my surprise he led the way with Steve number 1 coming behind me.

My brain was working overtime and my heart was beating pretty fast. It's not easy trying to keep an eye on two blokes when one is in front and the other is behind. My plan was that as soon as we got outside the door, I was going to punch Steve number two in the back of his head as hard as I could and then turn quickly to deal with number one. Luckily there were a few people in the way on our way through the pub and Steve number one ended up a few paces back. When we exited the door I couldn't believe that Steve number two took an extra couple of paces towards the street. This was like an invitation. I hit him with a lovely straight right to the lower part of the back of his head and he started to drop so my steel toecaps found their way to booting him in the head. I turned just as Steve number one was coming out and he looked stunned.

'What's going on?' he said.

'THIS.'

I landed a left hook to his jaw that knocked him clean out. This gave me time to stomp on the pair of them a bit and the landlady was telling me that that was enough. So I grabbed Steve number one by the collar and gave him a bit of a shake. He came round, although very dazed.

'You come round here causing shit again and you'll get more of the same, right?' and with that I smacked him with a big right hand. I stood up, smiled at the manageress and calmly walked back into the pub. I was shaking with adrenalin and my right leg was doing an Elvis impression but I don't think anyone noticed. The pub was silent. Everyone just stared at me in disbelief. I went round the back of the bar and put my jacket on because I had a bat and thought the two Steves would be back soon with some mates. One of the barmaids had called the police and handed me the phone. The operator asked what was going on and said something about a riot.

'Everything's okay, just a little scuffle, nothing for you guys to worry about.' I didn't want the Old Bill turning up asking questions.

Back at the bar the locals and the manageress were interrogating me, asking me what martial arts I did and how did I knock the two of them out so quickly. They really couldn't believe the two Steves had been done over so easily by this much smaller man on his own. I got about twenty handshakes before the pub emptied for the night. A patrol car came by and a police sergeant took a statement from me saying that Steve number one wanted to press charges. Steve number one turned up and he had a nasty split in his lip, but he couldn't remember if it was from a punch or a kick. Afterwards the policeman said that he would have loved to have seen them get what they deserved and he shook my hand. I had to go to the police station later on and get formally interviewed but that was a while ago and nothing has come of it. The policeman told me that the two Steves haven't caused any trouble since and that Midhurst is a nicer place because of what I did, which was good to hear. I did another few weekends there but there was no more trouble so the work ended. I was a bit of a celebrity and all the young lads wanted to shake my hand, and buy me a dink. I might pop up to Midhurst for a pint one day, and you never know, I might bump into some familiar faces.

Bernard Driscoll, South Wales

The local rugby team had been playing in a cup match. At the time there were a lot of police officers playing for the team and they have all come into the bottom bar minding their own business. A couple of guys who'd had a run-in with the police officers were drinking there and start taunting them. One lad then goes over and starts arguing with one of the policemen. I go over and give him a warning that if he carries on he's going out. A few minutes later, two of the doormen have gone over to him and asked him to leave. He's walked out quietly but when he's got to the swinging glass doors, he has swung around to hit the doorman. The door was closing and his hand has gone straight through the door. He's cut his main artery and fallen to the floor, blood pumping all over the shop.

One of the doormen can see he's in a bad way and goes down to help him. He wraps his arm with a bandage and stops the blood flow. The other boys who were with him started bottling the doorman yet the doorman carried on lying over this boy, saving his life, even with all these bottles bouncing off him. The paramedics turned up and they reckoned it was touch and go. Police turned up and took the doorman away because he had so much blood on him; he ended up getting locked up for a night for saving the boy's life. The boy ended up in hospital for a while and, ungrateful as he was, he tried taking the doorman on, but there had been too many witnesses and nothing came of it.

Ari Bolden, Victoria, Canada

Why do I get all the big guys? Have I done something to offend the god of Murphy's Law or something? I stand six foot one and weigh in at 185 pounds. In the bouncing world, I fall on the lower end of the size chart. I worked the front door of a tough nightclub for three years. I got tested by everyone, especially guys over 200 pounds. I am a damn good 'cooler' who can talk almost any situation down and I don't let guys get under my skin. However, there are those times that guys won't leave or take a hint.

I remember calling for the rest of the boys when four blokes were raising hell at our front door. I wasn't going to let them in. I don't need attitude in my bar. Go somewhere else. These troublemakers were there for one purpose: to fight. And they wanted to fight the bouncers. It takes a special breed of person to pick on bouncers. One either has to be extremely drunk, extremely dumb, or extremely tough. You never really know until the bell rings. So, I see these guys are ready to pounce when one of them takes a swing at the owner. I jumped the rope and pushed the offender backward. The rest of the boys were moving in to help but, like I said, I was the smallest of everyone, and the quickest, so I engaged the group faster than the rest of the boys. I sized up the situation and figured that these guys were all workout rats.

I felt a hand on my shoulder and spun around. I looked up. And up. The boys had paired off and I got stuck, as always, with the biggest out of the group. I sometimes wonder if they did that to me on purpose because it always happened. *Leave the really big guy for*

Sleepy, I would hear in my head. They called me Sleepy because I was known for choking out assholes. Hell, I'd been grappling for so many years that if I slapped it on, you're out in five seconds. The guy stood at least six foot five and was in the neighbourhood of 250 pounds. But I never feel fear. Or anger even. I always try to remain as calm as I can.

The giant was drooling at the mouth looking like a caveman without his bone. He put his hands on my shoulders. I figure he thought he could just wrestle me to the ground and smash me to pieces. The moment he did, I trapped both his arms. I guess he wasn't a big fan of Royce Gracie or the UFC because if he was he would have know what was coming next. I moved around him and put my foot in the back of his knee, pulling him back and to my level. I threw on the chokehold. *Five, four, three, two, one and you're out!* I remember dropping him to the ground, taking a few steps and then spitting on his unconscious body. The rest of the boys bounced the rest of the blokes. And the police arrived soon after. Not only did the troublemakers get beat down, they got taken downtown by the police. Sometimes, things turn out all right for us.

Douglas Gentles, Cardiff

Compared to when I first started working the doors, I now get an hour what I used to earn in a whole night. The money for this job is never enough. Thankfully every club I have worked (except Yates's) I've been able to earn extra while working the door (though never by selling drugs). Some weekends I could earn an extra £500 on top of my wages. The sad fucking thing is that all this extra money was just wasted; I never saved it.

Working the doors, people get to know you and after a while they ask you if you could do a little job for them or if you know of anyone that would be willing to do a little job for them. So opportunities arose to earn extra doing these little jobs, which could range from debt collecting to giving someone a smack or, if need be and if the money was right, giving them a damn good beating. Everything has a price and thankfully I know the people willing to do these things for a price. Many opportunities have arisen to sell drugs on the doors but that's something I never did. But I have got to know some drug dealers, who have employed my services to collect debts for them, normally from other smaller dealers. This was good money until the main players got nicked and are now serving long jail terms, so these days I don't do as much as I used to when they were free.

Years ago when I was new to working the doors, I found that some of the older women (well if you're nineteen and the woman is thirty-five I call that older) were willing to pay for your time. At that time, when money was all I was really interested in, a woman offering £50 or £60 for a quick shag was a good offer and one I was happy to take. This went on for about a year. I stopped because I was offered £300 by a middle-aged couple who wanted me to 'rape' the woman while the husband sat and watched. I did it for the money but it really made me stop and look at myself. I didn't like the way money was starting to take over my life so I never went with another woman again for money. I had many offers but that couple put an end to that money earner.

Peter Edwards, Chepstow

I was working in a pub with another bouncer when one of the regulars starts having some sort of fit. This woman must be about twenty stone and usually pretty quiet but she's on the floor going ape shit like she was breakdancing. We manage to get her into the foyer and now that she's calm, put her into the recovery position. The paramedics are called and we are just watching her until they arrive. After a couple of minutes she looks a lot better but still doesn't know where she is. The paramedics turn up and try talking to her. Her eyes are rolling in her head, she's dribbling and talking rubbish. The paramedics bring out this chair thing and put her in it. As they try to lift the fat fucker up, she goes mental and starts lashing out. Kevin, the other doorman, and myself rush over to help. We try to hold her but she's just too strong. She punches one of the paramedics and elbows Kevin in the mouth. The paramedics strap her into the chair and take her away. Kevin has his hand over his mouth and I ask him if he's OK. With that he spits out his front tooth, which she must have knocked out. I know I shouldn't have laughed but I couldn't help myself. Every time I looked at him and for weeks after, until he got a false one, I just laughed my head off.

Mickey Jones, London

I can remember once the boss of this nightclub paid us and gave us a bonus for Xmas. Turned out it had been a bad night for him and the money was moody and not worth the paper written on. When we asked him, he was unable to pay us all a bonus; instead we all finished at 11pm and went and sat in the club. Now, with over twenty large doormen sitting in the club you would think that there would be no trouble. Wrong. As the night went on we could see this group of blokes arseing around in the corner and the manager is talking to them. Turns out they were a group of bouncers and doormen from a nearby club who completely trashed ours a few months ago. This one came over and asked, 'What you going to do if we start in the club, guys? We have to have a word with the manager and it might kick off.' We sat there laughing and shrugged it off telling them to go ahead with what they were going to do. Little did we know they were going to slice him open. When we saw the blood we knew that there was something seriously wrong and we all jumped in to help the boss, who by now was on the floor screaming. Guess his pretty boy days were over. We managed to hold a few of them down for the police. Turned out our boss was passing moody money all over London. In the end the boss got three years and we all walked away with a nice pat on the back for helping off duty.

Anthony Thomas, Merthyr Tydfil

The trouble with punk rock nights is that you tend to have more accidents happen, with all the kids jumping around and that. This one guy fell on his hand, breaking his two fingers so bad that they were bent over the wrong way. A girl was sick next to him from just looking at them. I offered to bend them back for him but he wouldn't let me. I had to get an ambulance for him as he was shaking, may have been shock. Another girl on the same night stood too close to the live band on stage. The guitarist, who was jumping around like a mental, swings his guitar, which nearly takes the top of the girl's head off. No kid, it's as if someone poured a bucket of red paint over the girl's head. I take a look at it and she's got this great big hole in her head. 'It's nothing love, just needs a stitch, that's all,' I lie to her. Off she goes in another ambulance and she's stitched up and kept in for a few days.

Jamie O'Keefe, London

I cannot name the worst club I have worked for legal reasons, as it is still operating, but there were just two of us at a club licensed for about 360 customers that always exceeded 500. It had a no-search policy, so was a playground for drugs, weapons and violence. The worst thing was that it was non-English-speaking environment and culture. You could get stabbed up in a moment with no witnesses or support and a majority of the people were non-existent in this country so could disappear without trace. I was there for two years and had to leave in the end before I was killed. I went to Florida for a couple of weeks with my kids as I really believed that my time was coming very close and needed to think about my future. Another doorman who had dealings with this group was stabbed. The only reason I was able to last that long was that I had lost my kids, home and business through an ugly divorce and just didn't give a fuck about my own life. Time healed my head and I got on with things but two years had just flown past. So I woke up and moved on.

animals, bloody animals

EVERYONE HAS A different outlook on life, just as one man's heaven is another man's hell. A doorman can't predict what a customer or workmate is going to do. Everyone can change their mood at the drop of a hat. A gentle and caring person can turn psychotic for no other reason than a spilt drink. An eye can be ripped out and yet the assailant can then protest to the doormen about why he has to be thrown out of the venue. You can blame it on drink or drugs but at the end of the day there are individuals among us who are just ticking time bombs. It's a doorman's job to identify these individuals and sort out their problems before an innocent customer gets involved.

Anthony Thomas, Merthyr Tydfil

Myself and my mate Chris had just chucked this boy out for fighting and he decided to have a pop at me instead. He was an ex-bouncer who had done a fair bit of time inside and was known as a right bully. He had nearly killed another bouncer a couple of years earlier by punching him in the windpipe and leaving him for dead. He looked a right psycho and had the eyes to go with it. I just blanked him as he gave me all the usual rubbish about biting my face off. 'See you in the morning, then mate,' I tell him. He then said something about my house and family, which finally got to me. I said, 'Come on then, round the back of the pub.'

As we were walking I can see the sneaky fucker's going to go for me, so I hit him with a right hook as he grabs me. I'm pulling him to the ground as he's trying to bite me. I get him down and start stamping and kicking him in the head and face. His eyes are in his head and he's pissing blood from his mouth and face. Chris and a couple of boys grab me off him and hold me back and take me inside the pub, I can't imagine what would have happened to him if I hadn't been stopped. I had gone completely apeshit and couldn't control myself. About ten minutes later, I'm just starting to calm down when Chris tells me the prick is outside talking to the police and pointing to the pub. Turns out he was trying to get me done for assault. The police come and have a word but I think they knew what he was like and that he usually started the trouble. In fact they let me know how glad they were that someone done the guy over. A few weeks later I saw him walking through town. He put his head down and pretended he couldn't see me. I just laughed and realised that another bully has met his match.

Keith Price, Bexleyheath, Kent

I worked in a comedy club for three years. This one night we were clearing out the drunken remains of the paying public. I approach this guy leaning over the cloakroom hatch and inform him that it's time to go home. 'Fuck off, I'm talking,' was the last thing he remembered saying. I grab his jacket collar from behind and spin him around like the fast-wash cycle on a Zanussi. I was left holding his jacket and he broke the sound barrier as he was launched into the air to hit the stone floor face down. From out of nowhere another bouncer ran up and took a Beckham corner kick at the guy's head, then proceeded to drag him feet first and dump him out in the street.

On my way home later I had to step over him to get by. I felt as I usually do: no compassion for him whatsoever. I never meant to hurt him and it wasn't my fault that he couldn't afford a better fitting jacket. He ended up spending four days on life support and survived. I got the sack and 'Beckham' got twelve months' prison.

Kris Cermele, Tampa, Florida

Gang members can spoil any good club, that's why we try to stop them getting in. I've known gangs slowly take over a club and before long the club closes and the gangs then move on to the next one. Many clubs these days stop them getting in, which can sometimes cause no end of trouble. I worked the club doors with an ex-pro heavyweight boxer called Damien. He took no messing from anyone and apart from being a boxer he lifted weights, so he was a big, frightening guy. Three gang members tried to get in the club one night. After being stopped at the main door, the bravest of them took a run at Damien. By the time I got to where they all were, the gang member was sitting down holding his broken jaw. Damien had thrown a short, straight right hand that stopped the guy in his tracks. We managed to get the three of them out of the club, where they shouted what they were going to do to Damien first chance they got. They make all the usual slit throat and guns to the head hand signals, which we just laughed off.

The club finishes and I'm off home to my bed, must have been in bed about two hours when the phone rings. Damien's on the other end and he tells me to come straight round to his home. He sounds worried so I don't argue but drive over as fast as I can. I find Damien and his wife waiting for me, sitting in the kitchen. Damien tells me what happened after he left the club.

Same as myself, he jumped straight into bed and fell off to sleep. Must have been an hour or so later when he wakes up by something pressing against his throat. Looking over him is the guy whose jaw he broke and one of the other two that came to the club. Pressed against his throat is the barrel of a handgun. 'I'm going to kill you and rape your wife, then kill her as well,' he's told by the one with the gun. The other one is taking all the jewellery and money from the room that he can find. With this going on the third member comes into the room and tells the others that there is a child sleeping in the other room. They talk amongst themselves and the last one to enter the room tells the others that he wants nothing to do with hurting kids. They turn around and leave the house.

Damien informs me, 'I really thought I was going to die. I believed that they were going to kill us all. They must have taken about $20,000 in jewellery and money but I would have given them anything to get rid of them. Just felt so helpless.' He asked me what should he do and I told him to phone the cops and get it sorted that way. Well, he didn't and that week he packed his job in. Not long after he left the area and took a job with a building firm.

I didn't last much longer working on the club doors. One night as I walked up to the club I had to pass the usual crowd waiting to get in. Suddenly without warning this small guy runs up and tries to stick a broken bottle into my face. As I move he plunges it into my hand, severing nerves and tendons. A few regulars from the club manage to pull him to the ground and await the cops. All the time the guy's telling me that it was a case of mistaken identity and he was sorry. After surgery and two years off work I still can't make a fist or feel three fingers on my right hand. Been offered work behind the counter of a small shop and looks like I'll take it.

Wayne Price, Mountain Ash

Two guys in the pool room one night start to argue, so we run in to see what was going on. This one guy picks up his pint glass and rams it straight into the side of the other guy's head. The whole glass shatters

Out for the count: the end of a violent encounter in a nightclub and now the doormen have to pick up the pieces.

as it sinks into him, making mincemeat out of the side of the guy's face. He falls to the floor screaming and holding his face together, bleeding like a pig everywhere. The other one tries to walk away from it all so we grab him, take him outside and kick the shit out of him, leaving him unconscious on the pavement. This was all over a game of pool. There wasn't even any money on the game, just a stupid argument that ended with this guy's face being torn open.

Jason Dicks, Bristol

After years of working on the door in various towns and cities, I've been hit and attacked by many irate women. Most women will attack a bouncer knowing that as a man he's not going to retaliate too much. They very seldom want to have a go when you have a woman bouncer with you, as they know she will give as good as she gets. To make matters worse it can be hard to throw women out; you have to watch how you grab them or before you know it you'll be up for assault. A good trick that I picked up to part them is by putting your fingers up their nose and pulling back, or if they have locked on to each other's hair try slapping their knuckles. It usually works. I did try the knuckles trick one day but the boy with me got in the way and I ended up smashing his knuckles instead, very funny.

When a few women are fighting it's a nightmare. One night there was a free-for-all going on and there must have been about ten girls fighting. I didn't know where to start. At one stage I had two girls in a headlock, one in each arm, and dragged them out. I then ran back inside and got punched by one woman as another is kicking me. I couldn't help but laugh has they were going for it and were hitting anything that moved. I pushed them to the door and out into the street. The lad with me was fighting off two mental girls outside and ended up with a stiletto shoe in his head for his troubles. Nearly all of them were fighting, shoes flying everywhere, clumps of hair being torn out, handbags and shoes being used as weapons. It was bonkers out there.

We went back into the club for the last couple. I ended up carrying the last one out and she was punching lumps into me while swearing like a good 'un. If they had been men I would have broken a few jaws. The law turned up and arrested a few of them and they were still going for it in the police wagon. Both myself and the other guy I worked with that night went home black and blue. That's why we need women door staff, to protect us from women beating lumps out of us. Give me a gang of drunken rugby players any day.

Douglas Gentles, Cardiff

There have been so many violent incidents over the years that it's hard to remember many, after a while you get so used to seeing them that they become part of the norm. I have seen so many people get hurt for stupid reasons: standing in the wrong part of a nightclub, being too good a dancer, being with the best-looking girl in the club, so many stupid reasons to kick someone's head in.

One incident that sticks in my head is from working in Luigi's when it was new to me. We had a full club, guys from different parts of the city standing around trying to look tough, as they did week in, week out. This night all hell broke out, it seemed like the whole club starting fighting at the same time. There were six of us working and we were all over the place, throwing bodies out of every available exit. Bottles, chairs, even tables were going everywhere. The fighting was now both in the club and outside on the street; talk about the Wild West. My attention was brought to a young guy who was covered in blood; the blood was his own and coming from a deep throat wound. He had been glassed and the cut was the deepest that I had ever seen. I caught him just as he was about to fall. I tried getting him to the front doors but had to drop him as some guy ran at me with a bottle. After knocking him out with a punch that Mike Tyson would have been proud of, I carried the young lad to the front door and shouted for Paul, who was a first-aider. He came over and I went to call for an ambulance.

Most of the fighting was now being done outside on the street. The ambulance arrived quickly but the trouble we had now was that this guy's mates wanted to take him home. They didn't understand how serious his wound was. One of the ambulancemen helped carry this guy while the other had to fight this guy's mates to get him to the ambulance. It was the only time that I have ever seen an ambulanceman fight, a sight that has stayed with me ever since. The ambulance guy knew that this guy was going to die if not treated right away. I heard the following week that the guy 'died' in the ambulance but thanks to the skills of the ambulance crew, they managed to save him. Those ambulancemen were brilliant.

Over the years working the doors you see so many people get bottled or stabbed. You have to be able to blank these incidents out if you are to do the job. These days the incident mentioned above would not even raise an eyebrow in my books but at that time of my life, being new to the door, it stayed in my mind. The thing that scared me most about all that went on that night was the buzz I got from it. The feeling was amazing – I loved it.

Neil Lewis, Treharris, South Wales

There were four of us running the door to the club, two upstairs and two downstairs. It was a busy night and we all seemed to be buzzing with adrenaline, one of those nights when you all seem to be up for it. Halfway through the night I notice this guy coming in who was banned from the club. He had been involved in a big scrap a few months earlier, which had started upstairs and continued out onto the street. He was one of the main ones fighting and was the son of the twat who had started it all. As soon as I realised who it was I went up and told the head doorman. 'Don't worry,' he replied. 'Leave him stay in and just make sure you search him well before he comes up.' He told me the boy had been to jail for stabbing a copper with a screwdriver and was known for carrying knives.

I noticed he had a couple of his mates with him. Some were skinheads and they looked a rough bunch. Towards the end of the night they started pointing and staring at me. They hadn't realised that I could see them out of the corner of my eye. I was on my own for a bit and just stared back at them. I then walked over and asked the main troublemaker what his problem was. He answered, 'No problem mate, I'll see you later,' all the time smiling with this stupid, smug look on his face. I shouted back, 'Don't worry, I'll be waiting.' I could feel my blood boil every time I caught him looking over. I went and told all the other doormen that I thought I'd have trouble with him by the end of the night.

Thirty minutes later and he has started trouble upstairs; he has pushed his ex-girlfriend over a table of drinks. He was then grabbed by one of the doormen, who showed him to the exit at the bottom of the stairs, the boy was struggling and started throwing punches at the two doormen as he was being taken out. One of the other doormen and I had heard the buzzer go off and we had run outside the club entrance to see what was happening. The one that got thrown out then starts shouting, 'I want that fat cunt up there.' Now Lyn, the doorman he was shouting at, was a bit touchy about his weight. Lyn rips his jacket off and runs straight at the boy and smacks him straight in the face, busting his knuckles on impact. He split the boy's face open like a kipper and there's blood everywhere. It was a fair blow but the boy was still up, screaming at him.

As Lyn's looking at him, the boy starts scooping the blood into his hands from his face. He starts shouting, 'Right then, who wants some fucking Aids.' He then glances in my direction and runs at me. I launch a rear kick at him, catching him right in the balls. It still didn't budge him. Fuck knows what he had taken; I know bigger men who would have crumbled to the ground after having their balls launched into space. He grabbed hold of me and started rubbing his bloodied hands in my face and mouth, catching me with his nails as he did this. Then I blew it; I went fucking mad. I started punching him with all my might whilst holding him in a headlock. I kept punching the damaged area above his eye that the other doorman had opened up. Blood was squirting from it by now. I could feel it getting worse; in fact it felt like my fist was going into a big hole in his face, but I still didn't stop. One of the doormen tried breaking it up by launching a steel toe-capped boot at him but instead of hitting him it smashes into my knuckles, breaking them instantly.

None of the troublemaker's skinhead mates would jump in as they were too afraid. The other doormen split us up before the police came. The troublemaker gets carried up the street away from the club by his mates. We all had a good laugh later, winding up the doorman who had broken my hand, saying it wouldn't have happened if he had lost a bit of weight.

Jamie O'Keefe, London

For me the most dangerous people are the frightened ones. Out of sheer panic they will not think twice about stabbing you. This is what happens in most of the domestic situations where a momentary few seconds of anger, fear, adrenaline give us that emotional and biological ability to lash out.

Bernard Driscoll, South Wales

After moving to Birmingham years ago to look for work, my mate Tony and myself got offered the chance of working in the nights on the door in this club on the Belfry golf course. Tony had done a few months' bouncing earlier and gave me a few tips. It was a very organised club back in those days: there would be ten of us working in a club that held about 1,000 people on most nights. There were two-way mirrors all around the club and we would stand behind them; none of the people knew we were watching them and we would be onto the trouble before it started. There was also a bloke who controlled the CCTV cameras from his room and he would radio to us as soon as he could see something was about to occur. We also had a cracking set of boys working with us, including some of Birmingham's best. One of them was this big black bloke from Manchester, a right character who would stand on the door giving people one-word answers in his deep voice, but when it went off, could he fight.

We had been radioed that there was a fight in the club and we ran in and soon broke it up. We chucked one of the boys who had been fighting out of the club and as soon as he got outside he fucked off. About an hour later he has shown back up and is standing near the club doors, saying fuck all. I tell one of the doormen, 'He's going to kick off with us soon.' An hour later and he's still standing there, saying fuck all. Now the bloke who he was fighting earlier is on his way out and leaves the club. Next thing you could see was the bloke waiting outside pulling this great big samurai sword out from under his coat and slashing the man across the chest. He then slashes him again and then he went and plunged it straight in his guts, dropping the bloke to the floor. There are pints of blood pouring out of the bloke, who is now doubled up on the floor.

We always had a baseball bat at the ready in the foyer in case things ever got out of hand. One of the boys working with us only wanted to go out and fight the bloke with the sword using the baseball bat. One of the other doormen wouldn't let him out. He told him, 'Fuck them, it's a drugs thing and it's not our problem. It's outside the club anyway.' The police turned up pretty sharpish and locked the samurai nut up. We had all sorts of police turning up and asking questions for the next week. Never did find out what happened to them.

Keith Price, Bexleyheath, Kent

I worked this club in south-east London for the past seven years with some of the best doormen that I've ever met, and working the doors for twenty-five years I've met a few. One night there was this guy inside, leaning up against the wall leering at the women. Now some of these women have had bad pasts and no future, but that doesn't mean that they are there to just be shagged and abused. At least buy them a drink first. A couple of girls complained that this guy of Eastern European appearance was touching them up as they walked past. I approached him about the allegations and got a 'No English, no understand' answer, so out he went. No fuss, no arguments, end of, I thought.

At the end of the night a screaming girl ran up the stairs begging for help. Stilks, Cyd and myself ran down to see what was wrong. Outside was a woman with blood streaming from a gaping cut above her right eye, another woman holding her jaw spitting blood and some guy rolling on the floor, gripping his bollocks. I calmed them down to find out just what had happened. The refugee had approached one of the women and said, 'Let me come home with you so I can fuck you.' She told him she was married and he tells her, 'Then I fuck you quietly so we don't wake your husband.' Not bad for someone who couldn't speak English. The woman pushed him away, so he punched her, splitting her above the eye. Her mate rushed in to help and he punched her in the mouth, knocking one tooth clean out and it was later established that he had fractured eight others. The guy on the floor got kicked in the balls when he went to help the girls.

We went off looking for the refugee after we called an ambulance. Cyd found him hiding in a petrol garage nearby. He put his arm up behind his back and brought him back to the club for his trial. Unfortunately the defence didn't turn up so we, the prosecution, went ahead. He was found guilty and sentenced to a broken jaw, broken collarbone, broken arm, fractured cheekbone, severely bruised and swollen bollocks and a deep cut across his face as a permanent reminder. The sentence was carried out immediately because I thought he might have grounds for appeal.

His life was saved by a girl screaming that we were going to kill him and to stop. The police came and took away the remains after the girls insisting on prosecuting. I was arrested five months later for allegedly punching him and causing actual bodily harm. Five witnesses came forward and exonerated me, so I got one of those lovely letters that say 'Insufficient evidence to support a prosecution'. God bless the Crown Prosecution Service. They only charged him with assault because the women pushed him first and provoked the attack. Bollocks. He got three months but I don't think he'll father any children.

Richard Williams, Aberdare

I was working a club in Abergavenny when early in the night a fight broke outside the club. It carried on down the street and out of sight around the corner. Suddenly I could hear bottles smashing and women screaming, then dead silence. Ten minutes later a guy I knew as Steve tried to get into the club.

'Sorry mate, you can't come in,' I told him.

'Why not?' he asked.

'It's because your ear has been cut off mate. In fact it's only still attached to your head by a small piece of skin.'

I fetched him a bar towel and off he disappeared into the night.

Douglas Gentles, Cardiff

Weapons now are part of my everyday life. They are also part of the club scene, you just have to deal with them. Knives, stun guns and CS gas are the main weapons in Cardiff. Thankfully guns are still not that common; I know a lot of people that have them but they are not shown on the street. Most of the clubs now search and have metal detectors. I have had knives thrown at me while standing on the door and it is scary but I've carried a weapon since I was fourteen so they don't worry me like they do some doormen.

During the 1999 Rugby World Cup I was working in a club called Rosie O'Brien's. Australia had played and the city centre was packed. During the day a fight broke out between eight guys, so we go in and get five out quickly. The others are putting up a good fight but we get them out and as we do, one looks at one of the doormen and shouts, 'I'm going to fucking stab you, cunt.' Well the effect those words had on this guy was shocking; this doorman, a lovely guy, shit himself and two weeks later gave up the door.

One of my first nights working at Rosie O'Brien's I refused a guy who then pulled out a knife and ran at me. I put him through the bus shelter outside the club and kept the knife for a souvenir. He later came and asked for his knife back, saying he was drunk that night and was sorry. I refused him entry again and told him the knife was now mine. The silly prick threatened me with the police. I just smiled and went inside otherwise I would have ended up hitting him just for being so stupid.

Cass Pennant, South East London

I was at Kisses nightclub about 1983–84. I'll give you an idea what we were up against. We had taken the door over from Gary Mason, later a British heavyweight boxing champion. He kept in contact and took his hat off to us when he still found us there six months later. Want to know what a lovely area we chose to ply our trade? It was about a stone's throw from the North Peckham estate (where little Damilola Taylor died). That first few months of Kisses we had them all; it was open season to all comers and did they come! One night they all came, every individual or gang that we had barred or thrown out must have been on the street this particular night. I think the atmosphere had been building up for weeks. We used to try to unwind before we started work, as you had no chance after. We took to having a quick drink in the pub next door to the club. It would fall silent as soon as you entered and we'd get our drinks and look for a table amongst all these people making slit-throat gestures.

The night in question started early. Amidst a Bronx-style summer heat wave we refused entry to a big shot and dumped him on his arse, threw him out on the street with all his cronies and messed his white suit up in the process. He said he was coming back – they all say they are going to come back, just give me a fiver for everyone that does. Well, this night they must have sounded the war drums for a fair crowd was mobbing up in the street within the hour. We took one look and saw just about everyone we had ever had cause to deny entry to in the past six months. Whether they were all different mobs or one big gang, they had fire in their hearts and just one aim, to burn the club down. It was a real uprising that wasn't entirely personal, for we knew we had never taken liberties, it's not our way, and we'd only ever responded to those with the wrong attitude. This was a different scenario, this was a hate – directed to a club and what it stood for. They hated us because we would stop them, they hated the club owner because he was making money, and they hated the punters because they were a soul crowd with a different outlook to life. This was a hate mob with a huge chip and the Peckham High Street filled with bodies screaming, 'Burn it down, burn it!' until it reached a frenzy.

Then we saw him, our man, the dandy dude we had flung out earlier. Suddenly it went off and it was a bad, bad scene. As I say, this wasn't personal, this was a combined uprising from those that were outcast and disrespected on their own streets and the night-club was a symbol of all that. They really were after forcing their way into the club and razing it to the ground. The door is the first line of defence and we'd become the only frontline when they smashed through the main entrance doors with scaffold poles and axes, beating us back to the stairs. I had my full complement – six doormen. Nowadays clubs employ a battalion of security men.

The next set of doors led onto the dance floor and took you inside, so we met fire with fire. Tools were put into our hands, axes and squirt proving most effective, the baying mob versus a team that held the door together for six months without ever taking a backward step. For us it was life-threatening stuff in a part of London that was a no-go area long before they ever used that term at the city hall. For them it was simple: payback time to anyone that had ever upset them. Everyone fought themselves to a standstill but no one was tired because of the adrenalin rush.

In all were we relatively unscathed. From holding the second set of doors we were back dishing it out through the wreckage of what was the main front door entrance. They held the streets because there was that many of them but we still held the club and that was the job. More importantly, we were still in control of a serious situation that was not to our liking. This was far deeper than the routine problems that go with the job but we had done it and done it as a team. It was one of them where every member could see firsthand how each would cope if pushed beyond all limits. The experience of that night by way of what we learned from each other meant I could put any one of those guys on another door with a different team and they would shape up that team for me. That's the biggest compliment I could pay those guys.

Daniel Copeland, Essex

I had just finished my shift, must've been about 1 A.M., and as it was a Saturday I thought I would stay behind for a drink and maybe go on somewhere with the boys when they'd done their stint. I got chatting with some young lads at the bar. I had seen them a few times before in the club and they seemed tidy enough lads, just out for a laugh and trying to pull. I was talking with a couple of them when one of their mates came back to the bar white as a sheet. He told us that this bloke, about fortyish, had come onto him in the bogs and offered him £50 if he could give the young lad a blowjob. Poor kid looked like he was going to throw up; it obviously dented his male ego. His mates were well pissed off and decided to sort this nonce out…

I had my mobile on me so I gave them my number and said to give me a call if things got out of hand but told them to take the trouble away from the club. I couldn't really see them calling me, as there were three of them and one of him so that was that. The young lad went up to the pervert and said that there were some garages behind the club and he'd meet him in the derelict one in five minutes. He told his mates he was going and they'd follow on in a couple of minutes to sort the guy out. The pervert and the young lad left the club and his mates weren't far behind but they couldn't find him anywhere. They were getting really worried and called me on my mobile about twenty minutes after they had gone.

'It's okay,' I said, 'he's here with me at the bar and he looks fine so come back in because he's just got the beers in. I take it you lads got the pervert sorted out?'

'How did he pay for the drinks?' the guy asked me on the phone.

'With a £50 note mate,' I answered.

Then it dawned on me. *The dirty bastard!* No wonder his mates couldn't find him, he was too busy getting a blowjob from an old pervert for money. I think his friends' opinion of him changed after that. I didn't stick around to see the outcome, made me feel quite ill in fact. Didn't see them again to find out either as I had moved on to become an electrician … well it keeps the wife happy!

Douglas Gentles, Cardiff

One of the things that nearly put me off working the doors was one night at Luigi's. A big fight breaks out and all five of us working had our hands full dealing with it. We were outnumbered four to one. I'm on the floor fighting with two big sons of bitches, then another one of these cunts' mates jumps on my back and tries breaking my neck, shouting out loud, 'I'm going to break this bastard's neck.' It's the only time that I remember thinking, *what the fuck am I doing this job for?* Feeling the guy's hands trying to twist my head so that my neck broke and hearing his words so clearly above the music and other noise made me find an inner strength that enabled me to push up and break free. As I did, another doorman grabbed hold of the guy and threw him out. I got up and walked right into a right hook from another one of these guys. I saw it coming but couldn't move and took a whack right in the mouth. I got hold of the guy and dragged him out the club, making sure I knocked his head two or three times against the posts en route to the main door.

The police arrived and nicked those still fighting outside. I had a few cuts on my head and hands from the fighting and they wanted me to go to hospital. I refused; I just wanted to get home. I lay awake all night thinking what was I working the door for. The money was shit, I had a lovely girlfriend, so why was I doing it?

Jason Payne, Merthyr Tydfil

The boss's son comes to the house one night and asks would I work this club in Cardiff. I agree and off I go, not realising it's a gay club. I get down to the club and after a while on the door it dawns on me. As we were 'straight' we weren't allowed into the club area unless called to. There was a gay man and woman on the door with us and if any trouble started in the club they had to go in first, then if need be a few other doormen and myself would be called. I would stand at the front door most of the night.

I get a message that there's a fight by the bar and I was needed. I'm in there like a shot. I look around and this big lad is on top of another guy, battering him. I push through the crowd, grab him in a chokehold and drag him to the main door and throw him into the street. Now, this is what I usually do and I think that's the end of it. The guy comes back up to the door crying his eyes out. 'You hurt me just then, you big bully, what you do that for?' he cries. I just didn't know how to take it. He was sobbing his heart out, this big lad with a face full of tears. I can honestly say I felt terrible for him and I stood there saying sorry.

I didn't get much trouble while I worked at that club as they were all out for a good time. It was strange at first when I would catch two blokes kissing but they didn't bother me after a while, I'd just stand on the door doing my job. Now and again one would come up and ask if I was batting for the other team, but I'd let them know my bread wasn't buttered on that side.

This pretty woman came up to the front door one night and asked had her two friends come to the club. Having not worked there long I didn't know who they were, so I let her into the club to look for them. She found them and stayed in the club. I get called to the dance floor where I found the woman I had let in had smashed a bottle into her girlfriend's face, slicing her right open. There was a large deep cut across her forehead spouting out blood everywhere. The reason being, she caught her dancing with someone else. For a stupid reason like that she scarred the poor girl for life.

Wayne Price, Mountain Ash

A mate of mine and his son one night were having a bit of trouble with some guys in a club that I was working at. They were arguing and before long it all went up and I had to jump in and keep them all apart. One of the guys they had trouble with was a doorman who I worked with who was just out for a drink. The landlord tells me to get them away from the club, he was friendly with them all and didn't want to see them fighting. To make sure nobody was going to fight outside the club, I get the father and son in my van and drive them away. The father tells me to drop them at this hotel that wasn't far away. I walk with them into the hotel just to make sure everything had calmed down and that there wasn't going to be any more trouble. Little did I know that the hotel was the regular drinking place for the guys the two had been arguing with earlier.

I was just standing by the bar having a Coke when I notice faces appearing here and there and it now dawns on me that we had turned up amongst them all. I wasn't really on my guard because I hadn't done anything and had more or less been the peace-keeper.

This guy comes on to me and says, 'Tell your buddies not to cause any trouble in here.'

'Tell him yourself mate, he's sitting by there,' I answer.

I don't know what he said to him but next thing all hell breaks loose and the tables have gone over and everyone's fighting. They were using chairs, table legs and a few baseball bats came out of nowhere. It happened so fast that I didn't have much time to respond and a few of them jumped on me. It seemed like the fight was going on for hours, but in fact because it was happening so fast it was probably just a few minutes.

Next thing, I'm being woken by paramedics. I rip off the oxygen mask and tear the collar they had put around my neck way. I didn't know where the hell I was or what had gone wrong. The paramedic was screaming at me and I was staggering everywhere because all my coordination had gone. My head had been smashed in by something heavy and there was blood pumping from gashes all over the top of my head. I try to get up from the floor of the hotel and as I do I pull out a needle that the paramedics had inserted into my arm. I scream over to the landlord that I was going to come back and kill every one of the pricks that had jumped on me. It seems I had been smashed over the head with a bat or table leg and everyone just stood back and watched them kick into me when I was out. There were a lot of them involved in the attack but where was the sense of fair play amongst the others? I couldn't work out how they had just stood back and watched me get stamped on with all the blood pumping out of my head.

The paramedics want me to go to the hospital but in my temper I insist that I'll be all right and I drive myself home. I get in the house, wash myself down and lay on the settee. I wake hours later to hear my sister on the phone reassuring someone that I had in fact not been kicked to death. She told them, 'Well, he's got a head like a balloon but he's still breathing.' I try to stand but the whole room starts to spin around and I sit back down until I get myself together. Over the next three weeks I was getting dizzy spells and sharp intense pain above one eye. It all came to a head one day sitting in my sister-in-law's kitchen. I was talking to my then brother-in-law, Glyn, when all of a sudden I get a sharp pain in the head and become disorientated. Glyn seems to shrink down in size and is quite a distance away, then all of a sudden he's right back in front of me right up to my face, like some sort of acid trip, I expect. I start to rock in the chair and can't see out of my one eye. Everyone around thought I had gone completely mad as I looked right off it. I couldn't move the one side of my body so they rushed me into the hospital.

The hospital found I had blood clots in the back of my head and had to perform an emergency operation on me. I couldn't talk or move for a few days and found out that they more or less took off my one ear to be able to drill into my head to remove the clots. A while after I came out of hospital I get the same pain above my left eye and after being once again sorted by the hospital, I'm told there had been another blood clot which had burst in the back of my head so I was very lucky with that one as it could have killed me.

Steve Wraith, Newcastle

The job can be messy at times and it's not uncommon to see at least one broken bone or some blood spilled at least once a week. But you also witness some strange human behaviour. There are the exhibitionists who like a good shag in a dark corner of the club, or the druggie having a conversation with the walls, but the most distressing sight I have ever witnessed had to be the lad we suspected of snorting coke in the toilets. I kicked the door in and I could not believe what I was looking at. A male in his early twenties kneeling in front of the toilet with his pants around his ankles masturbating over his own shit which he had placed around the toilet seat. Sick or what? When he realized he had been rumbled he stood up and turned towards me and the lads and put his hand out to apologise. He had shit all over his hand and for once in our lives we all backed off till he'd cleaned himself up, then kicked him into the street.

Lee Callaghan, South Wales

I got picked to work at a club in Caerphilly because the local guys who had been working the door weren't doing the job. There were about six of us chosen to sort the club out. There were some big lads there and it wasn't long before I found myself struggling to get this big lump out. He had to leave the club and I was at the top of some stairs struggling with him when I decided to throw him down the stairs. He must have weighed about 16 stone and didn't touch the steps as I threw him. He crashed head first through a partition wall at the bottom of the steps. I thought I had killed him and ran down to check him over. He was cut up pretty bad with wooden splinters in his face and neck but other than that he was OK.

I got back into the club and things seemed to calm down a bit. Something happened in the club and a woman door staff went over to check it out. I followed her over. Before I could do anything this guy jumps up and smashes a broken Coke can into the side of her head. She fell back, with the impact of the can cutting a complete circle around her ear, and I sort of caught her. I then threw the table that the guy had in front of him out of the way and started to smash the fuck out of the guy using my elbows in close on his face. I dragged him out and threw him down the stairs. Every doorman I dragged him past kicked or punched him. At the bottom of the stairs the others laid into him and the prick looked like he'd been in a car crash. The woman we worked with left the club with blood pissing out from around her ear. She never came back to work after that. I think that women should be used to search handbags and the female customers but not to get involved in the fighting. It's not that some doorwomen can't handle themselves, it's because in my own opinion I'd be more worried about them getting hurt than defusing a situation.

chapter five
characters and top dogs

THERE ARE WORKMATES and customers that will always be remembered by a doorman, for a host of different reasons. A good doorman stands out, maybe for his courage, intellect or his sense of humour. There are also certain customers that can't be classed as run-of-the-mill or indeed be put into any category. Some of them are gangsters or 'faces' with reputations so fierce that none but the toughest bouncers dare cross them. Others are bizarre but unforgettable characters, part of nightlife's rich tapestry. Whenever a doorman looks back on his years on the doors, he will recall the characters and top dogs he has met along the way.

Big Jack, London

I must have seen all the 'faces' of the last thirty years come and go. It's funny how you don't realise the historic value of things until long after. I remember the Sixties as a more pleasant time but with loads of top-class violence. How the fuck that works I don't know! Must have been about my third night on the door, I remember these two rather small blokes came up to the door. They were all suited and booted, real well dressed men. They just stood there not saying a word. I think I was expected to know what to do. Anyway my pal comes to the door, gives them the red carpet treatment, then the thinner one shoves a few notes in my mate's top pocket and in they go.

I said, 'Who the fuck were them cheeky fuckers'?

My pal looked at me as if I had just fallen off a Christmas tree. 'What do mean, who are they?'

'Like I said, who are they?' I was starting to feel a bit stupid now.

'They,' he tells me, 'are Ronnie and Reggie Kray. But we just refer to them as the Twins.'

Oh shit, I thought. Of course I had heard of the Kray Twins, but I pictured them about six foot eight and twenty-two stone. I admit they looked similar but not like identical twins. Inside, they knew everyone, or rather everyone knew them. They had people keep whispering to them and pulling them aside. They looked very edgy and anyone who came within twenty feet got the benefit of the eyes. People were gagging for their attention, I think trying to win favour with them.

I saw Ronnie go into the toilets. Then my fellow doormen, who were closer, went running in as Ronnie casually walked out cool as anything with a sort of grin on his face. I went in and this bloke is on the deck screaming, with a neat slice down the side of his cheek. We walked out past what was in fact 'the Firm' and one of the door lads took him to the London Hospital opposite the Blind Beggar pub. Now knowing the score, I walked up to the Twins and said, 'Everything okay lads?' I got the same look and silence as I'd got on the door earlier. I took that as my cue to go. As I did, Reggie called me back and said, 'Jack, here, take the wife somewhere nice,' as he slipped me £50, a lot of dosh back then. How the fuck he knew my name and that I was married I don't know to this day.

I saw the Twins twice after that, before they were nicked. People were vanishing all over the place and nobody had seen Jack the Hat for ages. Everyone involved with anywhere that served alcohol knew Jack. The rumours were now more than that. We all knew they had done away with Jack and Frank Mitchell. I think the twins really thought nobody knew or dared to speak even though Ronnie seemed to want people to know and basked in it. In reality it was all a matter of time. Good or bad, we will never see their likes again. They were special. Gangsters can be special as well you know.

Cass Pennant, South East London

Since the original skinhead culture you've had gangs in large numbers. Even in the Kray era you had your firms and it don't matter who you are, you have to show respect both ways. If you've got a serious firm you can't stop them coming in legit; you must remember it's their club, their manor, they have every right. But you can't have rival gangs inside the club; the doorman has to stop that happening. That's why I always had one local doorman who would be our spotter. If it does occur, you pull in the code of respect and have a quiet word with each main face to say, 'Look, you can do what you like to each other outside but inside we get involved and we go straight in. Now we aren't your problem, so it's up to you guys whether you want a three-way brawl.'

The other situation is you will have a local firm moving in the club anyhow and the local face will insist he's a special case, with the old routine, looking for the confrontation that will have half the dancefloor coming to his aid. Apart from the obvious there's another way to handle it, where you give him his respect (and that's all that he is after) and keep the upper hand. You do an unofficial deal. He comes in, doesn't pay or get searched. In return he acts as policeman to his own firm. Inadvertently he has now made himself one of us and the ice is broken with that particular posse who you've got to live with every weekend.

John Garfield, Los Angeles

Many years ago I used to date a stripper and she was working at a small club in upstate New York, so I drove her up there. At the door, I ran into a former lightweight sparring mate who was now about 170 pounds and the bouncer. But he was no more than five-nine. It was a pretty rowdy place and I asked him, 'How do you manage to keep everybody in line?' There were some really big, loud rednecks in there. They looked like they'd like nothing better than to fight. He turned to me and said simply, 'None of these guys is willing to die.'

Peter Edwards, Chepstow

I've worked with guys from all over the country, guys who impressed me and some who were complete arseholes. Of all the guys I've met, Haydn Bennet was the best by far. He wasn't the best fighter, though he would get stuck in, he wasn't great at defusing a situation, in fact as a bouncer he was just an average sort of guy. But

Haydn had the biggest knob I have ever seen in my life. Not that I make it a point of looking at men's knobs but his was huge, a miracle of medical science. He had this trick where he always had a hole in his trouser pocket and would pull his dick to one side so his bell end would stick out. He would call some local tart into a corner of the club and say something like, 'What do you think of this love,' or, 'Look, I've ripped my trousers again.' All the other doormen new of his trick and we'd watch the girl's face as she saw the size of his dick. Girls who wouldn't give him the time of day as they entered the club would, after talking to others, suddenly try to make conversation with him. A few really got the hump if he wouldn't show it to them. He could have made a fortune as a porn star if he'd spent a few quid having plastic surgery on his face. Women would come to the door and ask which was the one with the massive dick. One guy even wanted to fight Haydn because he was under the impression that Haydn 'thought he was hard' because he had a big knob.

On one stormy night some customers brought umbrellas to the club with them. We had to make sure they were placed in the cloakroom as they could be used as weapons. This whale of a woman argues with Haydn that she isn't going to pay to put her umbrella in the cloakroom but will keep it with her all night. She then tries to push past Haydn, who blocks her path. After a few shoves and some good swear words, Haydn attempts to get her out of the club. She won't go easily and puts up a fierce struggle and I have to help him get the blue whale out. Fast as a mongoose she lunges at Haydn with her umbrella, which stabs him straight in the groin and he falls to the floor. I get the woman out and return to check on Haydn as the whale attacks the main door with her brolly.

Haydn is bent over and I ask if he's all right. 'I'm bleeding. The fucking bitch stabbed me,' he cries. He gets to his feet and puts his hand down his trousers to check his tackle. 'It's my leg, thank fuck it's my leg! She missed my dick but stabbed me in the leg instead,' he screams out. You should have seen the look of relief on his face as he continued with the words, 'It's the source of all my powers. Without it I'm just like Clark Kent. Thank you God, thank you.'

After a few stitches in the hospital he spent the rest of the night showing the scar to every woman who asked how he was.

No matter how bad life gets or how down I am, the vision I have of Haydn jumping around thanking God that 'the source of all his powers' was still intact cracks me up every time I think about him.

Douglas Gentles, Cardiff

I have always found that all teams of doormen have at least one guy who can defuse ninety-nine per cent of situations before it kicks off. Taffy was a six foot four, twenty-three-stone man monster who never failed to sort out a problem before it kicked off. I have never known anyone like him. He would see something starting, rush over and get between them, then start telling them jokes and before you knew it they were all laughing and everything was OK. He had a gift and stopped a lot of trouble with it.

Terry Turbo, North London

We were the top dogs in Camberley: Joe Johnson, Mick Rapley, Eddie Stokes, Ian Whitelin, Owen Gardner, Errol, Gary McCann, Brian Tuff, Paul Pinto and myself. We were all fucking lunatics then and some of us have got better and some a lot worse! Nearly all of the above are individuals in their own right and you wouldn't want to fuck with any of them. Since they brought in this silly registration system a lot of the people on the doors are two bob and would get fucked up if there was a really serious incident. We always got paid well. Now the wages reflect the quality of door staff: £7 to £9 per hour. Would you risk your life for that? And they take national insurance and tax as well.

I have met some hard guys in my time but Eddie Stokes is the scariest geezer I have ever met. He doesn't put it about but he's a martial arts wizard with no fear and supreme fitness. He could chase you for twenty miles and still torture you for hours. A really nice geezer but someone you would never cross unless you were clinically insane. I used to train with him in jiu-jitsu and he always used to have me limping home with tears in my eyes. He's the sort of bloke you'd really hit hard or slam in the floor and he'd just laugh like a madman and thank you for it. He set up his own class, which was just street combat, and he was flying in these masters in one-punch knockout techniques and pressure point striking, and they would spend the whole afternoon knocking each other out and strangling each other until the other person was unconscious. I always came up with an excuse so I never had to go!

The smartest individuals I have worked with are Boogie and Gooner, they both know how to talk to people and if it goes the wrong way they both have this uncanny awareness where they see things coming before they happen. They can defuse situations as well just by talking to people in a certain way. They are both street guys who are known faces and are greatly respected in and around London.

Carlton Leach, East London

Most of the lads I looked up to then were not what you would call gangsters, they were top boys of the football firms. Men like Billy Gardner and Vic Darke I had lot of respect for. Vic was older than me and I looked up to him, a hard, hard man if ever there was one. I would go as far to say that my first proper idol was Vic Darke, Vic was and is the most fearless man I have ever seen and I have seen a lot. Vic though, was not a doorman. The hardest doorman I worked with is Lou Yates. Lou was a monster of a man and so good and quick with his hands he never needed a tool. Lou had class. Give them a chance to walk away and if they're stupid enough to still be standing there, knock them spark out with one punch – job done.

The most dangerous person I came in contact with, I would say, was Tommy Adams (of notorious London brothers the Adams), who I really liked. This was when I was at the Paradise Club. We didn't know who they were at first but like most faces the Adamses were perfect gentlemen. But I must admit I was wary when they came in.

I never set out to be a head doorman. I had good, younger and fearless guys around me and because I was older and had all the experience I had learned from people like Lou Yates and the East End villains, I was the obvious choice. We expanded from there and

Soccer hooligan-turned-doorman Carlton Leach: 'I had spent years
fighting bouncers and now I was one.'

I formed security companies with my best mate Tony Tucker. Tony
was murdered in the Range Rover hit in Rettendon in 1995. Clubs
started wanting invoices and started wanting a more business-type
door, that's why security companies came about.

Darryl Taskers, South Wales
I've worked with a good few respected doormen over the years,
guys like Big Lee, Shirley, Curtis, Mad Morris and my partner
Sean. I have gotten to learn the job from just listening to them,
learning from their experiences if you like. Martial arts has helped

me quite a bit when the situation arises but the best tactic is to nip it in the bud before it kicks off. I always talk tidy to everyone when they enter or leave the establishment but if their attitude changes then so does mine. I was told years ago, 'When the shit hits the fan, get in hard, fast and don't worry who you have to hit, just get the fuckers out.'

There always seem to be new security firms around waiting to take over the club/pub where you work. They see the place running smooth and think it looks easy, never realising you've had to work hard to get it that way. They always talk the same old bollocks, promising the landlords cheaper prices and better boys to do the job. That's why the doorman's wage isn't that good, with all these companies undercutting each other. Most landlords don't give a fuck about the guys on the door, they just worry about what goes in their tills. They forget that we're the ones that look after them and their bar staff.

Douglas Gentles, Cardiff

Over the years I've seen various top football players out on the town, especially when Wales play an international. The singer Charlotte Church is always good for a laugh, she seems to think that just because she has millions that she's entitled to come into a club. Refusing her has always caused a great outburst from the young girl: 'Don't you know who I am?' or 'I earn millions, how much do you earn, wanker?' You never hear that on her records.

One of the celebrities from *I'm a Celebrity Get Me Out Of Here* (I won't say his name) has always been good for a laugh whenever he's been in Cardiff. One night outside a club called Rosie O'Brien he came along and asked for a light for his fag, then started telling jokes. He then takes a piss in the bus stop outside the club and while doing so starts singing at the top of his voice and shouting at every woman that walks past. He even flashed at two women and asked if they wanted a game. He was very funny.

The FA Cup being played in Cardiff always bring the stars out. One who caused problems for us was a famous female Radio One DJ. Her and a close female friend were in Yates's and after a while were asked to leave because they were winding up the guys and then started throwing shoes around the packed club, one hitting a member of the bar staff. The female with the DJ was really up for a fight outside the club, she was a right little troublemaker.

Robin Barratt, Manchester

The stairs up to this club were steep and we worked the door downstairs. After the initial rush it was tedious. Most people were in by about 11.30 and they didn't generally leave until the end of the evening. The manager, who started his career a few years earlier as a doorman, was a great guy. He didn't much like working this club and would often come down to the door to have a chat and smoke. He didn't really mind what we did; we could smoke, chat up girls, smack the odd customer for misbehaving, in fact the manager would often be the first into any violent situation. He still used weights and took steroids and quite often lost his temper. I think he missed his days on the door; he missed the action.

'Got a ciggy?' he asked us one evening. I didn't smoke. Mike looked down at the cigarette in his hand, and then up to the manager apologetically. 'Last one,' said Mike.

He searched his pockets for change, just about finding the right amount and went back upstairs to the cigarette machine, which was situated at the top of the staircase near the entrance doors to the club. We stood quietly on the door, not taking much notice until we heard shouting and swearing and banging. We thought it was a drunk customer causing trouble, so we rushed in and halfway up the stairs, coming face to face with the cigarette machine, which was teetering over the edge and just about to fall onto us.

'Fucking thing took my money,' yelled the manager. 'Move out the fucking way.' Like a scene from the *Keystone Cops*, we turned around and ran back down the stairs as the machine rumbled and crashed its way behind us, spewing its contents of cigarettes and change as it fell. Nonchalantly the manager followed, bent over and picked up a packet of Marlboro. Silently he opened it as we stood looking on, shocked, and asked for a light.

'Tell you what,' he said quietly, 'I'll have the fags, you have the money.' We scrabbled on the floor and between the tangled metal frame and plastic, picking up coins. 'Fucking customers,' said the manager. 'Bunch of fucking yobs, the lot of them. I expect I'll have to claim on the insurance for this.' We made a good few quid that night and the manager never lost any more money in any cigarette machines.

Rodri Cartwright, South Wales

I have worked with all sorts of doormen, including some of Wales's best. The funniest would have to be the Dazzler, who would shave abs muscles into his belly hair and always get his old boy out. Then there's Big John, who would make this other doorman walk around the club on a lead wearing big flower sunglasses, barking at the punters. Two of the hardest would have to be Tommo and Psycho, who against any odds would taunt each other who would be the first to use the radio for help. Neither would press it. We would get to where the action had been to find bodies everywhere with the pair of them back to back.

Cass Pennant, South East London

In my biography, *Cass*, I told of Mad Jaffa backing us up with a rusty hand grenade in a hostile pub in Peckham – yes, that place again. Crazy Dave was another who took 1,000 stitches once because he wouldn't take a backward step in a fracas with the Towners (E16). Then I had good mileage out of Harry the Murderer working Redhill and Reigate. I'd say to the boys, 'Get a problem with the locals, tell them I'm sending Harry down.' They knew who he was because he worked down there but I had to keep resting him because he'd go schizo on them. Although quite a funny lad to work with on the boring nights, he was a proper gentleman when not rubbed up the wrong way. We always introduced him as 'the Murderer' but he would swear it was just manslaughter. 'You're out of order Cass,' he would go.

There was a fellow called Vince who was the total opposite of his brother Crazy Dave (there were three brothers and he was the calming influence). He looked so unassuming, more like a white English salesman or city office worker. Never said a lot, never pushed the conversation and also wore glasses. He worked with nearly everyone who worked the door with me, in the very worst places. It didn't take long for any of us to know this guy was proper; he had it all without ever looking like he could. This was an effective weapon in the war on the door. Deft and skilful is how I would describe him but totally honest in how he operated, an expert in judo who knew the language of the street. When he passed away unexpectedly the whole door world paid its respects. I still miss the person he was, we all do. His name was Vincent Cornwell and unusually for my door he was a 'straight' guy, inwardly tough but also a true professional the way he worked a door.

Crazy Dave and his other brother Nick got me minding the opening night of Sam Fox's own wine bar, Sam's in Tottenham. She was a big Page Three star and I was a little over protective. Both Sam and her mum were down to earth and really nice. The place was heavy and as she moved around there's this guy – slim, normal build – who kept shielding her, sometimes discreetly, sometimes in my way, to the point I thought that if he was her agent he was acting in a funny way. I was later told the guy was Dave Lea, her personal minder who went on to mind many Hollywood stars. The guy was deadly in martial arts and respected by all. I should have been put in my place if he was her full-time minder but he showed me the true art of a pro minder, remain discreet always unless danger threatens, act as if you're not there and never take the star's limelight. This guy was a minder before ever the word celebrity was fashionable. What he had shown put me on good footing for when I later did work for Frank Bruno. Leave the bouncers on the door, let the stars be the stars, while you are their shadow, ears and eyes.

Bernard Driscoll, South Wales

I remember the first night with this doorman named Snuffer. I'd heard a lot about him and told someone to tell him to turn up for work at 7.30 in this nightclub. He turns up for work and asks this local boy who has had a few beers, 'Do you know where Bernard is?' The boy turns to him and smugly asks, 'Who are you then? The bouncer from Mothercare, is it?' Snuffer knocks the boy out cold. He finds us a couple of minutes later and explains what has happened. We go around the corner and there's no one there. I thought he was off his head, imagining things, but he insists, 'He was right by there, on the floor.' Next thing you could see is this boy coming out of the toilets carrying this guy who got knocked out. He then decides to come running straight at us and hits the other doorman with us. He then turns on Snuffer, who hits him from one side of the club to the other, all with body shots. By now he was screaming to be let out of the club and started coughing up blood. He went outside and ended up going in an ambulance. With that, Snuffer has finally introduced himself to us. He became a valued member of our team for the last couple of years.

Jason Dicks, Bristol

I was on the door with this girl bouncer Angie. She was really tall and trained as a kickboxer. She had been with us a couple of months and was doing well. Week after week she was throwing women out who had been fighting. She was even jumping in to help when the men were scrapping. This night one of the bouncers was bringing this girl down to be searched for dealing drugs in the club. As soon as he lets her go she pushes the doorgirl flying and goes running out of the doors. I was searching at the time and just looked on. The bouncer then turns to Angie and calls her a useless fucking twat in front of all the punters. As I'm on my way in to tell him he's out of order, as none of us would have expected the girl to have done that, Angie suddenly kicks him to the side of the head, dropping him to his knees. She then knees him in the face, smashing his nose up. I just about grabbed her off him before she stamped on his head. This lad fancied himself as a hard man but was now looking up at her from the floor, blood spread over his face. Angie was taken in a back room to calm down, as she was right up for a full-on scrap. He got up and I just laughed at him, as he had made a complete fool of himself. He asked me not to tell anyone about what happened. I've worked with some good fighters but never saw someone with as much balls as Angie; she was like a female Terminator.

Michael Jones, London

The man who lives next door to me, Bob, is an alcoholic and is always hanging around the pub I work in. One night after work I stayed on at the pub to have a drink with the boys. When I got home I could see a police car outside my house. I walked up and said, 'What's the problem officer?' The copper just laughed and said, 'If you live here then mate, Bob told me to tell you he was sorry.' I walked into the house and my missus was on the settee drinking a cup of tea, crying her eyes out. I spoke with the other policeman there who said that the bloke next door had walked into my house and pissed in my wardrobe, he then got undressed and got into bed with my missus. She woke up to get something to drink and I think she thought that I had lost a lot of weight. One of the neighbours the other side called the police as he thought I was killing her.

Douglas Gentles, Cardiff

You get to meet many weird and wonderful people but the one character that always sticks in my mind is the manager of the first club I worked, a guy called Ronnie Elvin. Small and tough, a boxer in his day, Ronnie would sit on the door and tell stories like no one I had ever known. At 10 P.M. every night he would go next door into Manwell's restaurant for a coffee. While he was out we would mess around with the barmaids, nick a few drinks and just act the clown. On his return we would stand to attention like a group of soldiers on parade. He would walk in and just know something was not right; the smiles on our faces always gave the game away, so he would chase us around the club punching us in the ribs. For an old guy he had a powerful punch. Ronnie never drank, he smoked at least forty a night and he would count the money in the till just for the fun of it, playing with the pound coins so much that it pissed everyone off, but we never said anything as we would know that he would call us over and when we least expect it, whack, right in the ribs – then go right back and start playing with the coins again.

Andrew Moffat, Edinburgh

We had this guy who came into the club years ago. He's dead now but I'll never forget him. He had a false leg but that never stopped him coming to the club for a good time. I could never understand how after only one or two drinks he'd get pissed up real fast and fall asleep.

One night I decided to watch him and found out he had a secret cavity in his plastic leg that he'd hide a small bottle of whiskey in.

Max Iacovou, Kent

I was put in as head doorman at the Squire in Catford and it was a 'clearout' job. Fuck me, clearout was not the word. The pub held about 350 people and 200 of them were trouble. We had one bloke who came in the pub called Arthur who was a proper crank, dressed in full Nazi uniform. He was a man of about six foot four with a big scar to the left of his face. He used to go behind the bar and help himself. I told him to get out from behind the bar. He replied that he was a barman, so I shouted back, 'Get out of the fucking bar!' He was obviously testing the water with me. The governor told me to leave him as he didn't want any trouble. I told him that our job was to sort out the punters in the pub. He then agreed and took my side after talking Arthur out from behind the bar. Arthur went outside, then came back and wanted to fight all six doormen. I said, 'You can fight me mate, as I'm the smallest.' Arthur walked outside, so I told everyone else to not come outside as it was going to be a one on one. Outside I asked Arthur if he wanted it but got no reply for a while. He then started telling me about some of the things he had done and how he has hurt many people. I snarled, 'So fucking what, are we going to have it or not?' I stood my ground against Arthur and he decided against having a go. Arthur told me I had a lot of bottle and after the confrontation he gave me more respect.

The Squire pub was so bad that the staff felt quite confident when we arrived. A barmaid called Sheriff always came to work with a small axe, as she was involved in a fight before and had lost half of her ear. One of the other doormen before us had his nose bitten off and he came back to work the door with us.

Dave Courtney, South London

You get different top dogs in different areas. The top dog in Newcastle may never have recognised the top dog in London, he may not have known who he was. It might be Mike Tyson and if you didn't know him you may want to have a go, because you don't know his reputation in a certain area. But of course, if you knew him, it's different. I respected them all. We are talking about an era when if you did have a reputation as a doorman, you had to be real tasty. You never had the privilege of fifty doormen working a club at the same time then; there were about four of you fighting for your fucking life.

chapter six
crime and
punishment

WHEN SOMEONE STEPS out of line they have to be punished; that's the doorman's code. If a bouncer turns bully, others will work out a way to stop him. If a customer oversteps the mark, then they have to be penalised. Years ago, when someone upset the doormen or customers it was normal procedure to take them outside and beat the sense into them. In this day and politically correct age, you might think this method is no longer used, but in every town and city there are doormen dishing out their own justice. Doormen are the judge, jury and the executioner on every pub or club door.

Jamie O'Keefe, London

I cannot tell you the worst thing I've done or been involved with because some serious shit went down and people got very seriously hurt using long-lasting, unpleasant methods to equalise things that escalated in a club. There was one incident though where some mug and two pals decided to pay me a visit at my home whilst my kids were there. That's low; you just don't do that. I was a lone parent bringing up kids and doing the door to try to support myself, and some drug dealers put pressure on me to let them sell drugs in my club. I'm the wrong guy to ask that sort of thing. One thing led to another and I bashed a few people up. Anyway, I got followed home one night or tracked down somehow and the threatening visit came. Luckily my kids were asleep so were hardly aware of the visit, apart from a bit of screaming when I resolved matters. They used my kids as part of their verbal threat and that was a stupid thing to do.

Not one of them was able to walk back out of my house. To cut a long story short, after I treated them to a face wash of boiling water and sugar made in the microwave, I phoned my pal Andy's number so he could hear what was going on in the background and in a short while he arrived and we gave them the full works. The boiling sugar solution is still cooking for a couple of minutes when it comes out the microwave and the sugar makes it stick to the skin. You don't fuck with my kids.

I didn't get any more visits. Must be something to do with my hospitality. Violence really sickens me and although it seems hypo-critical to say it, I have had to resort to violence to protect others or myself. The difference between me and most other people is that I do not make threats. I either do something and you won't even know until you feel the pain or I do nothing. There's no point in making threats, empty or real. Either serve someone up or don't.

It's my belief that anybody can do anybody, you just have to find a way. There is not a person on this earth that I could not put out of the game. Let's face it, if it took only one individual to take out President Kennedy, Gandhi, Malcolm X, John Lennon and the like, how the fuck are you going to stop me getting to you? However, just as I believe anybody can do anybody, I'm fully aware that I can also be done by anyone. It's one of the laws of reality. So what I'm saying is that if you fuck with me, there will be consequences. It matters not if you have the top 100 fighting protection team of gangsters or bodyguards. Unless you shit, bathe and sleep with then, one way or another I will get to you. Even if it's not me personally, it will still be done. I'm no gangster or hardman and do not want a reputation for being a vicious callous man. I want to be remembered as a fair person who people leave alone when they are trying to build their little empires.

Ian Hews, Essex

I get a phone call from a local club owner who tells me he has a problem with a new doorman he had just started who was a body-builder. There had been a scuffle between a couple of young lads and the new bouncer went completely berserk, knocking one of the lads to the ground and proceeding to kick and stamp on the lad's head. Nothing but a no-good, steroid freak, bully bouncer.

At the end of the evening, two of us went up to the club and smashed the doorman all around the dance floor, through the back doors and beat the fuck out of him in the car park. About forty minutes later the Old Bill turn up and arrest the two of us. Turns out the council had installed a CCTV camera in the car park, which picked up the both of us laying into the bully bouncer. The club owner explained what it was all about and after six hours the police decided to let us out with no charges. Must have been the only time the police have let me off with anything. The police sergeant said, 'Hopefully you've learnt your lesson, do it again and you will be nicked.' A week later they installed cameras watching the front door of the club as well.

Anthony Thomas, Merthyr Tydfil

I got in for work late one night, I'd been doing a boxing exhibition and was still pumped full of adrenalin. After the boys had asked how the event went, they told me that some dickhead had been playing up earlier and to watch him. This guy was the spit of George Michael, really loved himself and fancied himself as a fighter. I watched him prancing around the club, pushing his weight around and in general making a prick of himself. At the end of the night he's performing again, and when I tell him to cool down his girlfriend sticks her nose in. I put her straight by telling her to stick her head up her fanny, which for some reason didn't help the situation much. He then takes a run at me and throws a well-telegraphed punch. I land a right hand, which crashes into his mouth taking all his front teeth out. He goes flying backwards a lot faster than when he came running at me, blood splatters over his girlfriend's face and over the other doormen standing there. He's out cold and as the lads drag him outside his girlfriend is screaming at me because I was a bully and picked on him for nothing; in fact she said that all he was doing was talking to her when I attacked him. We kick her out of the club as well and after mopping the floor and picking up his teeth to add to our trophy collection, we get back on the door to be confronted by the police. Seems he wanted to press charges, so they spoke to the other bouncers and left. From what I gather he received a message the next day saying that if I was charged he would get a few house calls. Can't for the life of me think who may be responsible for informing the gummy George Michael of that.

Michael Rees, Bath

This local headcase turns up at the front door of the club and attempts to gain entry. He had been banned a short while before for carrying a knife and when the doorman tried to get the knife off him he got slashed across his hand. The headcase ran out of the club and when he got picked up by the police a few days later he had a cast iron alibi and witnesses to prove he hadn't been near the club. I inform him that he's not wanted in the club and that he's never getting in. After a few minutes of arguing he lets me know, 'OK, you fat prick, maybe I'll come up behind you one night and slash your throat with the same knife that I slashed your stupid mate with.' As I step forward to confront him he steps back and beckons me on with one hand while his other is stuck in his jacket pocket, no doubt around his knife. Of course I backed off and went back into the club. All night it was in my head to sort the prick out before he gets brave and comes looking for me.

I left the club late that night and as usual before I got home I stopped the car to get some grub. Just getting my chips and curry sauce, I noticed the prick outside the chip shop talking to his scumbag mates. I walked up behind him and before his mates could warn him I poured my curry down the back of his neck. He jumped around screaming like an epileptic chimpanzee. Everyone was watching as he tried in vain to get the hot curry off his neck and his back. The curry was red hot and burned him quite bad, which was what the fool needed to sort his head out.

What you must understand is that the more you let guys like that prick get away with things, the more they will push their luck with you. Some people will tell you that the scumbags see kindness as weakness and it's true, you have to fight fire with fire no matter what the risk you run of being pulled in by the police. The word then goes around that you're not the quiet type and will not take anything off anyone. I feel that every bouncer who works in a major city or a bad area has at some point to go looking to put closure on an incident that may have happened inside or out side a club.

John Robery, Enfield, North London

I always love going down the boozer and listening to the stories the experienced heads have to tell. One that has stuck in my mind happened in the mid-Seventies. Paul was known in the area as a bit of a tearaway and was the younger brother of a tough nut who had fought a few faces over the years. Paul was out one night in a Tottenham nightclub when somebody pointed out to one of the bouncers that Paul was 'the brother of the cunt' who smashed the shit out of one of the geezers on the door. As he was coming out, they proceeded in booting twenty shades of shit out of young Paul, who didn't stand a chance against so many.

Now, Paul didn't want to ring his brother to sort it out, he wanted to gain a reputation of his own. He rang around all his mates he had grown up with in nearby Enfield and met up in their local. Over a few beers they each chucked in a few suggestions. Some wanted to ask around and find out where they lived; another of his mates who was off his nut wanted to get a shooter and shoot them all. Not surprisingly they decided to fuck that decision off and put it down to just beer talk. They eventually came up with a plan that they all agreed on. There were fourteen lads altogether and each could hold their own in a scrap; they were called the Lancaster Boys because of the road they drank in. They decided to meet two weeks later in the Eagle pub, quite near to where they were going to do their 'army-like' operation. This was exactly a month after Paul got a bashing; he wanted to let things die down a bit before seeking revenge.

Friday came and they met in the Eagle at 7 P.M., psyched up and wanting to get the job done with. Over a few beers they talked about how badly they wanted it and fine-tuned their plan before setting off. The first part of the plan was to synchronise their watches! They did this and went into the club at 8 P.M. in threes, with Paul and his best mate staying outside to meet extra back-up to take care of geezers on the door. They nervously spent their hour before the big kick-off in the club, each in a different mood, from the unrelaxed whose arse was doing an aerobics session to the relaxed fucker who managed a bunk-up in the bogs with his bird! It was nearing the magic time of 9 P.M. and each of the groups positioned themselves in threes round each doorman. Nervous looks were exchanged between them as the tension built and they were getting ready to explode.

What happened next was described to me as 'the doormen all hitting the deck like dominoes'. Nine o'clock struck and all the boys sprang into action, bashing the bouncers with their nuts, fists, bottles and even fire extinguishers. More people joined in as this was an opportunity to give the doormen they didn't like a couple of cheap shots without any comeback. Paul and his little crew waited for the doormen on the outside to start to make a move inside before bashing the fuck out of them. Bouncers were kicked everywhere and one of the unlucky ones was chucked from the balcony, in what was described to me as looking like a scene from a cartoon; the dance floor split open and one unlucky bloke who wasn't fast enough was squashed by this nineteen-stone lump.

The boys made their escapes before the Old Bill came but stupidly made their way back to the Eagle to revel in their victory. Luckily no one knew this is where they escaped to and they could compare their war wounds and stories without having the Old Bill crash in on them. For weeks and months they expected comeback. It was too good to be true that their plan worked and they were getting away with it, but luckily for them Tottenham wasn't their area and they got away scot-free.

Daniel Seery, Birmingham

A well-known fighter around here had been picking on people as usual, only this time it was my brother. He used a baseball bat on my brother and gave him a right going over. As far as I was concerned he had made the biggest mistake of his life. Deep down I knew he had only done him over because he knew he was my brother. He was a regular at the club I was working at so I knew he would show his face around there. What I had in mind was to insure this bully had no face left to show.

It was Saturday; the bully would arrive soon. All night I had been waiting for the bastard to turn up. My stomach was churning because I had seen this man fight before and he was vicious. I kept looking anxiously at the faces entering the club and that's when I noticed him. I waited for him to enter closer. He took a slight glimpse at me and then looked away. He knew the score. As soon as he set foot in the club you could see the apparent relief on his face – but it soon changed when he felt his jacket collar being aggressively tugged. I tugged the bastard backwards, then span him round so he was facing me. I launched a right hook into his nose. His face twisted away, spilling blood, and another three punches went into his head. He dropped to the floor moaning. I went up to him and stomped on his head. He tried getting back up so I put a massive kick into the side of his ribs. CRACK. His ribs broke.

Some of the regulars noticed me fighting him and they were his mates. They started coming towards me. I didn't realise what was going on as I was still laying into his unconscious body on the floor. Suddenly I felt a very sharp pain into the back of my head. It temporarily stunned me. I turned around to see that I had a group of people running at me. I just thought *fuck this* and I started laying into everything that breathed. One bloke ran at me with full speed and knocked me to the floor. I had everyone kicking and stamping on me. I was still in a rage so I couldn't be bothered to defend myself; I decided to carry on attacking them, taking their best shots as I fought. Some big fucker leant over me, ready to put a stamp in my face. A quick, sharp toe punt to his bollocks had him on the floor screaming in agony. The other bouncers started dealing with some of my crowd until there was about five left. They were quickly gotten rid of with me still kicking at everything.

One of my friends leant over to help me up but I kicked into his jaw and knocked him on the floor. He sprawled back up and put me in a headlock. Then another friend grabbed my legs to stop me kicking at everything. An ambulance was called and I had to receive treatment for a massive cut on my head where someone had stamped on me. I'm glad the bouncer who I kicked in the head was a good friend, because if he wasn't I'm sure he would have battered me. I was quickly forgiven and we remained good friends. This just proves how you can develop a good friendship working as a doorman. You'll never get friends like that at any other job.

Ian Hews, Essex

Some of the German clubs that I worked were rough as fuck. One was in a small town near the border of East Germany. The town was well known for trouble because you had a lot of villains selling and smuggling stuff across the borders. You also had American and British soldiers stationed there, mostly manning the checkpoints. There was a lot of tension when all the groups got pissed up. It was a twentieth century outpost.

The club was open twenty-four hours a day. On this occasion it was a Sunday afternoon and was my day off work. I popped around to the club to pick up some cash. As I walk in, I notice there are Hell's Angels everywhere. They were taking over the place and being a right nuisance. Anyone who stood up to these guys would be a fool as there were too many of them and they were all armed and didn't give a fuck what damage they did to you, especially after a few beers.

As I was leaving, a guy walks out of the toilets with blood pouring from his nose and head. Two Hell's Angels came out after him, laughing their heads off at what they had just done. One of the locals told me that the slags had done the guy over just for the fun of it. I walked around the back of the club where the Angels had parked their bikes. Seeing the bikes gave me a great idea. I knew I couldn't fight them all, as that would be suicide, so I sought to smash up the bikes instead. I looked around and found a metal rod, which was quite heavy. It felt really good smashing the bikes, doing just enough damage so they looked a total mess but the fuckers could still ride them away from the club. Laughing, I quickly left the area.

Later that evening, I was on my way back to the club when in the distance I could hear someone shouting in German. I looked around and noticed a few of the Hell's Angels and it was me they were shouting at. They must have been 100 yards away. Suddenly one of the Angels pulls out a handgun and starts shooting at me. At that distance there was no way he could have hit me but I wasn't hanging around to find out. I ran like Forrest Gump down the road.

The following morning the one who had taken pot shots at me was found dead, shot three times in the head. It made all the national newspapers. Maybe one of the local villains took a dislike to him. Can't see why though, he seemed like a nice chap to me.

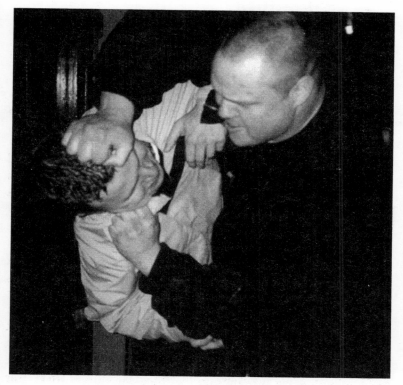

Sometimes the direct approach is the best.

Richard Williams, Aberdare

I was working Asylum Club in Ebbw Vale when right at the end of a busy night, just as we were locking up, it kicked off outside. This idiot came up to the door and started punching and kicking it, trying to impress us. He then proceeds to throw a haymaker straight at the small pane of glass that was in the door. Thing was that the glass was covered with a very fine wire mesh, almost like cheese wire. His whole hand went through the glass and when he pulled his hand back the wire mesh had travelled right up to his wrist. On my horse's life! The wire cut through all the bones and tendons in his hand. His fingers were hanging by threads, like slivers of raw bacon. There were even bits of bone and flesh attached to the wire on the window. Blood was squirting all over the shop and he screamed in pain, clasping his damaged hand. Myself and the lads finished locking up, had a good look at the guy's hand, then walked off home, leaving him there.

Stilks, Crayford

If someone crosses me and it's left unsorted then I'll track them down, especially the big, twenty-stone guys. You should see their faces when I knock on their doors at four in the morning. They open their windows to see me standing there shouting up, 'I'd like a word with you.' Usually they don't want to fight me; after all, one minute they are fast asleep next to their woman, the next they're face to face with a madman on their doorstep. Sometimes I just have to show them what I can do.

Douglas Gentles, Cardiff

I have had many bad experiences with the police. It's now at the stage of where we have a love/hate relationship: they love to hate me and I love to hate them. The one incident that finally banged the nails into the coffin of that last bit of respect I had for the police was an incident that took place in 2001 while working at Berlins. This guy was turned away for having too much to drink. He started mouthing off at the two guys on the front door, usual stuff, 'I'm going to come back and going to fuck you up.' About an hour later he did come back and tried getting in again, only to be refused again. Once more he starts swearing at the two guys on the front door. He even tried pushing his way in. He was there for nearly thirty minutes shouting and swearing at the boys. Another doorman and myself go up on the door, so there are four of us and still this guy is mouthing off, 'Fucking wankers,' and, 'I'm going to fuck you up.' People are walking past laughing at him.

I get on the police radio and ask them to send a unit to move this twat away from the door. I'm told that they have him on camera and they will get a unit down to us when they can. Now, this guy comes over and, pointing at each of us, tells us that he is going to stab us. Then he walks off towards the alley opposite the club. He makes it look like he has taken a knife out of his coat and is holding it behind his back. He now walks over towards us with the one hand behind his back and the other outstretched. He starts shouting at us to come and get it if we have the balls. He is really losing the plot. I'm on the police radio letting them know what this guy is saying. Still no unit available. One of our boys, Richie, moves out to his left and I move out to his right. Richie is trying to see if the guy does have a knife but can't tell, as this guy has his shirt hanging out at the back. Then, as the guy makes a move towards the two boys on the door, Richie kicks away his legs and jumps on him, taking him to the ground. I run over and jump on his shoulders and use my knee to pin his head to the ground. We shout at him to drop the knife. He then tells us that he doesn't have one. I get on the radio again and ask where the police unit is. I'm told they have seen everything and that a unit is en route.

When the police arrive, we let the guy up. The side of his face was cut from the pebbles on the ground; the council was relaying the ground and small pebbles were all over. The police let him walk off and then came over and took our details. A little while later the police caught up with this guy and got him to press charges against us for ABH. We were arrested the following week and charged. I decided to take the matter to crown court. I was banned from working in the city centre (the first doorman ever to be banned from working in Cardiff) and before the matter was finally over I had been to court twelve times for this incident. And why? Because the police were only showing the Crown Prosecution Service part of the tape, the bit where we take the guy down and hold him until the police arrive. On the morning of the trial, the police had to produce the full tape. This was played for the judge and to the CPS for the first time. The CPS were lost for words and the judge was furious with the police. He said the tape showed we had done nothing wrong. He slagged off the guy involved and wanted to know why he hadn't been charged with anything. He praised us for doing a hard job well.

This incident caused me get stress, it was the final straw for my girlfriend and we parted less than four weeks after. My kids thought their daddy was going to get locked up, I believe the police wanted us off the streets for reasons I can't go into. Any respect I had for them was gone. They are two-faced bastards; with one hand they shake your hand and with the other they stab you in the back.

Terry Turbo, North London

The Rex in Stratford was a nightmare when we first went there. There were people getting mugged, beaten up, cars were getting broken into. The next day I went up to Stratford and walked around the venue and found all the hiding places and escape routes that the locals used. When we worked there again, they didn't know what had hit them. We were constantly beating them up and ambushing them when they were trying to mug people. After about two hours we had cleaned up the whole place. The Old Bill came down at about 1.30 P.M. and asked to speak to me. I went out thinking *here we go, we're all going to get nicked.* I was so surprised when he pulled me to one side and said, 'We've been watching you and your guys on CCTV and although we find your way of working unethical, it bloody works. We haven't had one incident reported and last time you were here there were thirty.' I didn't get a community award though. Bit disappointing but there you go.

Anthony Thomas, Merthyr Tydfil

After working this club for a few months we lose the contract due to all the police inquiries and court cases. I end up working at the Vulcan Inn, which was known to be the roughest pub in town. I'm partnered by Wayne, who has been a doorman for over twenty years and isn't the type to mess with. A few weeks of throwing the scumbags out into the road and we more or less got the place sorted.

This one scumbag gets chucked out and threatens me with the big comeback, how I was now a dead man walking and he is on the way up to my house to do damage. I've heard this a zillion times but this piss-ant lived near me so he might just get brave enough. Later that night I get home to find out that he's been there shouting the odds to my girlfriend. There's a knock on the door and I open it to find him at the bottom of my path calling me out while clutching his baseball bat. I tell him that he's getting himself deeper and deeper into trouble and to leave before I really take offence. He runs straight at me with the bat and tries to strike a home run with my head. I duck the bat and rugby-tackle him to the floor. All of a sudden another scumbag comes out of hiding behind my bushes and hits me over the head with an iron bar. My head splits open and while dazed I'm forced to let go of the one that I'm holding. They are now both circling me trying to hit me with the bat or the bar. I'm thinking to myself, *I'm going to get that bat or they are going to put me away.* Even if I took a shot in the meantime, it was the only chance I had.

I reach out and the prick with the bat smashes my arm with it. It was the chance I needed and I'm on him, smashing him on the floor. I grab the bat and go apeshit stamping on him, and I can't feel the other one hitting me across the back with the iron bar because the adrenalin is pumping through me at a million miles an hour. I'm now kicking the fuck into both of them and it ends when they manage to run off with me in hot pursuit. It's off to the hospital to get my scalp glued up and to be checked over. While I'm there I notice the two piss-ants are already being seen to and are crying as they get stitched up by the doctor. I just started laughing and shout a few things over to both of them. Next night I'm back working the Vulcan with my head glued and bruises all over me. The police interview the two scumbags, who want to do me for assault but get charged instead and end up doing twenty months inside.

Tommy Meaney, Leeds

Working in London I was put with various doormen. Some were real gentlemen and some were out and out bullyboys. Being from a different part of the country, I didn't know who they were and had no idea if they could be trusted. You can usually tell within a few hours of meeting someone if they are genuine or not. The way they walk, talk or look at you can give you an inclination of what they are like. This one boy who I was put to work with was a bodybuilder and a right bully. I was only with him about two hours when there was a fight between what was basically two kids. He rushed in there and without even trying to part them he knocked one out and kicked the other in the stomach, which dropped him. I had to carry the poor fuckers out of the club. He's then bragging to a couple of other doormen how quick he'd done the business. None of them tell him how much of a prick he made himself look.

There was an hour to go and about four really big men were arguing over by the cloakroom. As I start to approach them I look for my back-up and he's nowhere to be seen. I could see it coming: it suddenly kicks off and I've hit the main one straight out through the main doors. I turned to have it with the others and they start clapping me. Turns out the main one had tucked the other three up with cash over something or other. The three of them went outside and beat him so bad an ambulance was called for him, but outside the club is nothing to do with us, I'm not a copper. I then notice old bullyboy creeping out of the toilets. He inquires if everything was all right. I looked at him and shook my head in disbelief. 'I didn't want to get involved because I'd already put two guys away and didn't want punters to think I'm a bully,' the gutless prick tells me. My head went and I grabbed him by the back of the neck and smashed his head into the exit door. He put up a bit of a fight but by now I was right up for it. I started stamping on his head until he was out. As the ambulance is getting ready to take the first guy away I call them over to take the bully bouncer as well.

I didn't see the guy for about a month, then one night I get out of my car outside my digs and suddenly the lights go out. I woke up in hospital with my head smashed up and my arm broken. From the marks on the side of my head the doctor could tell it had been done by a knuckleduster. Seems someone was waiting for me to come home and attacked me from the side. I still had all my money on me so it must have been a grudge attack, not a mugging. After I got out of hospital it took me just a few phone calls to find out that the bully from the club was bragging that he beat me in a fair fight, one on one.

I waited a week or so, then went back to the club to have it out with the bully. No sooner had I stepped back through the doors than the prick and a few of his friends jumped me and kicked the shit out of me. I woke up around the back of the club covered in blood and one eye completely closed from being booted in the face a few times. I had to hobble all the way home as I had lost my car keys and none of the taxi drivers would take me in the state I was in. Two weeks later and I was back home in Leeds, working with real doormen who I could trust and knew were watching my back.

Maybe in the near future I'll pay a visit to friends that I still have in London. Maybe I'll stop by a certain bouncer's house, show him how to really use a knuckleduster.

Jason Payne, Merthyr Tydfil

This drunken guy comes down the stairs of the club, pissed as hell. He falls everywhere and I have to pick him up to get him to his feet. With that he walks up to my mate Lee and for some unknown reason starts to twist Lee's nipple, God knows why. Quick as a flash Lee smacks him one straight on the chin, out cold, early night for him. Don't think he'll be twisting Lee's nipple again.

Wayne Price, Mountain Ash

Working the Thorne Hotel in Abercynon one night and we had four guys in who were pushing their weight around making pricks of themselves. My mate Hugh and myself get the first two out and the others don't want to know, so they follow them out the door. At the end of the night I finish and go off to get a Chinese with my wife (now my ex-wife). Walking down the road I notice this figure walking towards us. He seems to be heading straight towards me so I give all the food to the wife just in case. Sure enough the four guys who we had thrown out had followed us and this was the first of them. He comes straight at me and we end up on the ground with me on top sticking punches into him. His mate runs up so I grab him and pull him down and proceed to beat them both. With that I feel something strike my head and start to see stars. One of the guys, John, has hit me over the head with a steel bar but with luck it doesn't put me out. I put my fingers in the eyes of one of the guys I'm fighting with on the floor. I really push them in deep and he's screaming. I get off the floor and I'm still giving it to the guys I was fighting with as the other two run off. As it happens someone had phoned the police and they turn up and arrest us all.

Next day after having my head stitched up over the hospital I have to report to Aberdare police station, where I am charged along with the first two guys I was fighting. The police make a mistake in letting us out of the station at the same time. Soon as we get around the corner I give them both a good hiding. I then went looking for the others and found one of them in a pub and hit him all over the shop, so that left just the one who had hit me with the bar, John. He was a bit fast on his feet for me and I never seemed to catch hold of him for years. I just couldn't find him. A friend came onto me one day and told me that John had been kicked to death in Somerset, so I never did settle the score with him, but someone must have.

Michael Jones, London

I'm not proud of it but one night I hit out at my missus. I'm not that kind of bloke but I was so filled with anger and rage that I couldn't control myself. She was out and this bloke was harassing her. Instead of having a word with him, I left him, thinking that she would tell me if she couldn't handle it. At the end of the night this bloke was all over her. I had spoken to her earlier and she was OK. When I swapped places with Giorgio, the other doorman, all I could see was the back of him, and it looked like at one point they were kissing. I flew over and threw the boy around like a rag doll. When we got outside at the end of the night we spoke about it and she accused me of not trusting her and thinking the worst of her. I then called her a slut, then she really wound me up and I went to put one on her. Suddenly without warning she hit me in the balls and put me on the floor. I was a laughing stock for a month but I learnt my lesson. Never ever make them angry when they've got PMT.

Eric Jones, Edinburgh

We turn this local guy away from the club. He has been barred so there is no way he's coming in. He's quite a game guy and has been kicked up and down the high street in the past but still gets up for more. He doesn't know when to give up. At first he got our respect for that but seeing as he's a right arse when he's drunk, we don't tolerate him any more because he can ruin our night. About twenty minutes after he is turned away, I notice him walking across the car park. He is holding two large, empty brandy bottles and an iron bar. He stops to talk with a few of his mates in this car. Next thing, myself and my mate on the door get bottles rained down on us from this guy and all his mates. Of course none of them get too close to us. The guy I was with says, 'Fuck this,' and off he marches to recruit another doorman and to pick up two small pickaxe handles for good measure.

At this point the owner of the club comes out and tries to calm us down as we were going apeshit. The prick who started it all threatens to go around to one of our houses, which isn't on. If they don't like our job they shouldn't get personal or else we do the same. We all run at the group of guys, the car drives off and everyone scatters. We just keep hitting out with the handles and a few of them cop a couple of good shots here and there. One guy gets clipped and falls over, only to have a few more put into him before we go back to the club. There's no one left outside and the main one that we wanted was the first to leave the scene.

Must have been about fifteen minutes later when two guys I knew from the club come up to me and tell me that their mate has just been leathered. I tell both of them about the guys throwing bottles and that their mate was part of the gang. Eventually the young lad comes up and tells us that he never threw bottles but was too scared to leave the group in case they started on him. I'm a fair guy so I spoke with the lad for a while then got him patched up. Basically this young lad had got a hiding because of the stupid prick that started it all. After we patched the young lad up he seemed happy with his appearance because he said his injuries made him look hard!

Jamie O'Keefe, London

I was in a club socialising and came across some wanker who had mugged my mother two years earlier. There were three of them in all from Barking who knew that she was drawing six months' worth of her pension that she left aside to buy the grandchildren Christmas presents. She never needed to use her pension because I took good care of all her needs. It hurt me bad inside when I was not there to protect her when getting mugged. She was a frail old thing but coming from a tough Scottish upbringing she put up a fight and as a result got beaten up, had her teeth knocked out and had to go to hospital. However she was a forgiving person and made me swear on her life that I would not seek revenge. I kept that promise until she passed away. I'm a believer of what goes around, comes around. One of the three is wheelchair bound now and the other has lost his sight, both in accidental circumstances from what I can make of things.

The third went into hiding. It was just a matter of time because he was a junkie and they always surface. By freak chance I was chilling out in a club that I worked at and, although off duty, everybody in that night knew who I was. This wanker arrived and I was tipped off that he was in the building. I asked the other guys to leave him, as I wanted to sort him in my way. As the night went on the wanker made himself more noticeable and was bowling about like he owned the place. I walked over to him on the dance floor and landed a full-blast double palm slap to each side of his neck, in a clapping motion. It's my trademark technique. It shuts off your central nervous system for a few seconds, leaving you to do what you want to the person. It took me fifteen years to devise this technique, which is why I get so much money to teach it to people. Anyway I hit the wanker and he dropped like a dead weight.

I lifted him up by his hair and then slit the top layers of skin covering his throat. It looked like I was holding one of the heads straight off a guillotine. In reality I only slit a couple of the seven layers of skin in front of the windpipe and did not cut into the windpipe, artery or vein. When you have the training and knowledge that I have you know just how far you can go to cause either effect or damage. This was for effect. The girls were screaming, the guys were in shock and the other bouncers in disbelief. They expected me to smack him one but not cut his throat. The wanker wakes up to find his throat bleeding as I'm dragging him out the club and down a flight of stairs holding only his hair. My whole point of the exercise was not to just repay the wanker, because I could have done that outside. It was to set a standard in the club with all the other punters and wannabe gangsters not to fuck when I'm around. It's an old Chinese philosophy of 'slaughter a chicken to train a monkey'. The monkeys don't fuck about with you once they have seen you rip a chicken apart. All the local wannabe hard nuts knew nothing about the score I had to settle; all they saw was my serving up someone for getting a bit loud on the dance floor. It worked a treat.

chapter seven
drugs and dealers

THERE ARE CUSTOMERS who will take drugs. There's no hiding the fact because it happens in all clubs and pubs. As long as you have drug takers there will be someone who can see the money on offer and supply them with what they need. At some point a doorman will realise that it's a never-ending, futile battle. If they stop dealers working on the premises then the doormen have done their job but of course the customers who take the drugs will go to a different venue where they can get what they want. This has closed many clubs: no drugs, no customers. It's a hard choice for a doorman. If he does his job well he will eventually put himself out of work.

Stilks, Crayford

A lot of the new breed of doormen need drugs or a few drinks to give them courage on the door. Before they get up there, they have to be half pissed or go to the toilet all night for their powder. Up until I was thirty-four years old I had never taken a drug. I went to work in a place called Stars, which was a dangerous place to work. Anything could happen in there and shootings and stabbings were not uncommon. I told a guy I worked with that I felt tired and he offered me some charlie. 'What's that going to do to me?' I asked. 'It will wake you up a bit,' he informed me. On the way home I told him that it hadn't really done anything for me. 'Well, it got you through the night, didn't it?' and I then realised that it had indeed.

Before long we were both doing it every night, until he informed me that I was going through £100 of his stuff each week. This shocked me, as I didn't have a clue that just a gram was worth about

£50. We decided that we couldn't afford to take that much each week so we had to take it off others. If someone went to the toilet more than once in twenty minutes then we got in there and if there was more than one in the cubicle we'd go in and take their stuff. We gave them two options: leave the club or we would phone the Old Bill. Of course we wouldn't phone but they couldn't take the risk.

After a while we couldn't get enough and wanted everyone's drugs and by now we were taking their money as well. We were getting more confident in the way we were doing it and of course the owners thought we were great every time we threw a dealer out. One time we knew someone was taking drugs in the cubicle and we kicked the door in. Standing in front of us was this huge coloured guy who took up the whole cubicle. He was holding this knife covered in charlie up to his nose. I took one look at him and thought there was no way we were going to bottle out now. I said, 'Mate, you're not allowed to do that in here. If you don't give us a line each you're out.' The guy points this knife with the charlie on it up to my nose. I turned to my mate and said, 'Right then, you go first.' After we both had a line I informed the guy that he must not do it again. Now that was a close one.

After about a year I realised that I wasn't sleeping well and didn't feel good taking it any more. All the nights of tossing around in bed not being able to sleep seemed stupid now, especially with all the stupid thoughts going through your mind about your mates all being against you. I stopped taking it for about two days and I slept like a baby. It then dawned on me that the only drug that worked for me was sleep, never mind all the coke. In the end we cleared out Stars and shut it down. I learnt one thing from that and that was if you take all the drugs out of a club, you kill the atmosphere. Today I think that drugs like cocaine have to be accepted a little. If I find one guy going to the toilet to powder his nose, I don't get involved, but if two are in there then I ask them to leave. You can't stop the drugs entirely or the club or pub will slowly die off.

Ian Hews, Essex

There were some young black lads who had been coming to the club for a few weeks before I found out they had been selling drugs. I wasn't having any of that so I banned them all. Now the manager of the club had the same make of car as mine but I used to park mine down the road in a car park where the other doormen parked. They could keep an eye on them better that way. At about three in the morning, I came out of the club and there was this loud sort of whooshing noise. I looked over and the manager's car was engulfed in flames. The black lads I had chucked out of the club thought it was my car. I looked over at them, shook my head, got in my car and drove off laughing.

Lee Callaghan, South Wales

When you get a situation where drunks are involved, nine times out of ten you could push them over if it came to it. If they are drugged up you have a problem; they have so much strength and energy they always put up a fight. I've seen one doorman throw a haymaker of a punch, landing on a druggie's chin to no effect other than to break the doorman's hand. You can knock them down and they will jump straight back up at you. The only way is to drag them outside and choke them out, leaving them to come around.

Kris Cermele, Tampa, Florida

The first few weeks working the clubs I noticed that most of the doormen seemed a little hyper. They were always full of energy, running around and sometimes fighting six or seven times a night. I found the work hard, it was so hot in the clubs and having to physically throw people out is hard work, nobody seemed to want to leave the easy way. Noticing I was worn out, one of the other doormen put a small wrap of speed in my hand. It all made sense now, how the other doormen never got tired and worked so hard. After a while I started to take a few grams of speed or coke each night. It made me feel a lot better but it wasn't something I was proud of. I had gone from being anti-drugs and stopping it coming into the clubs to looking for the dealer who could sell me the best stuff.

I had to pick up the doorman who used to supply me with speed for work one night. I arrived at his home and he invited me in. As he took a shower he told me to get a cold drink from the kitchen for him and myself. The whole apartment was stinking. I declined the drink but went to fetch one for him. I noticed on his table in the kitchen there were a few spoons that had at some time been burned. That's when I realised the other doorman was a crack head, and I was going down the same road. That was the end of drugs for me, I didn't want to end up like him. I stopped taking powder and instead of getting up early each day I'd stay in bed and recharge my batteries. A good carbohydrate meal before work and maybe a sports drink if I needed it, seemed to do the trick.

Andrew Moffat, Edinburgh

There's not a club or pub that hasn't had a regular drug taker or dealer frequent. It's everywhere, no matter what you do it will always be there. A close friend of mine said to me once, 'Andrew, how do you feel about drugs being sold in the club?'

I thought the question over and replied, 'I hate it, I usually give the dealers a smack and hand the drugs in to the manager, who gets it picked up by the police.'

Then he asked me another question, 'Have you ever tried drugs?'

I said, 'Yes, I've tried cannabis and have taken speed years ago, to get me through the shift.'

'Then how can you smack someone for dealing if you yourself have bought some off a dealer, yourself?'

He was right, I was being a hypocrite, smacking dealers when in fact I myself had used their services myself. These days when I catch a dealer I hand the drugs in but no longer smack the dealer around a bit. The only time I do that is when they try to sell drugs in the club for a second time because then I know they are taking the piss and it gets personal.

John Churchill, Brighton

We often find hypodermic needles in the toilet, that's the men's and women's toilets. Burnt tinfoil which the smackheads use is a regular find in the clubs. There's nothing we can do to stop it because there's too much money for the dealers to earn. If I came down too hard on a dealer he'd just pay a few guys to sort me. I've known it happen and I'm not such a fool to think it couldn't happen to me. I know guys who back a few years ago were stealing car radios to make a tenner; now they're driving top-of-the-range cars, selling smack to kids. They make an absolute fortune. The police never seem to catch them because there's always some stupid prick carrying the stuff for them. This is why so many bouncers end up selling drugs. They can control other dealers by stopping them coming into the clubs, while the whole time make a bundle selling their shit.

Bernard Driscoll, South Wales

After becoming head doorman in one nightclub, I got asked to start my own company and take over this new club opening up. Things have changed so much through the years; before you would just get hard men who would go outside, fight and come back in and shake hands. These days, since the drug scene has taken over, some of

Door boss Bernard Driscoll: 'I've had my car windows shot in, front door blasted by a shotgun, telephone wires cut and had too many stitches on my body to count.'

these kids just don't care what they use. Things have changed so much, nearly every establishment has a doorman these days: social clubs, fast food outlets. Working in your own town always has its downside. I've had my car windows shot in, front door of my house blasted in by a shotgun, doors to my offices shot in, telephone wires cut, car scratched. I've been bottled a few times and have had too many stitches on my body to count. Most of it is down to drugs. One boy tried to come into the club one night and I told him he was banned from the night before. He genuinely didn't even know he had been in the club.

Micky Jones, London

The door has changed in the past ten years. There is a much bigger problem now with drugs and people having their drinks spiked. Drugs to me are the root of all evil; get rid of the drugs and the pushers and our job would be much easier. Once you could go out and leave your drinks; now you have to guard them with your life from fear of being spiked.

In London you get a lot of outsiders coming to the big clubs like the Ministry or the Palace to peddle their drugs. One night I was working with this doorman and he was talking about his niece and how stunning she was. She came to the club and stood chatting to us on the door for about fifteen minutes. She had left her things with her mate in the club. About thirty minutes after she had left us her friend came rushing out to get us, shouting that her friend had collapsed and could we get an ambulance. We run into the club and the doorman who was with me completely lost it. He's left me to deal with his niece who by now was in convulsions on the floor. He ran into the club in a right rage and grabbed hold of the nearest dealer and sparked him with a clean right; it took three of our boys to pull him off. He then calmed down for a while but you could see he was still thinking about what had happened to his niece and he charges back in, like a wild thing lashing out at them all.

After the police had gone, we were all sitting around having a drink and a smoke when the boss came in. The hospital had rung to say that the doorman's niece wasn't spiked but she had had a seizure and collapsed from dehydration. I'd like to say he felt bad about the hiding he gave the dealers but they didn't come back for a while, apart from one of them who ended up on the door with us. He was a right mouthy fucker, good for a laugh though. He must have spent more time in a police car than on the door with us.

I started working for a firm in London as it was the only way you were covered with the law. In a way it was a good thing as all the bases were covered. The boss I was working for at the time knew his stuff as he had studied law in college. He would do his best to get you out of any situation no matter what. I have been arrested twice but all charges were dropped the both times; they were for bully-boy drug dealers who on their own were nothing. The one I got arrested for was a dealer who was well known in London, he had sold an E to this little girl who was a regular to the club, an E that put her into a coma. I gave him the finest beating that I could muster and in turn he did a little stint in hospital. The police arrested me on the Monday morning and by the afternoon my self and the boss were in the pub. Someone else didn't like the dealer much though either – he's dead now.

Lee Callaghan, South Wales

If someone is suspected of dealing then we give them the option of being strip-searched or get the police in. Most will choose the strip-search, when of course we make sure there are two doormen present. One dealer opted for being searched and in the back room he took all his clothes off and we found nothing on him – until he bent over to pick up his clothes and a large lump of blow fell out from between the cheeks of his arse. Yuck! After laughing like fuck we let him out and put the blow in the confiscated box, which only the manager has the key for, and it's then handed in to the police.

Terry Turbo, North London

I was eighteen in 1988 and that's when I first got into the club scene. I started off as a punter then became an MC, then a magazine editor, then a rave promoter and then I went on to set up my own security company. My honest opinion, I'd rather be running a club or working on a door with 1,000 pillheads than 1,000 beerheads. The difference is the beerheads think they are all invincible and want to fight each other at the drop of a hat and the pillheads just want to be your best friends all night.

Martin Bayfield, Rhyl

If there's one thing I hate other than druggies and their dealers, it's bad doormen. I had more than my fair share of them when I worked in this one nightclub in England. It took us months before I knew we had a good team who we could all trust. The company that we worked for were putting different boys in who either didn't have the arse for it or were in with the dealers. It didn't take long to catch on and we would fuck them off, after a few weeks.

This one bouncer who was known to have taken the odd drug himself was letting dealers into the club and was on their payroll. In my eyes he may as well have sold the drugs himself to the kids and help put some of them in hospital. How some of them can sleep at night I don't know. So I pulled him into the office and had a word with him. He reckoned someone was shit-stirring and that he was straight. The following day, who do I see in a Tesco car park but him and one of the dealer friends chatting away. That night in work I pull him to one side and ask him again and he tells me the same, that he's not involved with the dealers. A week later one of the dealers was caught selling, and thrown out on his arse. About an hour later I can see this bouncer bollocking the other doorman about throwing the dealer out. By now I'd had enough; I wasn't about to discuss it again with him. I march straight up to him, hit him straight between the eyes and drag him out of the club. I learnt that there is no way you can talk to pricks like him. After all, he was probably making good money off the dealers. He was outside kicking the doors and screaming about what he was going to do to me. I just made sure the doors were locked and informed the other bouncers that he was not coming back in.

A few days later I popped down to the bodybuilding gym and I knew he was there as I checked to see if his car was parked outside. I approached him inside in front of all his steroid-freak friends and offered him out in the car park for a one on one. Of course he won't come outside but said he was drunk and didn't mean to argue with me. I could see he had no bottle and was a no good, drug-dealing prick. He later went on to become head doorman of another club.

Jamie O'Keefe, London

I've never been involved in the rave scene. It's nice to see young kids enjoy themselves but it's impossible to be involved in the scene without having some connection to the drugs side. Even turning a blind eye to the sale of ecstasy is being involved. Let's face it, a firm of conditioned door staff looking after a bunch of kids into love, peace and dance, is not exactly challenging work. I personally don't like working anywhere that makes you become complacent. I prefer an environment that keeps you switched on.

Most 'bouncer wars' are not about the door, as working the doors pays shit money. Hidden underneath is the control of drug sales, and that, to some people, is worth fighting for. I mean, call me old-fashioned but aren't door staff supposed to be ridding the clubs and pubs of the criminal element? The whole thing is a fucking joke. Drug dealers going under the guise of doormen. What next, vicars selling crack cocaine? You have to search hard to find decent door staff who take pride in their job, who are not bullies and do not endorse drugs. They are the real doormen.

We once went to an illegal drinking club in the West End where we could chill and meet other doormen we knew. It was in a three-storey building with the first two floors for our use. I didn't know that the third floor was a crackhouse where junkies and dealers hung out. I thought it was a brothel, so never took much notice. One night a guy ran in and said the police are raiding the illegal cab office next door so are likely to raid the drinking club. The security quickly bolted the doors from the inside. Next thing I know, the power went off and a petrol bomb came through the window and we were all trapped inside. We tried to get down the stairs but that had been set on fire as well. We all forced entry into the top level, which was a drug haven and not a brothel, only to be confronted with guns and knives pointed at us. They thought we were robbing them until one of the guys screamed that he was on fire. They let us past to the roof exit and we all got out. The fire brigade came out and nobody got hurt. It turned out to be a rival drug gang who wanted to burn the place down and all inside. I was just in the wrong place at the wrong time.

Douglas Gentles, Cardiff

There was never any real trouble with any of the raves I worked. The only thing that would happen is a few of the guys working would catch someone selling drugs, normally Es, and instead of handing them over to the police they would given the dealer a smack and take the drugs and money off them. Not being one for drugs, I would have a bigger share of the cash and let the other boys keep the drugs. A nice little earner while it lasted.

I was often told of stories about rival doormen fighting for control of the drug trade within a rave. I never saw any of that. I don't believe in doormen fighting against each other, not even for control of the drug scene. The market is big enough for everyone to work together and still make good money. It's just greed that stops it from happening. Maybe if there was a bit more working together between different teams of doormen from around the country then the foreign gangs that have taken control over big sections of the drug market would not have had the chance to move in so easily, as they have done. Every city up and down the country has the ability to form a strong team of working doormen. Joined together they would be one hell of a force.

Cass Pennant, South East London

Every club we worked was out of control and that's the only reason we were there, because we never worked for normal door money and we only worked the problem places. The West End was another country to us, it was where all the nice people went. The only security work I never felt quite in control of was these rave scene promoters working the illegal raves, because you could never trust the lies their own drugs feed them. I had a lot of behind the scenes shit with those guys.

Peter Edwards, Chepstow

I got an offer to go abroad to Ibiza and work in a bar a mate of mine called Steven had just taken over. The money was excellent and the digs were free, so I thought why not give it a go. After a couple of weeks I started realising who the dealers were. When I had a word with Steven, he told me to turn a blind eye as they were giving him a wage every week to operate in his club. I didn't like the idea of this because all the years I'd been bouncing I'd looked out to stop this kind of thing, but he was the boss who was paying my wages. After a while things started to get rough and very much out of hand. Steven was getting into a lot of things he just couldn't handle and now he didn't want the dealers in his club anymore. Of course the dealers took exception to this and started threatening him with guns and knives.

One of the main dealers turns up with his mates and attempts to enter the bar. I inform him, 'Sorry mate, you can't come in, you're no longer welcome in the club I'm afraid.' He said to me, 'Can I have a word with you outside on your own.' Over the past couple of months I'd got to know him quite well even though he was a dealer. I knew you should never leave the door to go outside with someone but I thought I knew him enough to talk some sense into him. He's talking nicely to me about how we were good friends and shouldn't argue. Then without notice he plunges this knife into my leg. I should have been ready for him but I wasn't. On instinct I threw a straight right hand that put him on the floor, not enough to knock him out but he was stunned for a while. I'm holding my leg with this knife sticking out of it, not a lot of blood showing at first but as I tried hopping away on it I could feel blood dripping all down my leg.

A few other doormen come out to help me and after they saw the knife they started coshing the dealer and his mates. I couldn't really help them but soon as they clonked a few on the head they all buggered off. I'm helped into the bar by Steven the owner, who sits me down and gets me tissues to hold over the wound. By now all of the other doormen are around me and a few of the customers are amazed to see this knife sticking out of my thigh. You know in those old Western films where the hero pulls an arrow out of his leg and everyone looks at him as if he's right hard? Well for some stupid reason I grabbed the knife and pulled it out. I must have looked really hard to everyone watching – until I fainted and fell off the chair.

It took some explaining at the hospital, telling them someone crept up on me and did it before I could see who it was. After a few days in a hospital bed and a few more at my digs, I limp over to the bar to see Steven. After asking how my leg was and how I felt, out of the blue he informs me, 'Pete, I'm afraid I'm going to have to let you go mate. A few of the dealers have been in and they're really not happy with you mate.'

'Not fucking happy with me!' I shout. 'I'm the arsehole who got a knife plunged into his leg. Can't say they're on my fucking Christmas card list.'

After a while I calm down and he explains that if I stay I'll be killed for sure. 'Pete, I'm telling you now for your own good, you will have a bullet in your head if you keep working here mate. For your own good I'm letting you go.' He put his hand in his pocket and gave me about £1,000 for my expenses and to say thank you. Two days later I'm on a plane going home.

When you weigh the odds up, you can't beat the dealers no matter what you try to do. You stop one, then another steps up to take his place. If you get too involved or cut off their business, you can end up done over or even killed.

Lee Morris, South Wales

I was knackered and just didn't want to be working on a pub door. I had been playing football in the day and my legs were really tired. There was a boy playing up by the bandit. I grab the boy and he goes nuts, throwing punches at me. As I wrestle him out of the pub, he still tries to fight me. 'Let's do it now,' I scream in his face, but he just fucks off instead. About half an hour later he comes back with two bottles and bottles the bouncer with me over the head. He then went for me. As I picked up a pint glass he threw the bottle at me and it hit me in the shoulder. I dropped the glass and ran at him. He was only small but he was pretty fit. I was cutting his face open with punches but he still kept getting back up and coming at me. He must have been on something as I knocked him down and he just kept coming. How I managed to stop him I don't know. The drugs had given him a strength that he didn't normally possess and made it almost impossible to knock the fucker out. Anyway the fight gets stopped and he goes his way. Not long after I caught up with him and cornered him. This time he was sober and had no drugs in him but of course he didn't want to know.

On another night I had just got in to work in this pub when I get told there's a boy in there smoking blow. Now this boy had a reputation as one of the hardest men in the town. I walked over to him and asked him to leave. He shoves me and says, 'Who the fuck are you? I'm not going anywhere,' and took his jacket off. He then starts squaring up to me. The other bouncers and I grab him and chuck him out and he goes for me. I spun round and hit him with a back-hander, followed by a left hook and he was knocked out. I gave him a good kick to make sure but he was still out. He came past the pub a few times making shooting gestures but nothing came of it.

Kris Cermele, Tampa, Florida

We had trouble from dealers getting crack and other major drugs into the club. We searched them and most of the time they still got their stuff in. We looked in their shoes, hair, pockets, everywhere we could think of, to no avail. I train on the weights when I manage to get some time to myself and go to this real classy gym not far from where I live. Training one day, I get talking to this guy who eventually tells me that he'd been in prison for three years and in the two years he's been out has become a born-again Christian. I sort of remember him from when he was a local gang member who used the club where I worked the doors.

I ask him, 'How the hell did you all manage to get drugs into the club?'

'Well,' he answers, 'we got our girlfriends to bring them in. We'd put them in plastic bags and the girls would put them up inside themselves. Then we'd retrieve them once we got into the club.'

I thought to myself, *there's no way I'm searching up there for them.* However you try to stop them getting drugs in, they'd find a new way. We were fighting a losing battle.

Darryl Taskers, South Wales

The drug scene has got much bigger. The people who take pills don't cause that much trouble, they're all usually loved-up, but when it comes down to drink certain people think they can fight the world. The thing is, drink don't make you tough, it just makes you drunk.

Most weekends we have gangs coming into the pub but I know a lot of the guys in the gangs and always make them feel welcome. It's very rarely they kick off but when one starts fighting you know the rest are behind them and then your work starts. With about ten lads in each gang and only two doormen working, you've just got to do your best.

Terry Turbo, North London

Every incident could potentially be dangerous but we never took any shit if we caught people selling gear. We'd hand them over to the police. You may not like that one but with all the 'doormen control drugs in clubs' rumours flying about, it's better to be safe than sorry. If we caught people mugging, we'd beat them up and strip them naked! If anyone wanted it, they got the kicking of their life but because of our reputation of being no-nonsense we never really had too many problems

Shaun Kelly, Ebbw Vale

I was on duty one night in this rugby club when I got called to a situation. This boy had collapsed and was unconscious on the floor. I could see he had taken something and that it just wasn't the drink that had done this to him, so I ask someone what's he taken. I get told he had taken the concoction of Ecstasy and the new drug that was doing the rounds called GHB. I had to think fast as he looked in a really bad way. I cleaned his mouth out of the spew and made sure his airways were clear. I then started giving him mouth-to-mouth until the paramedics turned up and took over. They put him in the ambulance and took him off to hospital. You can't just stand back, you must react fast. Over the years you build up enough experience to deal with most situations.

Jamie O'Keefe, London

Back in the old days, doormen would sign on the dole as unemployed but work for cash at night on the door. The licensing scheme interfered with that due to having to provide all personal details along with our National Insurance number. It's hard these days to get a good wage if you declare your income, so many do day jobs as well. There are also the few that deal drugs or take money from dealers to turn a blind eye to drug selling. People do whatever they need to do to pay the bills; it's just a shame that some will do things to profit from other people's suffering. Good door staff should get paid according to professionalism and not have to resort to other means to make ends meet. The good ones work bloody hard with being switched on, polite and taking crap off drunks all night and are mentally knackered after a shift. It's a thankless job and the professionals deserve more recognition and a wage according to experience and professionalism. I think it's a joke to expect them to do the job for less than £20 per hour.

dropping your guard

IT IS BETTER to be ready for the worst than be caught unawares. A good doorman is constantly aware of where the troublemakers are and what's going down. If a doorman lets his guard down then he's in trouble. If he underestimates how the night is going, he could be caught in a full-scale war. If he overestimates a troublemaker's ability then he will be too cautious and wary when the time comes to respond. A good doorman has to get the balance correct and that takes years of experience.

Ian Hews, Essex

I was working one of the biggest clubs in London, which had a licence to hold about 2,000 clubbers. One night this posh lad turns up from the local college and asks can he hire the club for the end of term disco. He estimated there would be about 3–400 students whose age group ranged between sixteen and nineteen. Everything was agreed and the club was booked for a Sunday, a night when the club was usually closed. We thought just five bouncers would do, seeing as all the students knew each other and it was a private party.

We ended up with over 800 pissed-up teenagers running around the club, fighting and puking up everywhere, young girls totally off their heads shouting and screaming at us, it was a nightmare. The club got wrecked and we spent the whole night running around breaking fights up. We learned a good lesson: always be prepared for the worst. I never worked another student party again after that one, thankfully.

Michael Vaughan, Newcastle

Sometimes we would get a mad rush of customers trying to get in the club. This would happen just as the pubs were starting to close, and got really hectic. This makes it difficult for us to search everyone coming in. We'd search some and just let the others past. It's the only way we could get things moving. I remember one girl getting her face cut open and the person who did it was an angelic-looking girl who one of the female door staff had failed to search. She had brought a small knife into the club with the sole purpose of cutting this other girl's face up. Just goes to show you can't trust anyone.

Cass Pennant, South East London

The most dangerous people were the guys that I worked with. These guys didn't work because they had to, they did the job because they were good at what they had to do; an elite, if you like, that came together to work the doors other security wouldn't touch because of the bad rep of those places. Sure, there were plenty of dangerous people we encountered. Some would be our own mates or others known to us. This was a respect thing and although we worked in small numbers (two to four) on average, often without radio communication, we would learn to move and link as one. We were almost telepathic in sensing when trouble was about to occur, or we were quick on reading trouble signs and reacting as a team.

Kevin Trottman, Liverpool

I was informed that this boy was dealing on the premises of the club. Another doorman and myself wait until the boy went to the toilet and after a quick search we found about forty wraps of speed on him. The police were called and the boy was arrested. A couple of months later, I was working in this other nightclub when the same boy came in. I called him to one side and told him it was a different club and if I caught him dealing I'd be sorting it out myself and not the police. He told me he was a changed man and was going straight. After watching him all night, I came to the conclusion that he wasn't dealing and was just out for a good night.

Earlier on in the evening, we had this live band playing and they left all their stuff at the back of the club. I clock the boy over by their stuff, filling his pockets as the band are up at the bar sinking a few bevies. I go back into the foyer and pretend I haven't seen him. I was by the main door as he came up, expecting me to open the door so he could leave the club. I smile at him and ask if he has had a good night. He answers that he's had an excellent night and would be back next week. 'I'm glad,' I tell him, 'but before you go, empty your fucking pockets.' He can see I'm not smiling any more and starts pulling stuff out of his pockets: drumsticks, mobile phone, lighter and a pair of trainers! The kid needed to be taught a lesson. I wanted to slap him around but he was so skinny I would have killed him. I just threatened him and put the fear of God into him instead. Maybe if I had given him a good beating the first time I caught him up to no good he wouldn't have tried his luck once more. These days I never give them a second chance. If they are up to no good then I ban them until hell freezes over.

Max Iacovou (left), author Julian Davies and Stellakis "Stilks" Stylianou

Jamie O'Keefe, London

I took a few uppercuts that I wasn't prepared for when I refused entry to a large female who said her girlfriend was in our club. She tried to glass me in the face with the drink she had with her and as I focused on defusing the attack, she stuck the fists in. Not only did I not expect it, she could box! The other security and manager were watching it on the CCTV and were doing a running commentary over the tannoy whilst having a good laugh. It was a nightmare because I don't hit females and just tried closing her down whilst shoving her out the doors.

Stilks, Crayford

Women are the worst there is when they fight. I feel they can be more vicious and violent. I've seen more glassings done by women than by men. Trouble is, you never know how to grab them because you can bet they would be straight down the police station complaining that you manhandled them and touched them up. Who's the copper going to believe when he gets a complaint, me or the woman? Now when I get two women fighting, I ask one of the other doormen to sort it, as I won't do it any more. I haven't got the patience to talk to the women who are fighting or the copper who may turn up and talk like shit to me. I'll let them kill themselves or let someone else sort it before I'd get involved. You just can't beat them because the moment you lay a hand on them they'll have you done.

Douglas Gentles, Cardiff

Young men out drinking, often trying to impress a girl or their mates, are always dangerous. The biggest mistake a doorman can make is to underestimate someone. Only a fool does it.

Andrew Moffat, Edinburgh

A lad who I worked with on the door for a while had an almighty argument with one of the female customers. I forget the reason but she was right up for fighting him. She tried to punch him but he moved and laughed in her face. Next thing she swung her handbag, which came down on his fucking head. Back he falls and lands flat on his arse. Turns out he hadn't searched her handbag, which he now found out by the lumps on his head carried a small bottle of brandy that she was sneaking into the club.

Ian Hews, Essex

Back in 1982 before they had hand-held scanners, we had to search everyone coming into the clubs for weapons by rubbing them down by hand. This old gent walks up to the door and goes to walk in. He's smartly dressed but his nose is spread all over his face, looking like he's done ten rounds with Joe Frazier. I moved to search him when he steps back looking me straight in the eye and tells me, 'You aren't touching me, so fuck off.'

'I ain't arguing with you pop,' I answer as I let him into the club.

About an hour later I'm walking around the bars and I notice the old boy sitting with two young girls having a drink. Every time I went past him he was chatting with someone else who would then get the old boy a drink. Over the next year he came up to the club every Thursday and Friday night like clockwork. He got friendly with us all and we eventually found out he was an old fighter who'd had over 300 amateur and professional fights. He would sit there in the warm all night, happy as a sandboy, getting free drinks off all the young girls. Glad I didn't argue with him: 300 fights, fuck that.

John Churchill, Brighton

It was coming to the end of the night and I had to go and check all the club fire exit doors. Most of the customers were gone and there were just a few getting ready to leave. I checked one fire exit and it was locked so I made my way over to one of the others. I stepped through the first door that led to a ramp, which had the exit doors behind it. Without warning, two guys jumped out of the shadows and jumped on me. I was too surprised to do anything and before I knew it they were sticking the boots in. A hard kick to the head and I was out with the fairies. I awoke to find another doorman shaking me and asking if I was all right. I managed to stand up and immediately threw up a mixture of my dinner, blood and my front teeth.

From what I gather, the other doorman had came walking down when he heard the exit door alarm go off. He didn't rush down because he thought it was just me checking it. I have no idea why those guys jumped me and to this day I don't know what they looked like. What kills me is that they may still be coming to the club and I probably have spoken to them politely.

Lee Morris, South Wales

I was working in this one pub and my mate Martin had come for a drink. He states, 'I bet there's hardly any trouble here.' He must have jinxed us, because as soon as he said it a fight has kicked off in the corner. We've grabbed them and I've hit this one in the ribs and he's gone down. I then felt something hitting my head but I was so hyped up I hardly felt it. I put my hand on my head and the blood was pissing out of me. We managed to get them out whilst fighting with them at the same time. They then fucked off before the police came. I shot over the hospital to get my head glued back together.

Cass Pennant, South East London

A guy who meant me serious harm turned up at my gym with a friend who said he wanted to talk. I immediately went for a sword I had stashed above the door, thinking, *what has he got?* His friend read my mind, he shouted, 'Don't!' Seems the chap came in peace. He gave me this metal dove he said he had made himself. What can you say to that? The guy walked off and I'd gone from hate to confusion. All-out gang war was off because a dove is a bird of peace. With all that had gone on before it, it took a while to sink in. One, it wasn't expected, and two, the geezer wasn't a crank, so what was that all about?

Andrew Moffat, Edinburgh

I'm forty-two years old and have seen almost everything there is to see on the door, from knife attacks to being shot at from a passing car. I have scars down my back from having a pint glass thrust into it and my right ear lobe is missing from having been bitten off by a hungry customer. Of all the pain my injuries have caused me I can put my hand on my heart and tell you the worst was when I was CS-gassed.

A customer left one of the clubs I was working at one night but on the way out he entered the staff cloakroom and lifted my jacket. He had got about halfway down the road when a girl from behind the bar rushed over and told me what he had done. I left one of my mates to watch the door while I went to catch the coat thief. He must have been a faster walker than I thought because when I got to where I thought he'd be, he was nowhere to be seen. Not wanting to lose my jacket, I walked a little further and noticed the thieving bastard arguing with two young lads. Before I could get to him a fight broke out between the three of them and the thief was by now wearing my jacket as he fought with them. I rushed in and broke it up just as the police pulled up. This wee WPC got out of the police wagon and told us to stop arguing and get off home. The jacket thief started to walk away, as did the other two. I made a lunge for my jacket and the WPC grabbed my arm while shouting, 'I'm fucking warning you for the last time.'

'Sorry love but I'm a doorman and this bastard just pinched my fucking jacket,' I try to explain to the WPC (who by the way was drop-dead gorgeous). Maybe it was the way I spoke or my tendency to wave my arms around that made her squirt some CS gas in my face. I have seen it used on the TV on them stupid Yank cop shows and always thought if that happened to me I'd just hold my breath. No fucking way. Straight away my eyes started to burn and just seemed to close on their own and wouldn't open. My nose started to burn so much that the only way I could breathe was through my mouth, which meant I was taking more of the blasted stuff into my body. I fell to my knees trying to drag air into my lungs. I tried rubbing my eyes (which I now know is the worst thing to do, as you end up rubbing it into the skin pores around the eyes) but that made it worse. Mucus was running down my face from my nose but I was in too much pain to worry about how I looked.

A few minutes – which felt like hours – later, my eyes started to clear as I started to breathe in fresh air. By now I was handcuffed and being marched into the wagon by the WPC and some giant of a copper who only got out of the wagon when I got sprayed. The worst was the jacket thief shouting, 'That's the way, keep the troublemaking scum off the streets.' I argued for about ten minutes in the back of the wagon before they took me back to the club to prove who I was. Before they let me go the WPC explained that she was waiting all night for a chance to spray someone and it was just my unlucky night.

Inside the club I checked myself in the mirror. My eyes where bright red and my face had started to blister where I had rubbed the chemical deeper into my skin when I started to panic. I found out later that the WPC was too close to my face when she used it. Next morning my face was full of blisters and some skin was peeling off around my nose. In the hospital waiting room some nosey old lady asked me what had happened. I explained that I was a doorman and said, 'Last night I threw some gypsies out of the club. Before they left they put a gypsy curse on me. This morning I woke up like this.' You should have seen the look on the nosey old cow's face, a right picture.

John Garfield, Los Angeles

I was walking along Third Avenue this one evening, past PJ Clarke's, a bar-hangout for the sports crowd and the media, and a booming voice hails me: 'John, John, over here.'

I looked over in the direction of the voice and I saw a guy as big as a building in a huge suit, standing in Clarke's doorway. He was easily six-six and over 350 pounds, and his barrel chest and tree-trunk arms were straining against the seams of his jacket. He was as big around as he was wide and his neck was like a thigh. He was like a collector from *The Godfather*. But he came away from the building and lumbered over to me. 'John, it's me, Mark, Mark Tendler.'

As I looked at him, I could see something about his features that was vaguely familiar inside that mountain. Then it struck me: I used to train with him at Stillman's Gym years before. But at that time, he was a tall, rangy heavyweight, barely 200 pounds. He explained to me that after he stopped fighting he became a powerlifter. For years he was a professional wrestler and now he was the bouncer at

Clarke's. We walked back just inside the entrance to Clarke's and reminisced about the good old days.

Over at the bar about fifteen feet away was an Ivy League-looking jock and his girl. The jock clearly had too much to drink and he said to his girl in a voice intended for Mark, 'See the bouncer at the door? He thinks because he's so big, he scares people. He doesn't scare me.' Now, the people in the bar are starting to inch away but Mark doesn't even look at Ivy League, he continues talking to me as if the guy doesn't exist. The jock raises the level of his voice. 'HE THINKS HE CAN PRETEND I'M NOT HERE. I'LL SHOW YOU WHAT A PHONEY HE IS. HOLD MY COAT,' he says to his girl. Everybody in the bar clears away, but Mark keeps talking to me without a hint of concern. I'm getting more nervous by the moment. The jock, full of bravado, heads towards us. Mark still doesn't acknowledge him. When the jock gets less than arm's-length away, Mark turns to him and says softly, 'If you hit me and I find out about it, you're going be in a lot of trouble.' The jock turned ashen and slunk away.

Jason Payne, Merthyr Tydfil

Two gangs kicked off one night while I was working in Pulsars in Caerphilly. We managed to get them all out and they continued to fight outside the club. A police van turns up and I'm thinking the police are going to lay into them, so I step back to watch the action. One copper gets out to stop the fighting. He was a sergeant but wasn't the biggest of guys. He jumps straight into the fight and starts to pull a few apart. These two lads were having a right old go and the copper grabs one of them. With that the other one tries to grab the copper, so I run in and push him away. I didn't notice another police van pull up behind us all. Suddenly two coppers grab my arms behind my back and within seconds I'm sitting in the back of the van with all the guys who'd been scrapping. The sergeant turns up and asks what I'm doing there. 'We saw him run up and try to hit you from behind,' answered one of the coppers. 'Don't be so stupid, he was in there helping me, get him out,' shouts the sergeant. Well, they let me go and the sergeant thanked me. But I couldn't believe how fast they got me in the back of the van, seeing as I'm six foot three and twenty stone.

Cass Pennant, South East London

The places we worked, Old Bill knew the strength and considered we were doing them a favour. There was a pub outside a South East London police station that didn't like the type of doormen I employed so I could never get this one onto my list. One day the landlord of the pub phoned me.

'Could you come down and run the door of the pub?' he asked.

'How can we? You know the problem with old bill not wanting us to run the door.'

Turns out the police had told him it's okay because fourteen of their officers needed hospital treatment after a stag party barney the night before. They'd had their go now they wanted us to go in.

Ari Bolden, Victoria, Canada

If I have learned anything in this business, it is never judge a book by its cover. Always expect the unexpected. Doormen are insulted on a nightly basis on a variety of topics. As soon as some sorry-ass yahoo has runs out of things to say about your mother, he'll move on to insult the profession. 'You must be real proud being a bouncer? I make more money in a day than you make in a week. I guess you couldn't get a real job you dumb lug. Besides, aren't you a little small to be a bouncer?'

As a doorman, I never advertised my background because the uncertainty principle works to my advantage. Let me tell you a little secret. This bouncer has his degree in ethical reasoning (philosophy), is working on his Masters in conflict resolution, is a certified private investigator, has written two books and started his martial arts career 19 years ago. I am damn proud of my accomplishments. So the moral of the story: never judge a book by its cover because the only thing worse than a tough bouncer is a smart one.

Phil George, London

It had been a nice night at the club, no trouble and we were all in a good mood. Must have been about 3.30 in the morning when the fire door exit alarm goes off. We went down to the exit to find nothing wrong and the alarm had stopped. About half an hour later one of us mentions that the manager hadn't been around for a while. We thought it best to take a look for him and walked all around the club trying to find him. Eventually we get upstairs to the office and the door was open, which was unusual because it's locked up most of the time. We had a look in and there's the manager lying on the floor all tied up. Don't know why we saw the funny side of it but we did: myself and the other doorman couldn't look at each other in case we burst out laughing. The manager says he's been robbed of the takings and they had only just left before we had found him, so there was a good chance they might still be in the club. We run back down into the club to hear both of the exits go off roughly about the same time; looks like whoever had robbed the club left by different exits. The other doormen join us and we split up, each group taking a different exit door. As my group get through our door we notice this guy walking away from the door and the club. We shout for him to stop and run up to grab him. We must have got just a few feet from him, when he turns around and pulls out his shotgun.

He looked at us and said, 'Would you like this?'

'No thanks mate,' I answered. 'See you again.'

We ran back to the club a lot faster than when we ran out of it, I can tell you.

Jason Dicks, Bristol

A strange thing is that the guys you think will give you the most trouble, don't. Then the guys you think you can handle easy are always the ones who fight like crazy. I've found the biggest does not mean the best. Put it this way: who would you want to have a one-on-one with, a big twenty-stone guy who doesn't know how to punch or a thirteen-stone guy who fights like Marvin Hagler? Most big guys are used to having their own way and their size often wins the fight for them before a punch is thrown. Smaller guys have to stand up for themselves because their physical size isn't going to help them. This isn't always the way it goes but believe me, I've come a cropper quite a few times trying to throw a small guy out only to find the fucker's laid one on me.

i'll be back

HOW MANY TIMES has a doorman heard the words, 'I'm coming back to sort you out?' After the effects of drink or drugs wear off, most troublemakers don't want to know. The last thing they want is to mess with the doormen who sorted them the night before. Every doorman knows this and that's why they mostly ignore the threats of comebacks. On the other hand, some do come back and you can bet they have back-up with them, if not in the shape of a few hefty friends then in the form of a weapon. You can't anticipate who is going to come back to haunt you but most good doormen will memorise a face in case there's a return.

Cass Pennant, South East London

Sometimes we got comebacks and carry-ons when they thought they would take advantage of our numbers. They'd come at us with everyone else from the local boozer or half the fucking estate, so a quick phone call to other clubs nearby meant we had teams that served as our cavalry call. We also had a few ringers posing as guests we used as footsoldiers. They'd be mates that could have a row without being built like doormen and were less obvious. We'd get them over if we thought we'd have a problem, on the promise of free entry and new birds to pull.

Peter Anthony, London

My first night on the door and I was standing outside with the head doorman and this bloke came up – I will never forget him as he has a big reputation. This bloke turns round to us, lifts up his top, and asks us, 'Do you want this?' Then he walked off. As we didn't know what he had shown us, we didn't know what to make of the guy. About fifteen minutes later he's back at the front door and again asks, 'Do you want this or not?' This time we look a little closer and realise he's holding a shooter. For some strange reason we stood our ground and told him to fuck off. Turns out what he was doing was testing the door to see if he could take over the club. A fortnight later he went to a club round the corner and shot the place up. We met him after and he was all right with us. I will never forget my first night on the door and having a gun pulled on me, I remember thinking, what the hell have I let myself in for?

Ian Hews, Essex

Four guys start a fight in the club so of course we throw them out. An hour or so later they return and lob two CS gas canisters into the front entrance. The fumes start to pour up the staircase into the disco above, which started a panic, sending punters running out of the club. A girl came running up to me screaming that her friend had passed out upstairs and she couldn't get her out. Two of us ran back up to search for the girl. With CS gas attacking the moisture in our eyes, making them burn and playing hell with our breathing, it's real nasty stuff indeed. We find the girl, carry her out and make sure she's all right. The police turn up and force us to close the club up for the night. The following week I'm looking at the local paper and there's the girl we rescued on the front page, explaining how heartless bouncers had thrown her out of the club for nothing and stopped everyone returning to the club. She got her fifteen minutes of fame and we get a bad name out of it all. Sorry that we went to help the bitch now.

Anthony Thomas, Merthyr Tydfil

Collecting entry money on the door one night and this guy I sort of knew from years ago turns up. He used to fancy himself as a fighter and was used to getting his own way. Turns out we had no change on the door so we let him in on condition that he gets change at the bar and to come back with it. A good while passes and he still hasn't come back with the cash. I spot him going and ask for the money.

He tells me he's paid and starts to give me loads of verbal abuse. For a crack, I let him act the hard man and pretend to back down to him. The other doormen are shocked, as usually I would have grabbed him by the throat by now. I tell the horrible bastard that he's right and I've made a terrible mistake. He thinks I've backed down so he's poking his finger at me and telling all who could hear what he's going to do to me. He goes to throw a punch and with that I'm on him, shaking him around like a rag doll. I'm now marching down the stairs to the front door dragging him by his foot. He's screaming and shouting to be let go, which I do after throwing him down the outside steps into the street. The other lads are in stitches and start calling me a rotten bastard for doing it. I explain that when I was younger I had seen him pick on smaller guys and always wanted to batter the bully.

The following week the same guy turns up and apologised for any trouble he had caused the week before. He seemed all right so I let him in and within two hours he's back from the bar confronting all us doormen to find out who had previously thrown him out. Once more he lifts his hands to me and before he can make a fist I've headbutted him out cold. He's then dragged out into the street to wake up with a very sore head. Funny thing is that he never came back the third week. Can't think why.

Jason Dicks, Bristol

Not many come back for a second go but why is it that when they do they always bring a few friends with them? I've hit guys who have deserved it and a few hours later they are back with their mates, even though it was only me that hit them. Another thing I find strange is that it's okay for three or four lads to beat the crap out of one doorman yet if it was the other way around they would be screaming that we were cowards and bullies. I got a right going over by a few guys years ago. I was outnumbered and working the door on my own so I didn't stand a chance. What I couldn't understand was that each one went around telling everyone that it was he who beat me fair and square on his own. It's as if they couldn't remember that there was a few of them and that they jumped me from behind. I think it's that they feel ashamed of what they have done and try and cover it up.

Marty Dee Donovan, South London

One of my most violent moments on the door was in 1995. I was working a club in Soho with two of us on the front door and two inside. We had just turned away two guys for being too drunk and they were now outside shouting abuse, as they always do. Then they were joined by three more that were to meet them in the club. The abuse got worse. Eventually one of them threw a dustbin at us and all of a sudden these guys were coming from everywhere. We fought for what seemed like ages and it wasn't until afterwards that I realised I had been stabbed. I also broke two of my fingers in the scuffle. One thing I remember most about that night was just how much blood can spill out of a wound unnoticed. At the end of it, it was them in the street unconscious missing teeth and having new-constructed noses. Although there were only two of us on the front door we were a good team, a team that was close and knew exactly how to handle those amateurs. Having a good reliable team is very important in this business.

Another night in a scuffle years later, I lost a testicle. Of all the things to lose! A guy grabbed my bollocks and pulled them like a bell rope. My eyes still water at the thought today.

Dave Courtney, South London

There isn't really a set of people who are the most dangerous but I would say the most active for fights would be the pikeys, the gypsies. Their life revolves around fighting; they love a tear-up, they don't even mind losing. If they lose they just come back with another couple of big lumps and start again. And naturally the more you do something the better you get at it. So the pikeys are naturally more up for it.

Neil Lewis, Treharris, South Wales

It had been a pretty normal night, no trouble whatsoever, not a boo out of anyone. It was chucking out time and there were about eight people left to get out. This twat then comes running in through the main doors shouting for his mates, who were just drinking up.

I told him straight but nice, 'We're closing mate, you'll have to wait outside for them.'

He then argues, 'Just leave me get my mates.'

I tell him a little firmer, 'Please mate, you'll have to wait outside, we are closing, now.'

He turns to me and says, 'Fuck you, you wanker,' and pulls out this huge torch. It was one of those ones the police use, a pretty heavy steel torch. He starts swinging it round like a *Star Wars* light sabre. It was quite funny just watching him. The other doorman, John, then comes to the door and tries to calm Daft Vader down. The guy has a right attitude and informs him, 'That wanker won't leave me in here,' still waving the torch at me.

I shout to him, 'Go home mate, come and see me tomorrow if you have got a problem.'

'No,' he yells, 'you stopped me getting in.'

He was starting to fuck me off. I still tried to keep calm and told him I didn't want any trouble. He must have thought I was bottling it and starts shouting, 'You're having it when you finish your shift.' The doormen then closed the door on him and we go back into the club.

His mates were laughing at him inside the club. One of them then says to me, 'Don't fuck about with him, he'll stab you as good as look at you.' I thought, *what, with a torch?* After hearing his friends brag him up, I was right up for it. I wanted to hurt the fucker now and thought, *if he's still outside he's having it big time.* About ten minutes later the other doormen and I get paid and we leave together. As soon as we get outside, the fucker ran over and shouted, 'Let's have it cunt.'

That's all I wanted to hear. My eyes were peeled on him looking for the torch. His hand went under his jumper and he starts to pull the torch out. I jumped straight on him like a mongoose on a cobra and put him in a headlock, taking him to the ground. I managed to get my one hand on the torch whilst the other hand was around his neck. I then went to work on him and started butting him with the side of my head, which was all I could use at that moment, until I softened him up. After about ten headbutts he was fucked but still kept fighting. I put my knee on his arm that held the torch, then started throwing big left and right punches into his face. He finally stopped moving.

I stood up and looked at him laid out in his own blood, but thought to myself, *I've got to finish him proper, make sure he don't come back with knives for more.* I dropped all my weight onto his face using my knee and held him there. Then I picked his torch up off the floor and started smashing him in the knees with it, then across the face. I was gone off on one and wanted to kill the fucker. Blood was spouting out from his face all over me as I kept hitting him with the torch. One of the other bouncers grabbed me and pulled me away and told me to fuck off before the Old Bill turned up. An ambulance came and took the guy away. Perhaps I went a little too far but he deserved it and would have done it to me given half a chance. I'd smashed my hand to bits and decided to keep a low profile for a while. I heard various rumours that the boy was going to do me for assault but nothing came of it.

Andrew Moffat, Edinburgh

You always get some wee twat saying he's going to come back to sort you out, but very few do. We had one lad come to the club and ask me to step outside to sort it out man to man. Before he could make his move I stuck a body shot into his ribs, which took all the air out of his lungs and made him double up and fall to the floor. Maybe I'm getting soft in my old age but I went and lifted him onto a chair until he got his act together. As he sat there he mentions, 'Fair play you beat me, but if you had hit me this hard last night I wouldn't have come back today.'

'Sorry son,' I replied, 'but I wasn't working last night, I went fishing instead.'

The lad looks around the club and says, 'Fucking hell, no! I'm in the poxy wrong club.' He had been thrown out of another club the night before and thought our club was the same one. Five minutes later another doorman came up to see if everything was all right on the front door. What he found was one bouncer and one bruised-ribbed lad, laughing and crying like school kids.

Ian Hews, Essex

A new club opens up in Battersea, south London, called Browns. The owners had spent a hell of a lot of money on the place. Among other things they installed a glass floor with a fish tank underneath it. It must have been about a fortnight after the club had opened up when some heavies arrived. After giving the doormen a beating the heavies demanded a cut of all the takings. The owner phoned us and asked us to take control of the door and to keep the heavies away, which we did. Over the next twelve months the club gets no trouble whatsoever and things are running great. The owner decides that we are no longer needed as the place is trouble free. He gets rid of us and employs a few local doormen instead.

A few weeks later the heavies return. After slapping the doormen around they start to smash the club up good and proper. Police are called, three of them end up in hospital and roughly £30,000 of damage is done to the club. I said to my partner, 'That must have been a lucky twelve months we had at the club then,' and we pissed ourselves laughing. Not long later the club closed for good.

Jason Payne, Merthyr Tydfil

This fight breaks out and as I'm in trying to break it up one prick takes a swing at me. Straight away I grab him by the throat and pin

Big Jason Payne, six foot three and twenty stone: 'We get threats all the time. Some you take serious, some you don't.'

him against the wall. He's trying to talk but I've got my fingers firmly locked around his windpipe so the prick just gargles. He's waving his wallet in my face for some reason. I take a look at it and he's showing me his warrant card. The prick was a copper. I let go of him and he proceeded to tell me what charges he was going to get me put on. I tell him straight, 'All right then mate, give me your name and number then, let's see what your sergeant says about you taking a shot at me.' He just walked off mumbling about how he would sort me out once he's back in the station. Prick never came back but it just goes to show that when the drink is in, anyone can be a complete arse.

Michael Vaughan, Newcastle

I've had comebacks and when they come they get it twice as bad as they did the first time. I'm not going to mess with them as they've only come back to the club for one thing, so I let them have it. One guy came up to the club door and offered me out after I had given him a slapping a few hours earlier for bullying some lad. I stepped out of the door, which I know I shouldn't have, only to find he has four mates waiting for me around the corner. A quick signal off me to the other doormen and they're outside standing next to me. I announce that it's going to be a fair fight between me and the bully, who shouts out that it is not fair because I have other doormen with me. He wanted to fight me when his mates were there, no doubt to jump in, but not when I had a few guys who would see fair play. The thing that got me was that not only him but his mates couldn't see what they were doing wrong. They thought I was the one not playing fair. Of course he wouldn't fight me and walked away shouting that the doormen were all 'wankers and cowards'.

Stilks, Crayford

I believe that a doorman who carries a weapon is frightened of something, someone or doesn't feel confident in himself. I don't carry a weapon and I don't think about getting stabbed or shot. If it happens then it happens. I was at a party once when I was about twenty-eight and some nineteen-year-old kids were playing up. I told them, 'Look, you're spoiling the party, now fuck off before I slap the lot of you.' They all left but returned half an hour later. Someone came up to me and said, 'Stilks, those lads you threw out have come back.' I marched up to the door and opened it, shouting, 'What the fuck do you lot want?' One of them was standing there pointing a sawn-off shotgun at me. I must have stood there for two seconds but it felt like a week. I could feel a cold sweat all over me and felt small against the shotgun pointed at me. 'Do yourself a favour,' I said. 'If you're not going to use that gun, put it away, take it home and we'll talk about this another day.' I stood back, shut the door and gave a mighty sigh of relief.

Aiden Redman, Huddersfield

It was about two in the morning and I was just leaving the Heaven and Hell club in Huddersfield. This group of men had been thrown out of the club when suddenly this one lad ran up and with all his might threw a brick straight into the eye of one of the doormen. The doorman was in fucking agony as he clutched his face. I enquired after the doorman a few days later because even though I didn't know him the incident frightened me. I was informed that he was in a hospital in Halifax and that very morning surgeons had removed his eye. It seems a very high price to pay for earning a few pounds on the door.

chapter ten
tactics and environment

EACH PUB OR club is different and the way each doorman reacts can be just as varied. Some employ wit to defuse a situation, others find a stronger approach to be better. Some are experts at reading body language or verbal cues, others simply hit first and ask questions later. When the shit hits the fan, each doorman has his own methods to put an end to the trouble. They find this by trial and error over years of being in conflicts. What may work on one customer may not work on another. A good doorman usually has a few tried and trusted methods that he can call upon when needed. He learns to adapt to the surroundings he finds himself in and also to the customer that he finds he has to confront.

Stilks, Crayford

One thing I learnt was that you needed certain types of doormen with you. First you needed doormen who would be happy just collecting tickets and watching over everyone. You then need someone who could talk on the main door, the type of guy who, if someone's wrong, he could make them see sense. Then there are the background doormen, the leaders, who don't collect tickets or get friendly with the customers. These guys are just there for one thing, to put a stop to the trouble. When it kicks off they are the ones who are the first in. You need good leaders or the whole team will break down. In my younger days I had to be the first one in, because I was the youngest and needed to prove myself to the bigger doormen I worked with. The last thing I wanted was for another doorman to get there before me and then ask me where I was when it started. As soon as it kicked off I'd be there running through the crowd. I probably started worse fights by pushing through the crowd than the fight I was running to.

I don't get scared because when something happens I react fast and don't give myself time to worry about the consequences. If you stop to think about what you are going to do, you won't do it. You have to go with that sudden burst of adrenalin that the situation gives you. If you relax and let the adrenalin come out of you, you won't react fast and you'll lose the battle. If the guy you have to face up to stops to talk with you and you talk back, the adrenalin you built up running through the crowd disappears and you have to psych yourself back up to win the fight. I don't listen to what they have to say and just do my job when I'm still psyched up.

The regulars tend to stand in the same places each night so I sort of memorise where everyone is. When the trouble kicks off I run to the area that I've been told it's at. Before I even get there I've got an idea of who it is because I know who is usually there. I always forget names, addresses and numbers but I never forget a face, so as I'm running up I'm thinking about who could be involved and the best way to handle them. I know if I have to jump on him or hit him one if he's a big one.

Richard Collins, Ireland

I have worked the door for over twelve years and seen things that would drive the ordinary man mad. Not just the scuffles that happen each night in most Irish clubs but the things that happen after work. If I told you them I'm sure that I'd disappear into thin air. The trouble with running the doors over here is that you never know who is connected. You could throw a lad out for fighting and later get a phone call that all your windows have been blasted in, scaring the life out of your wife and kids. Maybe you finish your shift and while leaving the club you find yourself looking down the barrel of a gun. I've known this happen to many of my friends. Drugs are not a big problem in the clubs that I've worked because if we found someone dealing their names would be passed on to certain parties who would take the law into their own hands.

Doormen were employed years ago because they looked thuggish and weren't scared to have a fight. All had strings of convictions for fighting. Now with all these door policies coming into force, the doorman is being replaced by a different kind of security, a politer, more reasonable doorman who may never have been in a fight in his life. I know that I'd rather work with someone who could handle himself than someone who wants to discuss with a customer why he wants to stick a pint glass into his girlfriend's face. Most new breed of doormen don't train. I wouldn't dream of working the door if I wasn't physically fit and had a good fighting ability. Most situations can be stopped without using force but you have to be prepared if it goes the other way. Most old school doormen I know carry a concealed weapon on them or on the premises where they work, a flick cosh or a knuckleduster being the favoured items. Better to have a weapon and not need it than to need one and not have one.

Other parts of the world have doormen who would just beat a punter up who'd been a pain and toss him into the street. Here we have to know exactly who we are dealing with before we give it to them, unless we are working alongside doormen who are connected, if you know what I mean. After all, if you dish out your own punishment then maybe it would come back to haunt you tenfold. There's something in Ireland that few outsiders know about; it's called a 'menu'. It's similar to the menu that you have in a café, where you can start with a cup of tea and prices will increase with the greater amount or quality of food you require. The menu I'm talking about is when you approach a connected person and tell them that you have a problem with someone and need to know the menu. This menu starts off with something like threatening said person, to the top of the list being death. Of course the price increases the further up the menu you go; you can't expect to pay the same price for a cup of tea in a café as you would a full breakfast, can you?

Let's just say I give some lad a good beating and I'm working on my own with no connections. The lad gets his money and goes to see a connected man who may read him off the menu. Of course the lad takes the risk that the connected man isn't a friend of mine. If all goes well the lad goes on his way and a few days later I'm walking up a lane and three or four guys jump out with sledgehammers.

They're not there to fix the fence posts – and that would be the last you'd hear from me, ever. It's as easy as that, therefore it's best to know who you're dealing with and how far you can push them over here in Ireland. I've known doormen get the word that they are in trouble and in the early hours of the morning they pack up and along with the whole family they leave town.

A doorman I worked with gave his ex-girlfriend a beating because she wouldn't go back with him. Her father went to see his connected friend and was told the menu. I was standing on the door and noticed a car about 100 yards from the club with a few guys watching us. When the other doorman left the front entrance to go to the bar for a drink for us, I was approached by an acquaintance who had been sitting in the car.

'Richard, how the devil are you?' he inquired.

'I'm doing all right, what brings you here tonight?' I asked.

'Just business, Richard. Why don't you go take a toilet break my friend.'

They had come to the club looking for the other doorman and didn't want me involved. I turned around and went to the toilet for twenty minutes. When I came back the other doorman was lying outside with his legs broken and his face looked like red jelly, all smashed in and swollen. He needed reconstructive surgery and never came back on the door again. A few of you reading this will say that I was a coward to have left him on his own. Well, I went to see him in hospital a few weeks after it happened and let me tell you he admitted to me that he would have done the same thing. After all, he's now walking again and working. If I had got involved and tried to stop the 'business' taking place I know for sure that I'd have had three or four guys smash every bone in my body with sledge or lump hammers, starting from the feet up. It's not about being a coward, it's about surviving and looking after your own family. You must realise that if they can't get to you then they will get to your wife and kids.

Dave Courtney, South London

My favourite weapon was the knuckleduster. My favourite tactics were: turn the other cheek, then jump out of a Transit van eight-handed with a bit of wood! Only joking. It was winning at all costs;

face was everything. If you lost you got sacked. Reputation did manage to keep you out of trouble up to a point, but the important things were:

1) Always make sure you were right in what you were doing. Make sure you can justify it to yourself.
2) Always get the crowd behind you. In other words, wait until the cunt has pissed off everyone else in the club before you give him a good hiding. Remember it's not the fucker rolling around getting battered on the floor you have to think about but the enemies and friends you make for the rest of your life once you've knocked all his teeth out.

Duncan Ferguson, Torbay, South Devon

I am not that big. If you line the doormen up where I work you'll find I'm about two inches shorter than the smallest of the rest and about four stone lighter. I haven't lost a situation (yet) but this isn't always to do with how I fight. Remember, why fight a bigger/smaller guy/girl if you don't have to? My views are that size doesn't make a lot of difference but mental aggressiveness and attitude does.

Lee Callaghan, South Wales

I was finding it hard to supplement my bodybuilding as the money wasn't going very far. My mate Clyde was running a few club doors and offered me work. I talked it over with my missus and we decided that it was the only way I could raise money to compete as a bodybuilder. I must have got into about six fights that first night but it didn't put me off the work. It's all a learning process, and you can't learn it by someone just telling you what to do. You slowly get to recognise the way a customer is going to react by his body movements. You can learn how to handle a situation by trial and error. Being polite and respectful is a good way to handle people but when they have drunk like a fish all night or taken a few grams of powder then the only thing that's going to work is aggression. You learn this by being jumped on by gangs, having punches thrown at the back of your head and rolling around on pub floors among the broken glass. We all have to go through this before we get wise to what situation we find ourselves in.

When things get on top and you have to get someone down fast, I found the best way was to go for the eyes first. You only have to flick someone in the eyes to buy yourself enough time to get them in a chokehold. When you have a lock on someone, just apply a little pressure and out they go. They're like putty in your hands once you choke them out. Most doormen these days know different choke-holds, it's the easiest way to get someone out. I often give them first aid after they've come around and chat to them to make sure they are all right. The best way to bring them back around is to pinch them on the back of the arm.

Kevin Trottman, Liverpool

A big fight broke out in the club while I was working. Two rival gangs were kicking off and the place went up. We were short staffed and I knew we couldn't handle them all. I ran up to one gang who had regrouped on the dance floor and told them the police had just come into the club through the front doors looking for them. I advised them to use the exit as fast as they could. I ran with them to the exit, opened the door for them to get out and slammed it behind them. The other gang of lads hadn't started it so I read them the riot act and let them see the night out in the club but kept a close watch on them all night. A good doorman has to think fast and sometimes you can put an end to things by using your brain instead of your fists.

Duncan Ferguson, Torbay, South Devon

You have to be more careful now than you ever did before. The 'new school' doormen are doing okay but the old school are finding it hard to change. Now there are cameras and so on you have to be more careful about what technique you use and about throwing punches. If you strike someone you have to make sure you can testify in court under the eyes of God that you felt threat-ened. If you punched someone in the back of the head and were caught on camera you are going to have a hard time trying to prove you were threatened. In order to be a good doorman I think you should adhere to the new rules but make sure you have a camera blind spot if needs be. We have two where I work and we can take people out to the exit where the blind spot is – though only if they deserve it.

Terry Turbo, North London

We always had great laughs but I never saw anyone defuse a situation with humour apart from the occasional, 'I'll be back with the so and so family from London, you've thrown out the wrong guy tonight boys, you're all dead,' to which we'd reply, 'If you really think that anyone is going to come to Camberley to kill us after the way you behaved tonight then you must be on drugs mate.' My way of fighting was to be polite but firm and if that didn't work I'd give them the magic elbow. Other doormen would use restraining holds and martial arts but for me that was too much fucking about.

Douglas Gentles, Cardiff

I learnt many things while working in the clubs and with the doormen I've been lucky enough to work with. Some things that I've learnt are:

1) Drink makes people bastards. They want to fight the world and you're the first one on their list.
2) Never trust a customer. Because of drink and drugs they can't be trusted.
3) Fighting and weapons are part of the job. If you're not willing to fight and use weapons then this job is just not for you.
4) You have to have a good team working with you. A good team will fight and die together. I'm willing to die for my team and I expect them to do the same for me. How many would die for me I just don't know but I'm not going to lower my standard because of anyone. I give 100 per cent.

Cass Pennant, South East London

There certainly wasn't a gun problem on the streets ten years ago, even though I was unfortunate enough to have a run-in with a gunman. I first saw the signs six, seven years ago when minding Frank Bruno opening nightclubs. I noticed the door security in Birmingham and Newcastle wore body amour. It had come to that. From London to the North, guns were now for real with the club set.

Duncan Ferguson, Torbay, South Devon

I often talk people out before escorting them out and find it more beneficial to the place I work. I used to throw people out, for want of a better word, but soon found the customers didn't talk to me and wouldn't tell me if they had a problem or if someone was doing something they shouldn't, like drugs in toilets. I now find that by them seeing me take a slightly less aggressive manner with trouble-makers, they often tell me things without worrying that I'll throw them out or get aggressive. I'm not saying don't throw people out or throwing out's wrong, merely that if they're not fighting, try and talk to them before you walk them. I find this method more useful, because people quite often come back and apologise or are more likely to come back and drink in there another night instead of them being scared to even walk past.

Kris Cermele, Tampa, Florida

Like most clubs, we had customers who were suited to the club and others who weren't; in other words we stopped all the ugly customers coming into the club. Customers would wait in line for hours only to be turned away when they got to the front of the line. We would use a megaphone to shout down the line informing customers what was permitted and what wasn't. I'd shout something like, 'Just to let you know the house rules, we have a dress code that is purely down to the doormen's discretion. We don't want anyone who is wearing gold or silver chains, white pumps, shorts, sandals, gang members, groups of guys, fat people, butt ugliness, hookers or anyone who is under the influence of drink or drugs. We hope you have a nice time and remember nobody gets in free. Thank you all for your time.' You would then witness the ones who knew they couldn't get in walk away from the line and leave to try and get in another club.

I know that this all may seem a bit harsh but if you had been in line wouldn't it be better if you were told straight away rather than wait until you were by the entrance, which could be an hour away? The clubs would employ well-dressed doormen to make customers feel like they have entered a nightclub which had both dignity and class. I'd always wear an earpiece connected to a central office, where one of the guys would sit watching the camera. He'd then bark out orders to us about who could and couldn't come in. His voice would echo in my ear: 'Too fat. Hookers. Drugged up. Assholes. Fags. Looks like my mother. Let her in, not her boyfriend. My girlfriend's sister, don't let her in.' Sometimes it would get confusing but this tactic made sure that about ninety per cent were of the type we wanted. There's an elite social strata at certain clubs which can be hard to be a part of, for just the simplest reasons. I've known customers be refused entry just because their hairstyle didn't fit in.

To be able to handle customers who have waited in line only to be stopped at the entrance, I'd say personality was the key. You have to be firm but not frighten away others who you'd like to become regular clientele. After all, the doorman is the first and last person you see when you come to the club, so he has to be a little flamboyant and reflect the club's atmosphere. It's like acting I suppose, where you get into character at 9 P.M. and by 5 A.M. you have to step out of it. We got offered everything to let customers into the club: sex, drugs, money and invites to private parties. Customers will do anything to get into a club that's hot. Every night a woman would offer to flash us to get in free or without having to wait. We also would balance the amount of women and men in the club. It would be no good us having sixty per cent of the club as men now would it. A large group of men would have difficulty getting into the club but a large group of pretty ladies would get in without much trouble. If I was trying to get into a club with my buddies I'd ask a woman to accompany me in and I'd buy her a few drinks for her trouble.

I can tell if I wanted a customer in the club by just the watch they are wearing. Flashing a forty grand watch could get you into all the top clubs, no problem at all. But women who are surgically improved can sometimes find it hard to gain entrance. A lot just come to the clubs hoping to latch onto a wealthy guy, and to be frank it's a little tacky to watch them parading around the club.

Regular women clientele are intimidated by the sight of a Boxtox and silicone-enhanced woman muscling in on their dates. You wouldn't believe how many face-paralysed Boxtox women I've stopped over the years. Some can't even get their lifeless faces to smile at the doorman to get in. It's like some sort of freak show.

Regular ladies would complain about us letting in so many ugly men, and the same would be said of the men. The doorman can sometimes be like a talent scout for a giant party. Some of the customers who find themselves part of the 'unnatural selection' get aggressive but no matter what they say, we must remain polite at all times. Even when calling us names like faggot, nigger and assholes, they always get a polite response from us. After all, in the last few years that I worked on the door about eight doormen in Florida had been shot at. I didn't want to be one. I could never sleep after someone had threatened me with being shot. That happened many times but thankfully they never kept their promises. If a fight broke out, after we got a good hold on the fighters we would be quite civilised with them. After all, in most vicious fights the winner ended up in jail and the loser in hospital so both were facing a bleak night out.

From experience you'd be able to tell a fake ID from a mile away. With every kid owning a computer and scanner it makes it easy for them to make. I remember one young lady coming to the club only to be turned away because she didn't look like the picture on the ID, and I then had to confiscate the ID Later in the night another woman wearing the same clothes turned up at the club wanting to get her ID back and in fact she looked like the photo on the card but I still wouldn't return it. She even called the cops and caused a scene until she admitted that she had lent the card to her young cousin. The cops really laid the law down to her about what she had done and she was forced to apologise. In the USA there's a jail sentence for anyone caught using a false ID so I think she was lucky that both her and the cousin were cautioned rather than locked up.

We had a chart of images at the club that showed what every ID in the States looked like, so we could compare them. On examining the customer's card, I'd check for the age first, then things like height, eye colour and spaces between the chin, nose or eyes. You can look similar to someone on the card but you could never have the same spacing on the face.

John Scriven, South Wales

I have noticed a lot of rivalry among door companies in my town: fighting for contracts, bad-mouthing other companies and other doormen to get the work. I don't think that that is the way to do it. Only one thing happens when these techniques are used: a person makes a lot of enemies. It's pretty much the same guys that stay on the scene. The guys that are working on the doors now have been doing it for years. Most probably they'll be doing it in years to come as well.

All doormen handle things differently, they all have different tactics. I have tried loads of different martial arts but the one I stuck with for longest was jiu-jitsu. Depending on the situation, I'll either walk them out, grab their face and run them out or stick my fingers up their nose and drag them out by the head. I don't plan any of it, I just grab and hurt whatever is available to me. I try never to punch them. Anyone who comes to the club playing up I treat them the same – as a scumbag, even if they are my mates. If they fuck about in the club then they are disrespecting me and I'll chuck them out just same.

Bill Daniels, Bolton

I have carried a knuckleduster with me for many years and have never even taken it out of my pocket. It gives me reassurance and makes me feel confident knowing I have it. If my life was in danger I would not hesitate to use it

Lee Morris, South Wales

One night in the Kooler nightclub this boy had kicked off on the dance floor. As I was splitting it up he turns on me. I catch him on the chin and knock him out. I started panicking as they couldn't bring him round. Then this other doorman comes over, takes the boy's shoe off and pinches his foot. The boy jumped up as if he had been electrocuted. Seems a good way to bring someone around.

Carlton Leach, East London

Any group of males is a threat: white, black, Chinese, whatever, they are a potential problem because you are outnumbered. If a group of twenty blokes want a row and only see six doormen, they will fancy their chances. Some clubs now won't let groups of males in. My opinion is that it shows weakness and lack of faith in the door team. I would much rather let twenty blokes in and show I'm not bothered. If they get rowdy then they'll find out what three or four top doormen can do.

We were used to working clubs and pubs with a couple of hundred punters, people were drunk and we were having six to ten fights a night. Then the rave scene happened. Next thing I know, we are working huge warehouses full of thousands of happy people and not one single bit of trouble. People started chatting and being nice to us. It proper freaked me out. Suddenly it was the love and peace bit like the old films of Woodstock.

Cass Pennant, South East London

There were some dangerous bastards that were quick to come at us with a tool. We had our own tools of every description and would pull them out of anywhere: above the cloakroom, under the foyer counter, over from behind the bar. We even kept a motor unlocked outside and within sight with everything stacked in the boot for any street or car park carry-on. Thing was, if someone was that dangerous they were not unknown to us. Somebody in the team would have done a bit of business with them in the past or they'd done bird together or something. There would be a way in to smooth things out because you never invite trouble unless you have to. Always remember it's a job of work and try not to get personal.

It was also very important to keep the heavy stuff going on away from the customers. The club would be empty within weeks if they saw how we sometimes had to go about business. It really was a thankless job, so you chose your moments when you are ready for a serious word with someone. Keep focused on that entry door. You shouldn't be bothered too much with what's behind you up on the dance floor; after all, it was you that let them in, remember!

Anthony Thomas, Merthyr Tydfil

There's nothing worse than trying to get someone out of the club and someone else interferes. I was getting some stick from this guy, and when push comes to shove I get him in a neck hold and start to drag him out fast. He's a big lad so I've got my job cut out, when his wife decides to help him. Stiletto shoe off and she's hitting me on the head with it. She was having a right old go trying to smash my head in with her size eight. I turn to her, still holding her husband, and every time she takes a shot I squeeze his neck a little harder and he starts to pass out. Eventually she realises what I'm doing and walks outside, where I throw her bully of a husband at her feet. He comes around and plays fuck with her. 'Are you mad, you stupid bitch? He nearly killed me because of you.' Then they disappear into the night. Such a sweet couple.

Michael Rees, Bath

One pub I was working at, the police must have turned up every weekend because of one complaint or another. Same old story each time: you'd get some twats wanting to take you on. When you oblige and beat them to a pulp, they end up wanting to press charges on you. One night when this big lad kicked off and I had gotten him out fairly fast, with not much trouble. I'm just getting him through the entrance doors when I'm struck from behind. I turn to look who had punched the back of my head but the assailant had run off. This distracted me long enough for the big lad to turn around and grab me in a bear hug. There's no way I can move my arms and can't risk us falling to the floor as he may land on top of me. You only have to take your eyes off someone for a second and a situation like this can occur. I should have known better.

He's taller than me so I bring my head slightly back and with all my weight behind it I bring it down on his nose, which explodes, blood and snot all over the both of us. He's down on the floor whimpering like a child, clutching his broken snout. I throw him out into the street and two coppers approach the door. They stop to talk with the lad I threw out and then walk in and start having a go at me for using too much force. A few choice words from both parties and

I'm taken down the station to be interviewed while the lad I hit is taken to the hospital.

Down the station the copper with the loudest mouth introduces me to the desk sergeant as 'a bully bouncer who fancies himself as a fighter'. I just remain silent and try not to make matters worse for myself, even though the temptation to shut the copper's mouth made it quite hard. Whenever you have a problem with the police, remain friendly and calm. I suppose if I had spoke kindly to them when they approached me I wouldn't have been locked up. I know other doormen who detest the police but one day they may find themselves needing a sympathetic copper down the station who could put a word in for you. As it happens the desk sergeant asks me how I like being a doorman. He was a straight guy who just wanted to get his shift over with. I thought, *right, now's my chance*, and start telling him how hard it is with all the drug takers and dealers coming into clubs. I then started talking about how I needed the money for my family and due to the lack of work available I'm forced into it. To finish up I recount how I managed to help two off-duty coppers from getting a good beating but the customers thought I was taking sides with the police.

I'm put in the cells for an hour, then released because the lad I hit didn't want to press charges. I strongly believe that talking to the desk sergeant politely saved my bacon. We sometimes get off-duty police in the club and always treat them with respect, even though it's not always the way they deserve to be treated.

Duncan Ferguson, Torbay, South Devon

Where I work, I walk about inside and I always make a point of going up to customers who are stood close together talking and say, in a nice, non-threatening manner, 'Having a good night folks?' You can tell from the answer what their mood is like. Customers will see you doing this all night and so they think nothing of it when I come up to them.

Arms out to the side is a big one, I notice. If they are talking and their arms are splayed out, and they are not talking about fishing ('It was this big') then get closer to them so you can hear what's being said. The best bet is to stop it before it starts. Go up and say, 'What's the problem lads/girls?' Stand so you're in the middle but not in between, so you can touch both their arms but are slightly behind them – it's hard to describe. Then settle the situation as best you can. Don't just stand there watching until they fight, then get nasty. This may seem like a good way to get your 'rep' but you don't want a rep, believe me. You will get a better name for yourself as being a nice polite guy who can calm down situations. As long as you muck in when it does get physical you will be okay. Let's be honest, anyone can grab a guy by the arms from behind or in a headlock and run full pace to the exit door.

Look at customers' faces, eyes especially. Not so you're staring them out, I mean when they are looking at someone, you look at their eyes. You can see if they don't like them. Something I have noticed is that people cut dialogue short and move towards you. When they drop to one-syllable words like 'yeah' and 'so' is when they are just about to attack. Talk to people. Once they know you they will come up to you and tell you things. The best doormen are the ones who stop the trouble before it begins. Work on your verbal skills. Learn to talk customers down, calm them down before they even kick off.

Carlton Leach, East London

My favourite way of fighting was using my headbutt. They used to call me 'Nut Nut' because I would always butt somebody. I also love a cosh and the good old knuckleduster but because the people I was working with, like Lou Yates and Danny Chippendale, were fighters, they always relied on their fists. Once this big lump fancied his chances with Lou. This bloke was huge, then in the blink of an eye Lou had sparked him. The funny thing was, he was hit so hard the guy was out cold, snoring! His mates scooped him up with a lot of difficulty and threw him on the back seat of a cab, still blowing out the Zs.

I respected this greatly, but as times changed the public started 'carrying' so we had to start carrying. I always swear by what we called 'red eye' or 'squirt' (industrial ammonia). If I have trouble with twenty people, a bottle of squirt is the best stuff. Lou had great humour and so did Danny Chippendale. They would try talking and joking first, but if that failed and the idiots overstepped the mark, they would be promptly taken out of the game. I thought this was a great way of doing things.

The door registration scheme was put in place to get rid of people like us. People started getting worried about having villains on the door but in the real world you had to have villains on the door to get the respect. At the end of the day, respect should start on the pavement, not in the club. You need to stop trouble before it happens inside. If you have fights in a pub or club all the time then you have a bad door, simple as that. I have respect for today's doormen and I am not slagging anyone off, but these days you have part-time doormen, men who use door work to supplement their main job. In the days I am talking about the door job was your income and reputation, it was very important. It's also impossible to have the camaraderie now when you are working with a guy you never knew before, he has no reputation and you only see him six hours a week.

As far as the police go, my attitude is this: if you are involved in violence you are, at some point, going to get nicked. There's no point moaning when you get pulled, it's part of it. I have to say the Old Bill I have dealt with have been fair with me. Nowadays doormen use the police far too often; any bit of bother and they are straight on the phone to the Old Bill. Special constables, that's what they are like these days. I think people take more liberties with bouncers now because they don't have respect for them. In the old days, people would know the faces on the door and who was behind the club. You would put word around the area that so and so or this or that family have an interest in the club. People would know then that if they came in that club and kicked off they wouldn't fucking get out again! Once you had spread the word, most of your work was done.

Douglas Gentles, Cardiff

The most violent and crazy person I know is me. I give 100 per cent and will die to protect a fellow doorman. Over the years, a number of occasions arose where a doorman I was working with felt the threat being made against him was too serious to ignore, therefore we would arrange to meet up later and take care of the matter before the nutter had time to come back and carry out the threat.

In my book, if you make a threat against a doorman then you're making it against all doormen. I believe in looking after your own. There are a lot of doormen now coming on the scene that are not worth a wank. Because of the police a lot of good doormen have given up working the doors. That's why I believe it's important that teams of good doormen must stick together and watch out for each other 24/7.

Richard Collins, Ireland

Over the years doormen have changed dramatically. One thing I hate is those big, stupid, puffed-up, black bomber jackets they now all wear. They look twice as big as they are and downright stupid. Also those stupid earpieces that they have in, I know they are supposed to help but I'd never wear one. What if someone runs up and punches them in the ear? Bet that would hurt.

Bernard Driscoll, South Wales

We had this bloke in the nightclub and he kept asking the DJ to play all these requests. The DJ says to him, 'I'm a DJ, not a fucking jukebox.' The bloke then lifts the DJ up by the throat with his bare hands. We ran in and grabbed him but this bloke was huge. I have him around the throat, a couple of the doormen have got him by his arms, but he threw the doormen off with ease. They grabbed him again and by now there are four of us on him. Another of our doormen, Snuffer comes running in. Now he was known as a knockout merchant, there weren't many who'd stand up after he had hit them. He's hit the bloke smack on the button, then straight down for a body shot. The bloke didn't even budge and tells us, 'If you leave me go, I'll walk out.' He then walked out without one bit of trouble and we thought that was the best way for him to leave. The guy was just too big and strong to drag out.

Jamie O'Keefe, London

One guy I worked with for a few years did nothing but use humour to defuse situations. Micky was a big lump who looked like one of those old school fairground rock n rollers. He was very into using weights at the gym so was a strong lad. Humour worked brilliantly for him. I would use psychology a lot as I never liked fighting on the door. It looks ugly and if it ever came to blows I would try to take the fight away from view of the customers or passing public. For example if I had a persistent prick who continuously would come to the door and give it large I would politely refuse them entry and that would mostly end it there but you would always get the twat who would take you for an easy touch due to your politeness. They are the ones that learnt the hard way! I think that my politeness and soft spoken non-aggressive side are one of my best weapons because it either prevents situations happening or for the tough guys it makes them over confident when they cannot detect aggression. They then let their own guard down quite a lot, then I will engage their brain with something like *'We have Oasis drinking in here tonight'* or something totally illogical like *'looks like it's going to rain sunny frogs if that bus is any longer?'* Whilst they are thinking *'What the fuck is he on about?'* I bang them one and it's all over.

If you're a boxer, when you get blasted in the ring, you know it's coming so you psych up for it and your physical and mental state is as switched on as possible for the battle ahead. However if you were totally relaxed on a beach, cinema, or whatever, you will be in a position of being 'off guard and unprepared for a sudden blow'. I've seen tiny guys and women bang big guys out using my technique of getting people to drop their guard. So that's the psychological side to the physical application of the stuff I teach and personally use. I dislike pain and violence so I try to ensure I don't suffer it or dish it out unnecessarily.

Kevin Trottman, Liverpool

When I have chucked people out of a club and they give me hassle I usually ignore them and put them out of my mind. If they've gone and pushed me too far I look for them over the next few days when there's no camera looking over my shoulder. Why wait for them to come to you? Confront them on their doorstep and I guarantee they will be different people. I've done a few house calls the following morning and it always turns out the same, with the people from the night before now turning into mice. It makes me laugh sometimes.

This one twat was a bit of a dealer, he threatened to cut me up and burn my house down. Now I knew he wasn't right in the head and might just carry out his threat unless I put a stop to it. I got up the following day and went for a run to wake up, but on this run I made sure I went past the dealer's house. I popped a duster in my pocket in case I got into a situation I couldn't handle. As I'm running past a local school I notice the dealer taking his two little kids to school. I knew he could see me so I wait by the school gates, as I didn't want to upset his kids; after all, they probably think he's the best dad in the world, never knowing the shit he sells in the local clubs. He leaves the school and walks towards me. As soon as he gets close he puts his hand out to shake mine. He apologises and puts it all down to the fact that he had drunk too much. I shook his hand but let him know that I didn't take kindly to threats, especially when my house and family are concerned.

I never had trouble with him from that day on. He always speaks politely and never causes trouble. I can't tell all doormen to do the same as it could sometimes backfire and the person you're looking for may have friends with him. All I can say is that it works for me, so far anyway.

Douglas Gentles, Cardiff

I was always the first in whenever fighting broke out, which it did six nights a week, often five times each night. When the violence was not aimed at the doormen there was no problem, we would just get hold of them and throw them out. If the trouble was aimed at us then we would fight using nothing else but our fists and if need be our feet, with the odd headbutt here and there. In those days we never used weapons; we didn't need to. We were good at our jobs. Later on I would need to use weapons while working the door or because of working the door; it was never a case of wanting to but having to. I believe the smartest individual is the one that goes home at night in one piece.

Michael Vaughan, Newcastle

There are a few good ways to handle a situation but I found that if push comes to shove, hit first. The CCTV camera is always on so I put my hand out as if I'm asking the aggressor to stop where they are, but if they deserve a clip I whisper so only they can hear me and call them all the foul names under the sun. Soon as they step forward, bang, I let them have it. Of course on the camera it looks like I didn't want to fight and the guy went for me.

I had to work the front door on my own one night and got offered outside by this twat whose ribs I had broken a few weeks earlier. He's outside with all his mates and I would have got kicked from pillar to post by them all. I tell them, 'I'll just phone a friend to back me up, I think that's fair lads, don't you?' Astonishingly they all agree. I then pretend to phone a local club and I ask for one of the big time gangsters from the area. You should have seen the look on the faces of the twats. They made their excuses and left, never to bother me again. Sometimes you have to use your brain and not your muscles on the door. Also real fighters don't come in gangs, they turn up on their own.

David White, Caerphilly

When Wales play rugby at the Arms Park on international day the whole of Cardiff would be buzzing with energy, you never saw so many people having a good time. The atmosphere was electric, with people dancing in the streets and all up for a good time, especially this one night when Wales won. We usually have a policy that we don't let rugby teams in; could you imagine if they all decided to play fuck? However, on this international day a large number of rugby players got in the club. They came in ones and twos so it wasn't until there was a load of them in that we realised they were all together. We get this happening with stag nights as well; they know they all won't get in together so they come in smaller numbers. I've played rugby myself and I'm sure that some of the rugby players who came on this one night played for Wales B team. There must have been about twenty of them in the corner of the club playing holy hell. There was ten of us working, five upstairs and five downstairs, but these were big lads so the familiar butterflies in the stomach started to kick in.

The head doorman radios me from upstairs and says, 'These guys are playing fuck in here, what are we going to do?' I told him,

'You're the fucking head doorman, you tell me!' Suddenly the emergency alarm goes off to indicate there's trouble somewhere in the club. We get directed to the gents' toilets where two rugby players are battering a few of the customers. Thankfully they hadn't joined up with their mates, so we grappled with them and got them out of the club. I ask the head doorman to phone the police so we can get the group from upstairs escorted out. He starts acting the big hard man and lets me know that we were quite capable of sorting it ourselves, even though the odds were stacked against us.

I don't usually carry or use a weapon but I slipped off to where I had my coat hanging up, and got my brass duster out of the pocket. I put my black leather gloves over it so nobody could say they saw me use a duster. I went around all our lads and told them it was all about to go up and to be on their guard. No sooner had I said that than the alarm goes off and we rush upstairs to where the rugby lads were. Seems the head doorman had gone to have a word with them and some way or another gets knocked out cold. One or two of the rugby guys have decided to kick fuck into the head doorman and the others are involved in various fights around us. Running up, I decided to tackle the biggest one first to get him out of the way. He just happens to be one of the guys sticking the boot into the head doorman. I smash him on the back of the head and he's poleaxed, lying flat on his face. I could feel the impact right up my arm as the duster struck the back of his skull. The other doormen are fighting with the rest of the team and I turn to find another rugby player lunge at me and grab me around the neck, trying to strangle me. We grapple for a while until I manage to sink my teeth into his hand. He lets go just as one of the other doormen hits him on the side of his head, launching him across the room.

Most fights only last a few minutes; if they've got a gutful of booze they are not going to fight for much longer. The fight started to die down, with some of the rugby players leaving the club and others dragging their mates out. I get back downstairs and before he leaves the club one of the biggest of them is shouting some shit about how we were a bunch of wankers. I step up close to him and he's ranting. I'm just focusing on knocking him out as fast as I can. He leans forward and I plant one on his chin. Again the duster connects with flesh and bone and another loudmouth rugby player gets dragged out. One of our lads runs into the manager's office and takes the videotape out of the recorder before the police turn up. The police take a few of them away in the wagon but don't ask for the tape, which would have been hard for us to explain. One of the coppers is talking to me about what happened when I realise I'm still wearing my duster. In fact my one leather glove has ripped open a bit and the duster can be clearly seen sticking out. I make an excuse that I have to check upstairs for a minute and quickly bugger off to ditch my beloved duster.

I think a few of the rugby players got charged but nobody came to interview us. If I had got caught wearing the duster I would have been in serious shit. I know loads of doormen who use them and take the risk of getting caught. If you ever see a doorman wearing gloves, look closely at his hands and I bet you can see the bulge of the duster. I know it's wrong but what are you going to do when some nineteen-stone, fit rugby players start to smash the place up? If you were in a club and some steroid gorilla wanted to stamp all over you, I bet you would thank God that the doorman was wearing a duster.

Jason Payne, Merthyr Tydfil

I'm walking around the club when I hear shouts coming from the main door. I run over and the other doormen had closed the door on someone who was still performing outside, banging the door and screaming about his ticket. I thought I'd have a word. I open the door and step outside, to be confronted by one of the biggest guys I've ever seen. I'm six foot three and I'm looking up to him. I had to stand on a step just to be on eye level with him. He's shouting at me about how he had a ticket and wasn't allowed entrance. He's red in the face and he's right up for it. If I backed down I'd have my hands full. 'Look, prick, doors close at 10.30, you know the rules, now fuck off,' I scream back at him. 'I'll just get my girlfriend then, if it's okay with you,' he whimpers. I let him in, he gets his girlfriend and walks out with his head down, not even looking at me. That's the thing with some of the noisy ones, they don't like it back in their faces. Sometimes you have to scream at them to get a point over.

Cass Pennant, South East London

Our favoured door method was to work to everyone's individual strengths, find your best pairs and work them within the team. One of the biggest lessons I learnt was always try and get the balance right of the team you operated. You need your diplomat, your psycho, your muscle bound, your linkman and your headman. What you don't need is a team of all leaders that can't be asked or told anything, a team of egos in other words. Don't matter how powerful the individual is you can use the character but not the ego for the team would be destroyed from within. The other thing learnt was try avoiding working your own manor because somebody always knows somebody close to themselves by which the nature of the job can bring you into a confrontation. Now, when that happens you can never be sure the door is 100 per cent trusted. Work off the manor nobody knows anyone or gives a fuck and everyone had got to get home on the same route. Using that method I swear we got through everything that was thrown up in front of us.

Andrew Moffat, Edinburgh

The security industry is changing the doorman image. We are no longer seen as muscle-bound thugs who beat up drunks but as club security who actually try to defuse a situation. I have young lads of my own and in the next few years no doubt they'll be going to clubs drinking. I would feel safer knowing that the doormen are vetted and properly trained. I know I belonged to the old school of doormen who just dive in there and get stuck into whoever is in the way. Over the years I've changed quite a bit. I try these days to resolve a dispute before it gets violent. If it does get violent I try to use the minimum of force to put an end to it. Numerous court cases and police visits have made me wise to the fact that I'm facing prison if I overstep the mark. Don't get me wrong, I still see the old red mist when it all flares up but I use my head more these days and try to talk them out of fighting rather than break somebody's nose then drag them out back for a beating. I would once chase someone out of the club and down the road to slap them around just for calling me a thick twat. These days I laugh it off. How would I feel if one of my boys when he's older insults a doorman and gets a kicking?

On more than one occasion I've given some lad a hiding because he was fighting only to find out later he was the one originally being attacked. I remember two young lads pretending to fight by the bar, just larking about. The doorman with me ran up and smashed one to the ground, knocking him cold. His mate tried to explain that they were messing around and got kicked in the balls. When the manager came over to see what had happened I stuck up for my workmate. The manager was happy and the two lads thrown out. These days I'd have a word with the manager and as head doorman I'd fire any doorman who overstepped the mark. Others may not like informing the boss that we have a bad team-mate on the door but I have to work with them, so I don't really lose any sleep over a bully doorman losing his job.

When a fight used to occur I'd run in from the side, punch the biggest one to the floor and stamp all over him if he was still conscious. Now I get them in a headlock as a restraint rather than a punishment, only ever putting on extra pressure if they still want to fight. When I started on the door I had a history of violence on my record already but due to changes to door policies I would never employ anyone who fancied himself as a street fighter as such.

Lee Callaghan, South Wales

Working the door of a big hotel when the manager came running up screaming for me to get someone out. 'He's high on drugs, just get him out,' he screamed. I confront the man and have to drag him out of the club. Outside he takes his glasses off and comes at me. I spent the last few years studying jiu-jitsu so I cupped my right hand and, throwing it straight from the hip, I smacked him straight in the ear. The idea is that the air pressure compacts when it hits the inner ear and disorients them; sometimes, as in this case, it knocks them out. Other doormen rush over to check he's okay. There's blood seeping from his ear and it's swollen twice the size. He wakes up and I'm ready in case he takes a shot at me. The only thing he can do is stagger around in circles, talking gibberish. This is the effect a good blow to the eardrum can have. Some people might think doing things like that to an aggressor is wrong; well, those people have never seen a doorman with his nose or ear bitten off.

Max Iacovou, Kent

I have learnt that no matter what the situation, never back down. Then you get your respect, because at the end of the day everybody bleeds and has a weakness.

temptation

A DOORMAN CAN be tempted in many ways: the options are almost limitless. It could be free drink, stealing entrance money, free drugs or women. Above all, it's women that can tempt a doorman the most. Many have lost wives or girlfriends from having a one-night stand with some pretty little thing that has caught their attention. Nobody can tell you for sure why certain women fall for the doorman: maybe it's the way they dress, handle themselves or just because of how dangerous their job can be. No matter what the reason is, the bottom line is that doormen will find this form of temptation hard to resist.

Steve Wraith, Newcastle

People often ask me what I get out of doing the door. Well it's simple. It's a means to an end. If you do six nights a week in a bar and club, say thirty-five hours a week at £12 an hour, you are pulling in more than some bar managers. It pays my bills, keeps a roof over my head and gives me money to spend on the finer things in life. I have had some laughs and met some characters as well, whom I wouldn't have otherwise met. Some doormen use the job as an agency and I would say I have worked with two of the worst offenders in living history. One of the lads has to this day over 300 telephone numbers in two cash bags of women he has bagged on the door, as well as Polaroid photos of himself and his conquests, just to prove he's no liar when it comes to telling the lads his tales. The other, who I shall call The Hawk, specialises in collecting souvenirs at the end of the night from the cubicles in the women's toilets. Still I suppose it takes all sorts.

Darren Withers, South Wales

While working a club in Istanbul called the Green Bar I met a doorman who I made friends with. His name was Rory and he was Australian, a nice guy but loved himself and liked to impress the ladies. He was always well groomed and the women loved him. I would turn up at the club in my gym kit to work but he always had his bow tie, black trousers and this white shirt, which didn't have a crease in it and was spotless. I couldn't work out why he went to so much trouble as the club was a right old dive, wallpaper hanging off the walls and the toilets constantly leaked sewage. If they asked me to go down the cellar to help move some barrels I would take a large stick with a six-inch nail in the end to kill any rats that came to close. This club was infested with the buggers. They weren't small either, some were like fucking pitbulls. I would find them everywhere; I even found one in my kit bag once and almost took it home.

One thing I learnt was never to touch anything electrical. The switches and the plug points were only held on by nails and most were hanging off the walls with bare wires showing. The place was a death trap, just waiting to catch some poor fucker out. One night I was at the club entrance talking to the barmaid, who also worked as a local hooker, and she was telling me about some of her customers. Out of the corner of my eye I could see Rory chatting to two local girls who had come from the dance floor just to speak to him. Rory was giving them all the chat and the girls were loving it. Fair play, he could pull the girls. He stretches his one arm out to lean against the wall, maybe just to look cool as he chatted up the girls. What he didn't realise was that he was about to put his finger on the bare wires of the light switch. With a loud crack his fingers touch the wires and before the lights in the foyer go off, Rory is propelled across the room to crash against the opposite wall, unconscious. I take one look at him lying on the floor looking like Don King and I join the barmaid in laughing our heads off. The barmaid actually pissed herself, soaking wet, and worked the rest of the night without a care in the world. Rory was okay and the two young girls looked after him all night, fetching him drinks and making a fuss of him.

Ian Hews, Essex

I had a few doormen working for me at a night club in the West End. The owner had an office and a two-bedroom flat in the actual club so if he pulled a bird or got too pissed up he could stay the night and not worry about going home. The second bedroom was spare so he let it be known that if anyone wanted to use it they could, so now all the doormen were queuing up to use it and couples were going in there nightly. About eighteen months later the club got raided. When the police searched the owner's office they found a secret camera. He had been sitting in his office filming everyone, and apparently he was selling the tapes abroad. He later got two years in prison. The doormen became porn stars only they never got paid for it. The police must have pissed themselves going through all those tapes.

Brian Richards, Newport

On the door you get to know which girls you can and can't mess about with. These two turn up one night and we are all just messing about having fun. This one girl's not a bad looker and she tells me she's the best blowjob in Newport. 'Okay love,' I tell her, 'I'll have to put you on a scale to see how good you are, one to ten and all that.' The girl's right up for it so after letting the guys on the door know where I'd be, we walk around the corner and position ourselves behind some parked cars. I'm leaning against this one car having a great time, when I notice this woman on crutches watching us. 'Excuse me,' she shouts, 'can I have my car, the one you're leaning on?' That sort of put a dampener on things so we went back into the club. I'm smiling like a Cheshire cat as I enter the club and my mates are laughing. I watch the girl walk up the stairs to the top floor and proceed to kiss my mate Peters, who hadn't a clue to what had just been going on. He comes down to the door and I let him know that the girl he's been kissing had two minutes before been giving me a blowjob. Of course he didn't believe me, but later the girl told him. To say the least, he wasn't happy.

Terry Turbo, North London

We got a shag nearly every night when we worked. I don't know what it is, birds just love big naughty geezers that get them free drinks all night and then escort them to the fire exit when they are plastered and let them have it. Fuck knows why, they just do.

Chris Hanstell, Wanstead

I used to work with this bloke called Damian, he was all right, the genuine article, took no shit but was quiet and a gentleman. This girl had been really going on at him to take her out and he found it hard to resist, knowing full well she was with someone and had a young kid. On the first occasion a date was set up his conscience got the better of him and he didn't turn up, much to her annoyance. One Saturday night she came with her mate to the club we were working. They turned up at happy hour and were getting well lashed up. She kept coming to the door giving my mate a hard time about standing her up and he felt really bad about it so said he would take her home at closing and talk about it on the way. When they got back to her place, her mate was still with them and they stripped off (all pissed up they were) and offered him what every bloke wants, a threesome. Casting aside his guilt seeing pictures on the wall of her kid and her dad – the kid was with the grandparents – he saw no reason not to and happily obliged. Whilst getting jiggy in the bedroom, they didn't hear her kind-of-ex-boyfriend come into the flat. He obviously heard all that was going on and stormed into the bedroom, right off his box on something or other, threatening to let off a CS gas canister right there in the bedroom. Well, my mate wasn't having any of it. He jumped on him, tackle out and all, and beat shit out of him. Then calmly got dressed and took himself home. Turns out the bloke was a well-known drug dealer in the area and that his girlfriend and mate often did that sort of thing.

Douglas Gentles, Cardiff

Working at Rosie's one night, a young girl was outside the club chatting to us. Then for some crazy reason she started crying and stripped off, totally naked, and started coming on to me, saying she just wanted to be loved. The people at the bus stops outside the club then started giving me shit because of this girl. All the while the other doormen were telling me to take her downstairs and fuck her in the cellar. Not that I didn't want to but there was just no way the people outside the club would have allowed that girl out of their sight. Finally the police came and took her away.

Stuart Mayley, Epping

I was being a bit of a silly boy really, been working for my guv'nor for about three years at a club near where I lived and I knew full well not to mess with him – and I never intended to, but his daughter was fucking gorgeous. He had this big pad out Epping way, the sort of gaff we all dream of, trellis outside with ivy climbing up to the higher windows, et cetera – picturesque stuff. I had been getting really friendly with his younger daughter, who he was obviously fiercely protective of, for two months following up to this event. We'd had a few nights out on the quiet and I was falling for her in a big way.

One night she called me on my mobile while I was working. Knowing her old man was working too, she told me to come over to her place for some 'hot love'. I told the head doorman that I felt like shit and needed to go home, which went down like a lead balloon; nevertheless he let me off – I could live with that. I called my mate Dan to come with me to be a lookout as the last thing I wanted was to get caught out and lose my income, not to say my kneecaps. Dan sat outside in his motor while I scooted up the trellis to her bedroom. I told Dan to give me three rings if the old man turned up early. Sure enough, he'd turned up earlier than normal, the big automated gates opened up letting him through in his big fuck-off black BMW 7 Series and Dan straight away tried my mobile. He got my answer phone. He sent me a text, but still no response. In a blind panic he stood by the house boundaries chucking up stones to her window. Still nothing – we were far too busy to notice.

He went back to his car and just kept redialling my number, knowing full well if he didn't warn me I would come out in a wooden overcoat. All of a sudden the window flew open and the nets blew out as I made my attempt to escape, stark naked. I would rather have died from the impact of the landing than let her dad get his hands on me. I took a rough landing and started to leg it across the front lawn to Dan's car. As luck would have it they had an automatic floodlight system and all lights were on my scared arse. I have never run so fast in my life – I expected a herd of bloodthirsty hounds to follow. I got out, how I don't know, sheer fear I think. I went to work the next evening, half expecting to have my gonads put in a vice and a lamp shone in my face, but nothing. Somehow we got away with it. Needless to say, we decided mutually that it was far too risky to carry on seeing each other. Thank God she never said a word about it.

Darryl Taskers, South Wales

It was quite dead out one night and there seemed to be more girls out than boys. This girl comes on to me and grabs my dick. I took her around the corner of the pub and we go at it. I must have done everything to her but shag her brains out. I've then noticed that opposite the pub the CCTV camera was fixed on us. That wasn't going to stop me and I was still right up for it but all of a sudden she wanted to stop. She must have been camera shy.

Another night in the pub, this boy and girl were starting to feel each other up. He gets his hand down her knickers and she's got his knob in her hand. I was looking at my mate, whose face was a picture, and we started laughing. Next thing you know, she's gone and sat on top of him. It was now time for us to go in and chuck them out. I said to my mate Shaun, 'I wonder if they'll lend me that tape tonight when I go home.' He turned round laughing and called me a right pervert

Jamie O'Keefe, London

Women putting themselves on offer to doormen? It happens all the time. It has never interested me. It's a bit like firefighters going out to put out fires and, whilst there, shagging a girl or two. Still I suppose people do whatever floats their boat. There's no harm in two single, consenting adults hooking up if that's their thing but when you get doormen cheating on their partners and drunken women in clubs cheating on the old man who's at home looking after the kids, then that's bollocks. You're either a professional doorman/woman or not. You're either faithful to your partner or not.

Martin Bayfield, Rhyl

I don't like working with women but sometimes you wish you had one on the doors with you. I remember getting a call to go straight to the club's ladies' toilets which is not something I relish, there's a funny smell in there that always turns my stomach, sort of blocked toilet and perfume smell. The other doorman with me, Ian, goes in first and I stand outside trying not to get involved. Ian comes out and insists I give him a hand. Inside there's a girl on one of the bogs with her knickers and skirt pulled down to her ankles, eyes rolling in her head, talking gibberish and looking like something from a *Zombie* film, froth dribbling out of her mouth. I wished I had not insisted that we had no women working on the door with us. Me and my big mouth.

I remembered the girl from earlier and she seemed sober and even talked to Ian for a while. He said she wasn't known as a drug taker, just a bit of a tart. We get her an ambulance, as we had no idea what to do with her. About an hour later the girl's mother is at the front door, ranting and raving like a loony. She wants to know why her daughter is lying in a hospital bed after having her stomach pumped out. The girl was in a pretty bad way. She threatens to sue the club and wants to know how her fifteen-year-old daughter got in the club anyway. I didn't know she was fifteen and realised that the woman must be in a right temper, seeing as her daughter had just had her drink spiked with Ecstasy. The mother was pointing and screaming at me as if it was my fault.

'Look,' I shout, 'we helped you daughter and have done the best we can. There's a notice on that wall behind me telling everyone to beware of having their drinks spiked. You're trying to blame me rather than blame yourself for being a bad parent. You must have known where you daughter goes on the weekends and anyway why the fuck are you not in the hospital watching over her, you old slapper? Now fuck off.'

With that she swears and stamps her feet a little but fucks off into the night. I have a word with Ian and we try to find out which prick spiked the drink but didn't get anywhere.

'Thing is Ian, the girl's been coming here for about a year now, and I have never known her to take drugs. After all she's only fifteen and seemed a nice girl in general.'

'Fifteen! What do you mean, fifteen? She was the one I fucked in my car nine months ago. I thought she was eighteen at the least,' he screamed at me.

Could you imagine if the girl's mother decided to sue the club, not only for her daughter getting spiked but getting nailed by the doorman as well?

Michael Vaughan, Newcastle

Sometimes before I start work I have a pint with a few friends in my local pub. It relaxes me before I go into battle. You may think that sounds like I'm a drama queen but it can get to be a proper blood and guts war on the doors some nights.

This one night I get to talking to an old flame of mine. We sort of re-kindle things a little and step outside the pub, where she pulls me into the alleyway. I'm a little bit worried about getting caught by the wife, seeing as I only live around the corner, so we try to think of somewhere else we can go. I knew the club that I worked at would open up early for cleaning and stock checks before the night started, so off we hurried to the club. We get there and the junior manager lets us in. Leaving my lady friend in the foyer I manage to persuade him to let me use the cloakroom for half and hour. The rest of the staff wouldn't be arriving for an hour so we had time.

At the back of the cloakroom I make a makeshift bed out of all the old coats that had been handed in over the years, lost property. We are going at it like porn stars, feeling safe that the junior manager was in his office and the rest of the building was empty. She gets on top of me and is riding away like Willie Carson when the door swings open. In steps the new cloakroom girl, who had come in early to learn where all the coats had to be placed before the punters came in. The girl I was with was still going like a good 'un until I asked her to stop and pointed to the girl standing mouth open and frozen to the spot. She was a friend of my wife's sister. I had to spend ages begging her not to tell anyone. She agreed and didn't open her mouth for a while. Then she gets fired for bad timekeeping and within a few days my wife calls me on the mobile requesting I come home straight away from work, as she had a problem at home that she couldn't tell me on the phone.

I get home to be confronted by my packed bags and my PlayStation behind the front door waiting for me. After trying to deny that I shagged some tart (my wife's words) in the cloakroom for what seemed like hours, I finally admit it after she tells me her sister has told her all the sordid details. Knowing things were over and divorce was imminent, I decided to come clean, so to speak. I inform her, 'Right then, you old fucking trout. If things are over then you better phone your mate and ask her about the blowjob she gave me when I gave her a lift home last year. Or was the mean bitch too drunk to remember that one?' Well, that seemed to do the trick as after six months I'm still out on my arse. Let that be a warning to all you bouncer superstuds out there.

Lyn Morgan, South Wales

You wouldn't believe some of the stuff that goes on in a nightclub. Some of the girls who come in just don't give a fuck. This one night

The experienced trio of (l to r) Neil Lewis, Lyn Morgan and John Scriven in classic white shirt/black trousers combo

was a charity night and people were chucking money into a hat doing stupid things. All of a sudden this other doorman and myself had this strange request. A bloke comes onto us and asks would we suck his wife's tits whilst he took photos. Obviously we obliged, seeing as it was for charity. He really seemed to be getting off on it.

This other time this doorman was winding this girl up about shaven fannies and vibrators. She says to him, 'I'll show you both later.' The boy now thinks his luck's in and after a while she comes up to him and rams her mobile phone in his face. It was one of these ones which takes photos. She had only gone in the toilet and used the vibrator on herself and took a photo. The boy's face was a fucking picture. Once we were winding this girl up and she offered to take my mate out the back of the club for a blowjob. We gave them a couple of minutes and then went to see what was going on. The girl takes the boy's cock in her hand and looking at the doormen says, 'Why don't you lot grow up.' She then carries on sucking him off without a care in the world. The boy's got his arms crossed, cool as fuck, laughing at us. We all went back into the club jealous of the lucky fucker.

Carlton Leach, East London
The girls do come onto doormen a lot, I think more in the old days. We were all suited up and there is an aura and class about a dicky-bow doorman. Now the doormen look like the punters. Maybe it was the fact we looked liked gangsters.

Douglas Gentles, Cardiff
Women do love doormen. I've lost count of how many women have come on to me. I'm no prize but still I have never had a problem with women. Every doorman I know has at some time had women offering themselves on a plate. Even if the doorman is fat, thin or ugly, it just doesn't matter. Having sex in a club is normal these days. I do believe that some people even want to be caught shagging in a club. I have been caught a few times either in the cloakroom or at the back of the club. Thankfully the times I was caught, either by the manager or by the head doorman, nothing was said. They all do it at some time.

While I was working at a club called Berlins in Cardiff, I would often stop girls to check ID. One night a young girl of about eighteen was refused for not having ID, so she offered me a blowjob. I just couldn't believe it; she was a lovely little thing, sexy as fuck. Thinking she was just trying to wind me up, I called her bluff, took her down the alley opposite the club and, fuck me, she bent down and starting sucking me off. She took it all the way.

After that night I found out that quite a few girls were more than happy to suck you off if you let them into the club. After I split from my girlfriend I took up every offer and made up for lost time. I also found that many girls were more than willing to suck you off or even fuck you for just giving them a lift home after the club. It seems that some girls get a buzz from telling their friends I shagged the bouncer from the club last night. I have also found that some girls won't give you the time of day when they are with their friends but you get that same girl alone and they are all over you like a rash and more than willing to spread their legs. Sounds crazy, I know, but that's what I have found out working the doors, especially when I worked in Berlins nightclub.

Next to Luigi's club there's a church with a small graveyard at the back. During my time at Luigi's I don't think a night passed without someone shagging in there on top of the graves. I've lost count of the number of people that I have caught over the years. Luigi's closed ten years ago and the place was reopened a few years back as Club X, a gay club. I hate to think what goes on in that churchyard these days.

Mickey Jones, London

I have never really been a ladies' man, but this one night a young lady turned up at the club. She was a nurse at the local hospital and she could remember me from visiting this girl who'd taken an 'E' in the club. The end of the night came and she was stood outside on her own waiting, so I asked her if she wanted a lift and she said yes. I explained that she lived near where I walked the dog in the night and would she mind if we picked him up. My dog humped her leg and bit her yet she still wanted the lift. Seven years later the dog's still humping her leg and I still can't get her out of my house.

Wayne Price, Mountain Ash

I was working once in a place called Ballys bar in Neath. I'd work all hours at the club, often starting about 2.30 on a Sunday afternoon and work right through till about three o'clock Monday morning. This one Sunday the night was going well, not much trouble and it was coming to the end of the night. There wasn't many left in the club, can't have been more than about fifty, when I was approached by two guys that I knew called Patrick and Steve. Patrick asked me to have a look for their wives as they wanted to go home. The four of them always came in together and were all good mates. I walk around the club and then I take a look in the ladies' toilets. I open the door and shout in to see if there's anybody there. I get no reply but I notice the middle cubicle is locked so I'm thinking someone's in there. We often found people who had fallen asleep drunk in there, so I shout again and once more I get no response. I stand on one of the empty cubicles' toilet and take a look over into the locked one. To my shock there was Patrick and Steve's wives both going for it. The younger and prettier of the two was on the toilet, legs in the air, and the older, rougher-looking one had her face buried between her legs. I was stunned to say the least, having never been confronted with a situation like it before. I coughed to get their attention and waited for them to come out. When they did the pretty one asked me not to say anything as their husbands had no idea whatsoever. Of course I couldn't tell them. I wouldn't have been able to have kept a straight face.

Eric Jones, Edinburgh

It was my first night at the Eros Club. A few of us get called to go to the disabled toilet. Nothing else was said so we made a beeline straight for it. We get there to be confronted by one of the lads, Derek. He whispered for us all to be quiet and gets out a 10p piece, which he uses to open the toilet door. Inside there's a bloke sitting down with his trousers around his ankles. On top of him there's this girl completely starkers going hell for leather. The guy sees us and pushes the girl off and puts his clothing tidy, then walks past us all, smiling. We were all laughing and in tears. The girl wasn't bothered at all and collected her neatly folded clothes and got dressed. As she left the club she got a standing ovation from all the door staff, which did embarrass her a little. Must admit she had quite a body on her, mind you.

Kris Cermele, Tampa, Florida

Some of the guys from the gym seem to think that working the club doors gets me loads of attention from the ladies. It can do but seeing as we work well into the early hours of the morning, when I leave the club the only thing on my mind is getting to sleep. At the gym or a party I may meet a woman and arrange a date, which is okay. You have to think to yourselves what type of woman is it that gives a doorman her number at the club. It's hard to find someone to go steady with; every woman you go steady with thinks you're screwing every bitch that comes to the club. The regular women visitors stay at the club till about four in the morning and that's mid-week as well. You can guarantee they have no jobs and are just looking for a meal ticket.

After breaking up with my woman I moved back with my parents for a short while. My father's blind so my mother was glad to have me around to help out. On this one occasion both my parents went away for the weekend to stay at my uncle's farm. They couldn't take my father's seeing-eye dog with them as my uncle had cats, so apart from the dog, Ben, I had the house to myself. I'd been flirting with this pretty little thing for a few weeks and after a few drinks she agreed to come home with me after I finished work. I hadn't really had time to talk with her that much but she looked superb. At my home we got to grips with each other and things were looking great when my dad's dog Ben came into the room. To get our attention he started to roll over and sit up and beg.

The girl I was with says, 'My, what a smart little doggie.'

'Yes,' I agree. 'It's because he's a blind dog.'

'Oh. How does he find his bowl?' the dumb bitch asks.

From then on I made my mind up never to pick up girls from the club. From the gym, library, beach, anywhere – but not the club.

Cass Pennant, South East London

Women do come onto doormen, to the point that to keep the boys' minds on the job in hand I exercised a 'no slush' rule whilst on duty.

We worked in small teams and could afford no weakness with any of us going soft on the night. One girl broke the defences, well two, because I met the wife, but that was off work and the other way round. This other girl used to pass me love letters in big pretty pink envelopes to pass onto this particular doorman, which I did right in front of the lads every time, and we would stand there while he'd open it. Boy did we give him some stick to embarrass him. He had the last laugh though because he married her.

Every lad would be in there just to pull a bird but the doorman could take his pick. The best answer I got to what the attraction is came when one said it's because when a doorman was suited and bowed he looks different to every other man there. Bond, James Bond. Now, if you bear in mind it wasn't like the pretty boys you get from the gyms nowadays, you know we had some guys that looked like the growlers they were, I've got to go with that. As for sex, just keep an eye on the one who decides to work the fire exit door all of a sudden. Then send one of the boys round the back to put the car headlights on them as we all pile out to take a look five minutes later. Shagging like rabbits.

Andrew Moffat, Edinburgh

I'll admit I've had sex with women and the only reason is because I'm a doorman. I have a cauliflower ear, broken nose, bad breath and piles. Do you really think I could pull some pretty girl if I wasn't a bouncer? It would never happen in a million years. A bouncer is a fanny magnet, no matter how he looks. I've spoken to women for only a few minutes then it's off down to the fire exit for a complete 'body search'. I'm not stupid to think it's my Brad Pitt features that gets them frothing at the gash.

the tossers you meet

A DOORMAN MEETS more than his fair share of tossers in his line of work. If it's not the idiot who wants to fight the world, it's the dickhead he is sometimes forced to work with. There are people out there who think they can get away with murder with a bouncer and will always try to push their luck. Some tossers are easy to spot, others remain hidden until the moment they reveal themselves to be one of the worst problems a doorman can have. Tossers are everywhere and a seasoned doorman can spot one at 1,000 yards.

Darren Withers, South Wales

I worked a place called Club Guzel in Istanbul, Turkey. We got about 850 to 1,000 people through the door each and every night of the week. The club was situated right on the divide of Europe and Asia so got to be a meeting place of East and West, where downtrodden Turks could pretend to be rich Europeans if they could afford the £30 entry fee and £10 for a glass of watered-down beer or cheap Turkish vodka. A good tip for tourists would be to smuggle in the contents of their hotel mini-bar, save them a lot of cash.

I had a good team of doormen working for me who I could really depend on if things heated up. All that is bar for Ahmet, who was the biggest horse's arse you could ever meet. He was a fair lump, a twenty-stone Turkish steroid monster who believed he was invincible. None of us ever saw him fight but really believed at first that he could do the business when provoked. After a few months of sorting the trouble out, myself and the others began to think Ahmet wasn't all he was cracked out to be. He was never around when the big boys were fighting and always the first in when the small ones were. I noticed that he always walked slowly when the real trouble started but was like a champion sprinter when anyone under ten stone was having a go. A young Turkish guy pulled me to one side one night and told me, 'That guy Ahmet can't fight, he couldn't beat a one-legged man who was blind and only had three minutes to live in a ten-minute fight.' Things started to make sense and I began to watch Ahmet a little closer.

Myself and Ahmet were watching the door one shift and I had to listen to Ahmet 'the magnificent' brag to the local girls for hours. He told them he was the hardest man in Istanbul, he could bench-press 300kg and owned the club but only worked the door because he loved to fight. In truth I was being paid £110 a night, my team £60 a night and Ahmet was getting £30 for ten hours' work. That tells you how valuable he was to the club. It must have been about 12.30 at night when this little Chinese guy comes to the door. The guy was about thirty-five years old and immaculately dressed. You had to admire the time and effort he had put in before coming to the club. The conversation Ahmet had with the guy went something like this:

Ahmet: 'What you want?'

Chinese guy: 'I'd like to enter the club, please.'

Ahmet, trying to impress giggling girls stood just behind him: 'Club is full, you no come in.'

Chinese guy: 'But you are letting others in, why not me?'

Ahmet: 'You're not coming in, yellow head, the Chinese restaurant is just down the road, you go there.'

The little Chinese guy looks up to Ahmet and tells him, 'I'm not looking for trouble, I just want to dance.' With that, Ahmet the Great reaches forward to grab the guy and impress the girls by throwing him out into the street. In a split second the guy leaps up and kicks Ahmet full force in the chops. No kidding, the guy looked harmless but could fight like Bruce Lee. Ahmet falls to the floor, out cold with his jaw busted open. I'm leaning against the wall laughing my tits off. All the time the little guy is asking me can he come into the club. I wave him on and in he goes to dance. I had to lift Ahmed up and get him sent off to the hospital. I made sure that little guy had free drinks all night. I must have told that story 1,000 times and still I laugh my head off while I tell it.

Bernard Driscoll, South Wales

I've worked with quite a lot of celebrities. I think a bloke who should really have a mention is Martin Kemp. Most of them used to be so full of themselves, you could see most of them just didn't want to be there, but Martin Kemp was different. He sat in this room with his manager and this young handicapped girl came to the club with her mother for an autograph. I went in and explained to him and he asked for her to come in. She ended up in there for half an hour having photos and he just couldn't do enough for her, he genuinely had time for people. Not like fellow *EastEnders* star Barbara Windsor, she was so far up herself it was unbelievable. She was opening this club in the town and she was five minutes early. Instead of going in and meeting people she made her car go around the block again. Two hours later and her time was up, she wouldn't even wait a few extra minutes to sign about five people's autographs.

Another famous soap star who had turned up to do an appearance was out of his head. We opened his car door for him and he fell out into the gutter. We told him we didn't want him like that; he then went away and came back later. When he came back he had to mime to his record live but was just looking up at the air without his lips moving. What a complete and utter tosser.

Ian Hews, Essex

One night I'm walking around the bars of a club, just making sure everything was okay. Suddenly this geezer comes up to me. I remember him because he used to go to my old school. After a short conversation he then tries to tell me what an easy job I've got and it's just money for old rope. Must have been about an hour later when a fight starts and he gets a glass rammed in his face, slicing him wide open. I thought to myself, *yeah mate, easy money*. Funny that he never did come back to the club after that.

Lee Callaghan, South Wales

It is always the tossers who cause the most trouble who are the ones who come back to the front door insisting they want to come back inside. They just can't be thrown out and leave it at that, they have to make a big song and dance about it. Week in, week out, we get the same arseholes causing trouble in the clubs and then pleading innocent with us later on when they find out they're banned. It's all right when they pick fights with smaller lads but when a doorman throws them around a bit they're always the first to fetch the police.

Dave Harper, Reading

One night, my son's mother's ex decided to come to the club where he knew I worked. Seems he was annoyed at me for going out with his ex. Me being me, I opened the door for him and his friend, told them where to pay, et cetera. After a while he decided to try and provoke me. I wasn't having any of it so I ask him to step outside, because I don't like people pissing me off. I told him, 'It has been a year since you split from your ex and you haven't grown up, so just go home.' He walked towards me and started to poke me in my chest. I told him, 'Don't do that,' and before he tried to do it again he was on the floor holding his mouth. His tooth came out and he had a fat lip. Like I said, I don't like people pissing me off.

Jamie O'Keefe, London

I put an exploding paint can in a room that a doorman would hide in when it kicked off. It turned out that he was being sucked off by one of the gay bar staff, which came to light when the can exploded and they ran out with pants down and covered in paint.

I have also had a lot of dealings with bullies. They think they are the dog's bollocks in their own little kingdom. But where else can an untrained, unskilled, uneducated individual get a job without any experience and then be left in charge of hundreds of people? I used the door money to put myself through college, to educate myself and try doing something with my life. Had I liked being a doorman I would have been the best that I could be at it. Others have no desire or belief that they can make a better life for themselves and just get into a rut. In all walks of life people abuse positions of trust and door staff are no different.

One wanker I worked with slapped a girl one night for no reason and in my opinion there is no excuse to justify physical violence towards a female. Anyway on his way home one night after that incident he got pulled over and had his face put to a car radiator hose with steaming water coming out of it. I think that there was a bit more to that situation happening than just a slap.

John Scriven, South Wales

I was watching this right prick bullying this other kid in the pub one night. The kid came over to me and asks, 'Will you sort this boy out for me, he just given me a few clips in the toilet.' I hate bullies and went over. I put my arm across his chest to have a word with him and he grabs me by the throat. I've then lost my head and grabbed him by the throat and charged him the whole length of the bar. I then dragged him over the bar, smashing glasses everywhere. The other doormen grabbed him off me and launched him out of the pub. The other two doormen thought I had knocked him silly, although I didn't hit him with one punch. He was falling about outside and started shouting death threats as he was walking away. I ain't seen him since though, just like all the others who leave death threats.

Clark, South Coast

Any doorman who has been working in one town for more than a couple of years gets to know the faces, people who it's just best not to let in. Some of these people, usually male, are feared throughout the community as dangerous and nasty nutters. Very few of them have done any more than glass a couple of innocent student types or knock out a smaller guy who didn't want any trouble in the first place. You also get the football hooligans who get their reputation from fighting in gangs and getting banned from going to see their team play. Some of these people live on this reputation and love the fame that it brings them up the pub or in a club. Trouble is they end up believing their own hype and after a few beers and a bit of nose candy can give you a lot of grief.

One such celebrity, who has been causing trouble for well over ten years (the time I've been on the doors), will have to remain nameless, as I'm still working and he is still on the loose. He got his name from creating havoc at football matches and was apparently the leader of one of Britain's hardest soccer gangs. In fact I was told that he was the hardest bloke in my town. He's got a book out too, telling stories of football violence and such like. He's about six foot three and weighs in at around sixteen stone, so he is pretty intimidating. Let's for argument's sake call him Nobby. Anyway, one night early in the evening a group of undesirables, seven or eight, stroll up to our door, where at the time there was just John, the head doorman, and myself having a little chat. I notice that one of them has got tattoos so I quickly tell them that, 'I'm sorry guys, but there are no visible tattoos at the weekends, but if you try the place down the road you should be fine.' Instantly a couple of them started to smirk and begin the usual banter we get when we turn scumbags away.

'Why's that then mate?' one of them asks.

'Well, the owner has a rule that he doesn't want people in here showing their tattoos off,' I explain to him.

He responds, 'That's fucking pathetic, you're just a fucking wanker, are you going to let us in or not?'

Then one of the groupies pipes up, 'Anyway you bald prick, he could knock you out with one punch.'

I've heard this a fair few times, but I'm always realistic in my answer. 'Possibly,' I reply, changing my look to a more serious one.

'Come on then, let's go round the corner and have a straightener,' Nobby says. 'He'll knock you out with one punch, you cunt.'

Now our head doorman is pretty good in situations like this and is well known with the lowlife in our town, and after telling a few of the group that he doubted Nobby could knock me out and anyway we didn't want any trouble and this and that, the group left for another club nearby. Quite a few other clubs let Nobby in because of his reputation. We *don't* let him in because of his reputation.

Hours pass and closing time comes. Everyone begins to leave when who do you think appears across the road? That's right, Nobby and his crew. A few of them looked full of courage (beer) and a few looked full of energy (coke). It just so happened that I was on the door again with John, so we clocked them as they started crossing over.

'So if I come back next week with a long-sleeved shirt on, are you going to let us in?'

'Nope,' was my reply. I knew they only wanted to wind us up, and to be honest, looking at their body language it seemed that they were more wary of us. One of them then makes John an interesting offer: 'I'll bet you a grand that Nobby can knock him out with one punch.'

'Look fellers, no one wants any trouble, it's the end of the night, let's just all go home and sleep it off, eh?'

Usually I am the diplomat and John is the one willing to react. This all went on for a couple of minutes, with a crowd of maybe forty people gathering to watch, when I decided to call their bluff. 'Tell you what, you've got a lot to say but you're not doing much. So how about doing something or just fucking off from here.'

John looked at me very surprised.

'Who are you talking to, you bald prick,' Nobby asks.

'You,' I reply. 'You're supposed to be so hard but all you're doing is talking.'

'Come round here then and let's have it,' he screams.

'Don't be a wanker, we're not in the school playground, if you want it so bad, come and get it.'

By this time Nobby didn't have much choice. His group was all telling him to go and knock me out. He started to walk around our railings and towards me. I could hear a mate of mine telling me to get my hands out of my pockets, and what a nutter Nobby was, but I was in that zone. Nobby got about five feet away when my left hand came out of my pocket, fist clenched, and BANG! By the time Nobby hit the floor I was already treating one of his mates to a lesson: 'Don't try and Judas-punch me or you'll get a slap.' I happened to turn round and a dazed Nobby was coming towards me again. I threw a punch and this time he dropped to my right hand. He had been knocked out twice in about two minutes. So much for reputations.

There was a bit of a scuffle with his mates, who didn't really know what to do. In fact I swear one of the younger ones was trying not to cry. Finally a police car came. Nobby and his mates then tried to get me nicked, which goes against the grain a bit. I got into a bit of trouble for this from the council as they had filmed it all on the city camera and I had to go and explain my actions, as I struck first. At the end of the meeting, the licensing officer said that he knew who these people were and that he had had to call me in to have a word because of procedures, then he shook my hand and congratulated me on a terrific punch.

Old Nobby has now told all his mates that I caught him with a cheap shot as he was walking past the club, or that six doormen filled him in. He's been back a couple of times, apparently tooled-up looking for revenge, with lots of back-up. One of his associates said to me a while back, 'You know he's a nutter Clarky, and you don't want a bloke like that finding out where you live and coming up your house, do you?'

My reply was quite simple: 'Nobby really doesn't want me going up his house either, does he?'

Daniel Seery, Birmingham

About a year back, I got called by my head supervisor and he told me there was a new chap who had just joined us as a doorman. He asked me to show him around and help him settle in on his first day. I told him, 'Okay then, no problem mate.' There was though. The new kid was twenty-five years old and about six foot five and sixteen stone. I told him a few tips and we got off to a good start. He seemed all right, but halfway through the night a young girl started giving him very sexy looks indeed. All of a sudden he felt he needed to impress her and started acting the hard man. About an hour later I noticed he was missing from my right-hand side, where he had been all night. When he came back I was very angry.

'Where the fuck have you been?' I asked.

'What's that got to do with you, you nosy twat?' he replied.

In normal circumstances I would have knocked the living daylights out of him and informed the door supervisor of his stupid actions. Being as it was his first day I thought I'd give him another chance. About twenty minutes later, I noticed him coming out of the toilet with the same girl again. 'Right, this is the last time. You fuck around once more and I'll have you sacked,' I shouted at him. But I said it at the wrong time; his new girlfriend was with him. He couldn't lose face in front of her could he?

'Yes I bet you will, and if you do I will break every bone in your body,' came his cocky response.

Oh, his girlfriend liked that, didn't she? I lost my temper and launched a single punch into his face and this big man dropped like a fly. You should have seen the look on his and his girlfriend's face. He got back up and started swinging at me. One punch connected but had barely any weight behind it and didn't really hurt me at all. I put another one into his lower jaw and he dropped yet again. This time he didn't get up. I thought, *this can't be right, a big lad like him out that soon.* I looked him over and he was in Sleepsville. Of course I told my superiors of his actions and they sacked him immediately.

John Scriven, South Wales

We had this right arrogant prick in this one night. He played for one of the local rugby teams and was chucking his weight about, bumping into people. I gave him a few chances until after a while he looked at me and then puts his feet up on one of the chairs. I thought, *you cheeky fucker.* I went over to him and ripped the chair out from under him and I started yelling at him, which makes him go quiet and walk away.

After a while we had this complaint from this girl that he had grabbed her. She then showed us the marks. I went and told him and he denied it, so I informed him that he's got to go. He agrees and starts to walk out. One of the doormen had heard the emergency button go off and came from upstairs. He came running in and grabbed the boy in a headlock. The boy now tries to get out of it so the doorman ran him straight into the door handle, smashing his head open. The boy then walks off and builds some courage up outside. He screams out, 'I'm bringing my brothers back tomorrow.' I shout back to him, 'You can't do it yourself then can you?' and he shouts back, 'No, I can't,' which I thought was a fair answer. I caught up with him in another pub in town a couple of weeks later and he shit himself and was offering to buy me drinks all night.

David Rudd, Beaconsfield

There was this cock bouncer who was going out with a girl my mate had known all his life, they were family friends. My mate was talking to this girl outside the club and the bouncer dragged him away and threatened him with a beating if he ever spoke to her again. Now what makes this bad is that my mate was in a wheelchair at the time, having been smashed up in a car crash. You name it, it was either broken, cracked or fractured, he was a right mess. I went mad when I heard about this but my mates told me not to bother. Anyway it wasn't long after that the bouncer packed his job in and left town. Maybe the next person he bullied was the wrong one.

Stilks, Crayford

If I get guys who I know are bullies or are looking for a fight, I stop them coming in. I try to be diplomatic about it and tell them something like, 'Look mate, I like you, you've never done me any wrong, but you can't come in here. I'm forty-five now and can't be bothered to have a fight with you in about half an hour's time. I can't wait here watching my back waiting for it to happen, I really can't be bothered. If you want to have it we'll do it now right here because if you go inside I know what's going to happen, maybe not today but it will soon and I'll have to watch my back in the meantime.' I let them know that they can come in when I'm not on the door but as long as I'm there they don't get in.

It's us doormen that risk our lives each night protecting innocent customers who want to have a good night out and not feel uncomfortable. We do the job that the police can't do. They can't put a copper in every club or pub so it's up to us to look after the place. The police should ease off on us a bit, knowing that our job is hard enough as it is. Years ago you could give some bully a slap and the police wouldn't want to know. Now, you'd get someone challenge you and when you beat them they are off to the police straight away. At the end of the day they are just bad losers who think that they have lost the fight but won the day by grassing you up.

Neil Lewis, Treharris, South Wales

We had this dance night called Pulse, it was going well but attracted a lot of scumbags who were banned from other clubs. We also had this new doorman working with us who had bounced in one of the bigger clubs in the city. He thought he was the main man: he knew everything about everyone and everything. He used to brag about how he had done this and how he had done that, he'd coshed people, CS-gassed them and a lot of other bullshit.

This one night there's an incident in the club and he's gone to deal with it. He didn't radio any of us because he thought he was Jack the Lad and could handle anything. The first I knew of the trouble was when I saw the bullshitter laid flat out on his back and this guy standing over him ready to kick the fuck out of him. The other bouncer, Scrivens, shoulder-charges the guy into a corner, then smashes him with some damaging punches. The guy slides down the wall and collapses to the floor on his knees. Scrivens is still hitting him with powerful right hands to the face. I jumped in and pulled him off before he did some serious damage he would regret later. I dragged the boy down the stairs and got him out. I was covered in the guy's blood as he was split open and bleeding.

The other bullshitting bouncer all of a sudden lost all his zap and we didn't hear much from him all night. He no longer thought he was the bee's knees as he tried to make us believe, but we already knew it anyway. You can always tell the ones who can't do it. They're the ones who talk more about it.

Cass Pennant, South East London

In our first night down in lowlife city, we kept the peace inside the club but rival gangs clashed outside after. Knives were used and two kids looked in a bad way. Our instruction from a club operating on police guidelines told us we couldn't go out and intervene. Fuck the club rules, we went out and got in the middle and separated the warring parties so that my mate, Mr T, could administer first aid. When the ambulance came with Old Bill they said Mr T's quick action had saved a life. The kids were really in bad shape but what was sadder was the club promoters were only worried about their nightclub licence, that's why we weren't getting a response to call out the emergency services from the club phones.

James Collier, Kettering, Northants
The security company I used to work for ran most of the doors in my town. Some pubs had their doormen starting earlier than others, hence we would stand at a pub and chat to our mates before our shift started. One night I wasn't due to start till eight o'clock and I dropped in to another pub looking for my best mate Wayne. I met up with him but he wasn't looking very happy. He said, 'There's about thirty to forty travellers in the pub looking like they are about to kick off.' Wayne is a huge bulk of a man and at the time was wearing an eye patch from recently losing his eye (he now has a false eye). He was working with a guy called Darren who is one of those 'shouldn't be a doorman' guys. You all know how it is these days, you need so many doormen in a town due

Some customers just don't want to leave: they'll grab hold of anything to resist being ejected

to regulations and the companies pay you peanuts, therefore you can't fulfil the requirements of every pub, so they end up employing anybody. Darren was a nice guy, but just didn't have what it took to be a doorman.

The three of us were chatting when SMASH, a window was broken. We looked in and the travellers weren't just fighting amongst themselves but were throwing glasses at each other and everywhere. Now it is best to leave these folk to fight but the few other punters and staff were at risk, so Wayne went running in and I followed. Needless to say I was shitting it as, no exaggeration, glasses were flying in all directions. I walked in with my arms waving to deflect any low-flying glasses. I did actually deflect one, so it's a good job I did this. I looked behind me for back-up and all I could see was Darren running up the road.

Wayne went into the middle of this and gently separated the two main fighters and asked for a chat. The group of travellers split at this point and half of them left the pub, tossing a few glasses as they went. Wayne then chatted to the other group, with me standing alongside him. First there was aggression at him but he must have commanded some respect, maybe due to his appearance, and they soon apologised. Darren had gone to get some of the doormen from the other pubs. A few turned up but waited at the door, which in my opinion wasn't true back-up, as the travellers could have turned on us at any minute. Then one of the other doormen walked aggressively up to Wayne and one of the travellers, who had now made their peace, and said, 'What's the fucking problem then?' Oh no, bad move. Why this guy Paul, usually a good doorman, had to barge into a situation he new nothing about and try to take over, I'll never know. From his comments things got a bit heated again and I had to calm it by removing Paul so the travellers could see we were 'on their side'. We resolved it and the travellers finished their drinks and left. Darren left working the doors after that night and the situation reinforced to me that there are in fact few colleagues on the door you can trust 100 per cent.

Dave Shaw, West London

I was given the task of showing this new mush the ropes. Alarm bells rang when he arrived, shirtsleeves rolled up and strutting up to the door like Clint Eastwood. I decided to leave 'Clint' with the other lads for a bit and take a well-earned break. When I got back, Clint was nowhere to be seen. I asked the lads where he was and I get the full story. The lads said they had let a chap go in, although he was not strictly following dress code. He proceeded to the restaurant and ordered himself a bottle of champagne. Well, our man Clint took great offence; not only had this guy been let in and been overlooked, but champers to boot! He swaggers over to ask our customer who the hell he thought he was and informs him that if he would just step outside, he would put him in his place. Turns out – to his surprise, not ours – that the guy he was offering out was a very highly respected London gangster, out of prison that day and wanting a quiet drink to celebrate. The last we heard of Clint he was in ward twelve!

Bernard Driscoll, South Wales

I had been working this one night and there had been ten of us bouncing. This boy had been chucked out a couple of times and kept coming back offering the head doorman out. After a while the doorman went out. They had a fair fight and the doorman won. About an hour later the bloke comes back with this policeman and he wants to do the doorman for assault. The policeman then asked me how many doormen were working and I told him nine. He then asked could I send them out one at a time so the bloke could identify him. The doorman who had done it was by now hiding in the club. The other doormen came out one at a time and the boy was counting them. By the time he got to the ninth, he said to the policeman, 'How many is that?' and the policeman replied, 'That's the last one now.' All of a sudden the boy starts screaming out, 'That's him, that's him.' He then told the policeman that the same doorman had beat him up the week before. The doorman's face was a right picture. He ended up getting charged and arrested for it. It ended up getting thrown out of court as the doorman wasn't even working the week before – he had gone to a rugby international in Scotland with the local fire brigade, which records showed. It made the boy look like he had made it all up but it had been his own fault for picking the wrong doorman. Not that he would have found the right one.

Ian Hews, Essex

One Saturday night I'm working this club that was absolutely packed out. All the regulars and other clubbers from miles around had turned up because a famous pop group was going to appear for about an hour, performing some of their songs. This was on a normal club night, so this publicity stunt was good for the club and also the group. The place was a sellout. I'm on the front door watching the crowd waiting to get in when this group of lads push past me and try to get in without paying. I stop them in their tracks and politely ask, 'What the fuck do you think you're doing?' The one in the front, who has a big cassette player pressed against his ear, looks at me as if I'm some kind of dipstick and says, 'I'm the drummer in the group and these are my mates.' He then attempts to push past me as if I don't exist, which was a big mistake. Clutching him by his jacket I throw him out through the door back into the road. Of course he's now shouting that he wants the manager and that I was a prick who he was going to make sure got sacked. I shout back at him, 'You're fucking banned mate, there's no way you are getting in here this or any other night, now piss off.'

He's now on his mobile telling his manager how the nasty doorman won't let him into the club. The rest of the band were already in the club and waiting for him to turn up. The manager comes down to the front door and informs me that the prick I was arguing with was the drummer and I must let him in because the band can't play without him. The manager was just as arrogant as the drummer and thought he had me by the balls and that I must do as he says because they were holding all the cards. Well, they were wrong; when I'm on the door I'm the one holding all the cards and the prick was not getting in.

The prick didn't get in. Mind you, the group did play for an hour, only with someone else playing the drums.

Bernard Driscoll, South Wales

We take one guy out of the club for causing trouble and I go to get his coat for him. As he passed by me he saw his chance and stuck the head on me on the way out, and ran off. The CCTV had filmed it and the police were called. He comes back an hour later, screaming with one of the ex-doormen from the club that he's going to have me after work. As we are leaving, he has gone onto the door girl, giving her shit. I've called him on and he's run at me throwing punches. I've hit him to the floor. He says he doesn't want any more so like a fool I let him back up. He then starts mouthing off again and I've hit him over the bonnet of a car. He threatens me that his brother's a policeman and he's going to get me done. All of a sudden a couple of his mates have jumped in to join him but I was with good doormen who had my back covered, thankfully. One doorman was putting them all away: he headbutted one, then knocked another two out. Another prick went to go for him and the other doormen knocked him out as well.

A police car turned up and the police were talking to us. The door girl went to leave the club, thinking the trouble was over and she was safe. A couple of boys now jumped in front of her car and tried to drag her out. We ran at them and it went right up. The doormen with me were knocking them everywhere, there were murders. At least eight guys were on the floor all fucked up and we didn't have a mark on us. Loads of police then turned up and told us to get out of the town.

We went to work the following week and nothing came of it. A month or two later, I get a phone call saying I'm getting taken on for a GBH. I thought, *you cheeky fucker, I was getting your coat nicely and you have headbutted me and now want to take me on.* Mad world, full of arseholes.

Peter Anthony, London

This happened about four weeks into me working the door. This group of fifteen lads was in the club and we had a bit of trouble with them during the night. One of the doormen, who was a bit steroided-up, went up to the lads and took a bottle off one of them, for some reason. This started them all to have a go against us outside the club. There were only three of us but we were giving it large and giving them a right battering. There were only a few who could come through the front door at the same time, so we battered each of them as they ran up to get at us. It felt good when the last of them hobbled off into the night, knowing we stamped our authority, and the regulars respected us for not backing down.

Must have been about two months later, I walk into the club to find them all playing pool. Turns out the boss had let them back in, without telling us. The boss said there will be no more trouble off them and if there was he would sort it out. Things were going okay until these six or so guys came in, stood by the bar and kicked off with the troublemakers from before. The six blokes absolutely fucking hammered them, claret everywhere, absolute carnage. One guy was on top of one of them just butting and butting him, splitting the guy's face open. We just stood there and didn't get involved, just turned our backs and pretended we didn't see anything and let them get the hiding of their lives. When it finally came to a stop we had to carry about ten unconscious troublemakers out. Didn't look so tough now, did they? We spoke to the guys who did it and found out they were army lads who didn't like to be messed with. They were cool as you like and seemed like real tidy lads.

The boss turns up from his hiding place in the cloakroom and asks us why we didn't stop it. I shout at him, 'You let them in, and said you were going to stop it, so why the fuck didn't you, prick!'

Bernard Driscoll, South Wales

This other night I was working in this nightclub when another doorman and myself were called to an argument between a couple of boys. We've gone running in and broke it up when from the side of me I've been smashed across the head with one of those big, chunky glass ashtrays. I've gone straight down on one knee and my head's been opened right up and has started spouting out blood everywhere. The boy then attempts to put it in the other doorman's face. He knocks the boy out cold first. The other doormen chuck the rest of them out. My head was now in a right mess and was banging for the rest of the night. The next day we get phone calls from the police saying that one of their sergeant's sons had been beaten up in the club and they wanted to know what had happened. I felt a lot better after telling the sergeant what his son had got up to in the club with the ashtray.

Mick Harris, West London

I was working on the door for this gypsy party when a load of them that had been to support their man at an unlicensed boxing show came in. They had made their way back to the pub for a celebration after a very convincing victory. The lads were full of high spirits and in a fun mood, not looking for trouble or anything like that. They had the fight on tape and were setting up the video to watch it again. Later on, one of my lads let in this bloke who had been at the sherbets all day but seemed okay. The gypsy lads had said not to turn people away unless they were in a right state – so that was a bit of a slip-up.

The tape goes on and cheers go up. A nice tidy fight by all accounts, no doubt who was in control. Anyway, this bloke who'd had a few started to kick up. 'Fucking pikeys, all fucking wankers, that bloke is fucking rubbish.' He must have thought it was a regular night and the fight was on the telly. Anyway 'that bloke', as he had called him, was standing right at the front in silence, examining his earlier performance. He turned and walked slowly up to this guy. By now there is silence and all heads are turned towards stupid drunk mouthy bloke. He now has that *oh fuck* look all over his boat. Next thing he is out cold, face down amongst the footprints and stray dry roasted nuts. A shout of 'rewind it' goes up and all turn back to the video. After about half an hour he gets up off the floor and stumbles out with that *what the fuck happened* puzzled look on his face.

Jason Payne, Merthyr Tydfil

We get told one night that there was a gang coming down soon to sort us out on the door. I know most doormen get told this every other night but, just in case, we got tooled-up, as you do. We have all got coshes and anything we can throw away fast. For the last few weeks this prick had been coming to the club and while the punters were coming through the front door, he'd take a swing at one of the doormen. The doorway was quite small so he'd throw the punch from behind a few customers and fuck off before one of us could catch him. I'm standing a little further outside the door than where I'd usually stand and I see him amongst the regulars lined up trying to get into the club. He doesn't know he's been spotted so as he gets close to the door he throws his usual punch, but this time I lean back and cosh the fucker on the head. He drops to one knee, then holding his head he creeps off, shouting that the doormen had split his head open using an axe, of all things. Well, that seemed to do the trick. Haven't heard from him in a while.

James Collier, Kettering, Northants

I hate the presumption that most doormen are thick. These days many of us have other jobs, in fact some are well educated with degrees. Although I don't wish to sound arrogant, I am educated myself and am a clinical health professional with a degree. I also lecture on nutrition at a university as well as do research. The one thing that annoys me when working is being looked down on, it's just plain rude. Anyway, you know the sort, the posh punters who think they're better off than you are. There was a group of males and females and a couple of the lads had had too many Babychams and were getting a bit boisterous. Two of us went over to have a word and ask them nicely to calm down. We were confronted with abusive comments and it was implied that we were of low intelligence. My mate laughed and said, 'Well James isn't fucking thick.' A posh girl said, 'Of course he is, just look at him.' I am a bodybuilder, so am well built and have a shaved head, but according to these girls' dangerous presumptions this also meant I am of sub-average intelligence.

A few insults were thrown both ways, then a debate kicked off and it turned out that this girl reckoned she knew a bit about health and keeping well. She was into all the alternative therapies. I questioned her about a few things and it led to her to comment on a few unscientifically validated supplement therapies she thought she knew about. This was a bad move as I criticise theories for a living. I proceeded to shower in a load of names of enzymes and metabolic pathways of why her theories were unsound and how the processes she was talking about couldn't occur due to simple physiology. In the end her friends were laughing in support of what I was saying, and she went red in the face and shouted, 'Oh fuck off!' to me and stomped out the pub like a spoilt little rich girl who couldn't get her way. When her friends left after her, we had a chuckle but then I told my mates that in fact I hadn't even heard of some of the supplement therapies she was on about and I had just completely made up the metabolic crap and physiology I had spouted. I just said what sounded plausible. I wasn't going to be outsmarted, even if I didn't have a clue!

Dave Harper, Reading

At a club where I was the head doorman, I left these two guys on the door. This particular club suffered with local young black guys who think they have the right to walk into a club without paying, for some reason. One guy in particular walked straight through and I told the guys to get him straight out. He was getting rather leery about it, so I went up to him and asked him to leave. He didn't want to go, so I grabbed his arm just by his armpit, where I squeezed him tight, and literally threw him out of the club. He then started to give me his Jamaican accent talk. I told him don't bother coming back, so he decided to pull out a knife. I told him, 'If you're going to use it, then use it.' As quick as I could, I disarmed him and pushed him hard back against the wall, grabbed his neck, and gently stroking his face (really taking the piss now), said, 'Hey boy, piss off. Don't ever come back here.' So off he went into the night.

Tommy Meaney, Leeds

I've worked in various clubs that have had good managers and a few bad ones as well. This one manager used to cook us steak and chips before we turned up for work; this other one used to make us buy our own drinks, a right horrible fucker. The horrible fucker finally came to an end with the help of myself and two other doormen. We had only been working with him for a few months but were having a right guts-full of him. He told everyone that my mates and myself were his bodyguards, putting our names around as if we were looking after him.

This one night we noticed a lot of people were going to the toilets and being very ill. We later found out there had been a bad batch of pills going round in the club. The police were on to us, as a couple ended up in hospital. Now, if it's one thing I hate it's drug dealers, I utterly despise the work-shy bastards. I had a word with

bouncers

one of my mates and he went in there undercover and found out who was doing the main dealing in the club. Where we work has a fifteen-foot wall by the exit doors, so as he's on his way out I smile at him and say goodnight. I suddenly grab him and with the help of Big Phil, the other bouncer working with me, we take him out the exit doors. I ask him who he is dealing for and he says he can't tell me or he'll get in trouble. I grab the skinny fucker by the legs and hang him over this wall, head first. I've got one leg and Big Phil has the other and it was hard to hold onto the dealer as he was squirming like hell. He starts screaming crying and yells out who he's dealing for. Turns out it was our horrible nightclub manager, so I gave the dealer a slap, smash his mobile phone up and send him on his way.

Now we'd been collecting money on the door all night and Big Phil and myself agree to split it between ourselves. It was a few hundred quid in all. I walk up to the manager and ask for a word with him in his office. I inform him that I caught some lad dealing in the club. He tells me, 'How dare the prick deal in my club, I hope you gave him a good slapping.' I then tell him the lad's name and you could see his face change when he realised it was the lad who was dealing for him. I pounced on him and dragged him onto his desk and proceeded to beat fuck out of him. As I'm hitting him I'm letting him know that we knew what his little game was. He squealed like a pig and had the cheek to offer me a partnership with him. Before I left him crying like a baby, I told him that the actual owners of the club better find someone else to manage it for them, because I'd be coming back the next night and if he was still there he was going head first over the wall. We left him with no bouncers on the door and 300 people in the club. Found out he pressed the fire alarm to get them all out just after we left.

Eric Jones, Edinburgh

After Brannagans I made a sensational return to Eros. It was that sensational that the crowd decided to have a kick-off in my honour. We must have been throwing guys out of fire exits for about ten minutes. That's a long time when there are about twelve doormen involved. At the end of the night all the door staff had a chat and all I remember Rob saying was, 'Well you'll all now realise that Eric is back!'

Things were going fine for the next seven months, then I once again lose my job there. It was over a punter trying to strangle one of our lads. The punter was a big strong lad so I decided to choke him out, see how he liked it. Before we got him out through the door he must have been choked out about four times. He was a heavy bugger to carry out as well. The powers that be decide to sack me; seems I was a little too heavy handed. The doorman who was earlier being strangled came outside and thanked me for saving his life. Work that out if you can.

Michael Jones, London

This bloke had been leaning over the balcony in the club. Now upstairs they had notices warning everyone not to lean over the balcony. Nearly everyone listened, but this night we had a group of boys in who were upstairs laughing and joking about. All of a sudden I heard this loud thud directly behind me. I turned round quick only to see this bloke lying on the floor, all crumpled up. He had hit his head on the table on the way down from falling off the balcony and he was in a very bad way. We managed to clear the pub and the area around him. The ambulancemen then turned up and said we had done a good job by clearing the area and not moving him. Two days later me and the boys were on the door and this bloke in a leg cast and neck brace starts walking towards us. The cheeky bastard had only come down to the club to accuse us of pushing him over the balcony.

Tommy Meaney, Leeds

I stayed with a friend in London and got some door work in one of the big clubs in the West End. The money was really impressive and a lot of the celebrities came there, who fucking loved themselves. Some of the things they got up to would shock you. We could have gone to the papers nearly every night with some of the stuff we saw going on there. I couldn't tell you how many times my jacket pocket was stuffed with notes to keep my mouth shut.

This one night this group of celebs had been to an awards ceremony and then moved on to our club. One of them had been playing a boxer on the TV and you could see it had gone straight to his head. He's strutting around banging into people, so I ask him, 'Come on mate, calm down a bit, you don't want to spoil your night?' He answers me, 'Do you know who I fucking am, you fucking prick?' I was stunned for a minute, as I had only seen him act on the TV and thought he was a nice person. I ask him if he knew who I was.

Before he could reply, I inform him, 'I'm the bouncer who knocked that actor out.'

'Which actor?' he asks.

As he said that I plant one on his chin that sends him over a table and flat on his back, out cold. A couple of his mates came along and took him to the toilet to sort him out. I knew the manager would want to see me and was certain I'd lose my job. As I walk in I've already thought of a lie to tell the boss, but he was only concerned with the papers getting hold of the story. If they did the actor would have been finished, as his reputation would be in tatters. I was told that if I shut my mouth I could keep my job, and returned to the front door just in time to see the actor getting in his taxi. I did think about going to the papers but why mess someone's life up for a few hundred quid?

Steve Wraith, Newcastle

The new breed of doormen coming through nowadays are by and large a big joke. One new starter woke a punter up in the bar and instead of throwing him out, told him to finish his drink and leave when he was ready. The same lad spotted a punter bringing a bottle of pop into a bar, which is not allowed. He stopped the lad, took the bottle and had a sip. Satisfied there was no alcohol in it he let him in with the bottle!

Jamie O'Keefe, London

Most managers I've had dealings with have been tossers. They make demands that you smash and bash certain customers, many claim to be former bouncers, and they stick you up on offer if the going gets tough. They just abuse door staff as a replaceable commodity. They are interested in making money, having a fiddle and acting like they are very important people. They interfere unnecessarily and always cut corners by having too few door staff to keep things safe. I've only found a couple of decent ones who realise what a shit job door staff have at times.

Mickey Jones, London

I'd been trying my hardest to get off the door but it is like an addiction. In twenty-five years I have been puked on, knifed and have had guns pulled out on me, amongst other things. If I had to give anyone any advice, the best would be: don't trust anyone. Doormen will be the best friends you will get, but they will also turn grass and stab you in the back. One day the Social turned up wanting details of how long we had all been there and which of us were claiming benefits. Same as any other doormen, we gave them false names and addresses, which usually got rid of them. But they came back to us again. A lot of us ended up with fines and money to repay the Social. There was this one bloke who worked the doors with us for years and apparently, instead of taking a chance getting caught, this bloke grassed the lot of us up. We never saw him again. Guess he wasn't as hard as he looked.

we are at war

A DOORMAN CAN find himself embroiled in a 'war' over one spilt drink or a cross word. It can start small and burst into a wild fire if unattended and not stopped straight away. A doorman can anticipate a fight happening but can't tell how it will end. Some troublemakers are not just hoping to even the score or get vengeance; they want to see the doorman hurt, maybe even killed. On top of that, door wars have become a feature of the past two decades, as the security industry has become organised. Some of the firms that appeared have dubious backers and are little more than private armies prepared to use any tactics to take over the doors in their town.

Douglas Gentles, Cardiff

There were a few people running teams years ago but they were so far up their own arses that I never had anything to do with them. A couple of the guys working the doors back then are these days running them. There seem to be more companies popping up from everywhere. Most tend to give up with Cardiff after a few months though. These companies employ doormen who have no experience and without it they don't stand a chance. Some firms have been known to send in teams to various pubs and clubs specially to start trouble, week in, week out. Then when the pub or club has had enough of their present security company, the 'old' one comes back on the scene and, as if by magic, the trouble stops. But from what I gather this goes on all over the country.

I have never really been involved in any bouncer wars. A few times while working in Luigi's we had teams of other doormen come in and before the end of the night they would start fighting, but they were always sent packing. I believe that all doormen should stick together. I hate it when a doorman on a night out with his mates starts a fight in another club. To me this is breaking a golden rule. If any doorman from any part of the UK comes into a club I'm working and they let me know they are a doorman and prove it by showing their card then I will let them in free of charge. In return I expect their respect while in the club. I'm totally against bouncer wars, I know they go on but as I see it there are enough people out there that want to give us a kicking without doing it ourselves.

There have always been gangs around. The thing that has changed the most about these gangs is the fashion. As more American TV has been showed in the UK over the last fifteen years, the gangs have followed the gang fashions from the States. Along with these fashions goes the weapons; it's cool to have a gun tucked into your trousers or a knuckleduster in your back pocket. Of course a gang inside a club causes problems for a doorman, especially if one or two are involved in a fight. Many times we've had fights with gangs; these days it's just part of the job.

As for people who try to get in without paying well that just don't happen in the clubs I work. There have been those that tried and it has ended up with fighting between us and them but if they don't pay then they don't come in, end of story. People like that can just fuck off and play their silly power games elsewhere. I always try to work with a good team behind me, guys that are not bullied into letting someone in for free because they are scared of the person and what they are capable of doing. A doorman working on his own or even two doormen working might have no choice against a group of guys refusing to pay. I guess some doormen would turn a blind eye but thankfully I've never worked with any that have.

Ian Hews, Essex

I was working this big club in Ilford, Essex. It was 7.30 on a Friday evening and I had just parked my car up and was walking along the main road to the club. This was in the early Eighties and there had been a lot of animosity between security firms offering doormen to the different clubs. It was trouble all the time and everyone was expecting it to go off. As I approached the club on the opposite side of the road, four toerags from another firm jumped me. Now these aren't your local idiots, these are guys getting paid to do you in and they aren't messing about. I did the first one and was trying to survive against the other three when I heard a big bang. For a second I thought a shotgun had been fired. I quickly looked over to where the bang had come from and saw Danny Benn, brother of Nigel Benn the famous boxer, who came flying out of the club. He had seen the fight taking place, had come running down a staircase and smashed through the fire exit doors (the bang) to help me in this fight, which wasn't going my way.

Now Danny Benn is built like Mike Tyson. He is a big, powerful lad of about eighteen stone. In his eagerness to help me he has forgotten about the main road and run straight across it without stopping to look. A car has hit him head on. He goes up in the air but luckily lands on his feet. To cut a long story short we gave the four would-be thugs a good hiding. We went to cross the road back to the club and there was an old geezer parked up with the front of his car caved in. I looked around and there's Danny rubbing his arse. The old boy was standing there scratching his head in total shock. I went over and apologised to him and said if he got a quote the club would pay for all the repairs to his car. He never did come back. Fuck knows what he told the insurance company: the bonnet had a great big imprint of Danny Benn's arse in it!

A few days later Danny got badly stabbed in the club and was rushed to hospital. When he came out he was stuck indoors for a while. One night his friends decided to take him to a house party. They put Danny in a wheelchair and push him round to this party. This is one of the old East End terraced houses and the party was upstairs, so rather than cart Danny upstairs where everyone is dancing, they leave him in the front room. There's Danny sitting in his wheelchair with a couple of beers having his first night out since his stabbing when the wooden floor joists gave way and the whole floor collapsed on top him, along with about sixty partygoers. The newspapers got a picture of Danny sitting there, still holding his beer can, after two tons of flooring had landed on his head. He went on to make a full recovery, I'm glad to say.

Keith Price, Bexleyheath, Kent

I get asked to do security for a twenty-first birthday party at this restaurant/disco. It was situated in a real shitty part of Kent, bit of a *Concrete Jungle* meets *Changing Rooms* sort of place. The evening was going along quite well. There were two of us on the door and another mate turned up to give a bit of moral support. So there we were me, Glen and Hughie. Hughie got pissed, Glen and myself just got bored. I thought, *what the fuck, we're being paid so let's make the most of it.* We then proceeded to rob the wine cellar, making trips back and fore to my car.

As the night wore on I noticed about a dozen invited guests who I didn't like the look of. I asked the kid whose party it was about them and he said it was okay. I could sense that maybe he was frightened of them but, after all, they had been invited. The biggest one came over and said, 'I've seen your mate nicking the wine and I want some, or I'll grass you up.' Glen told me and I told the bloke to fuck off and mind his own business, no one likes a grass. Another one of the crowd comes over and told me that I was okay but my mate was a bit of a cunt and I should have a word with him. Fair enough, I told Glen that we should leave the wine alone as we had enough to open up our own bar. During the night I threw a few kids out for taking drugs and generally thought the night was going well, with the exception of the dirty dozen who were starting to get on my tits. I didn't like their attitude or their behaviour.

Just before closing time, about ten to midnight, Glen went to the toilet. Ten minutes later and he hadn't come back so I went to check on him. I found three of the dirty dozen punching the fuck out of him in the toilets. I gave them a few kicks and punches as I pulled Glen out. He was screaming that he'd been stabbed but after a quick check over it turned out that he had just been winded. Next thing I knew it was like a Wild West brawl. One older man got punched in the head with a bottle and a girl got slashed across her face. Hughie came to his senses enough to grab hold of one of the ringleaders and hold on to him like a bucking bronco. I threw Glen behind the bar to protect him and started to throw the spirit bottles from the optics at the attacking crowd. We were cornered like rats.

The biggest and baddest of the bunch stepped forward, ripped his shirt open and shouts, 'Right who fucking wants it?'

'I do,' I shout back and launch myself at him and his mates, spraying the lot of them with ammonia. They cowered and screamed but I was just getting warmed up. I snapped off a chair leg and started whipping, kicking and punching anything that moved. I was like Michael Flatley on acid, after all my life was in serious danger. One of them smashed a glass ashtray down on my head. Now I was really mad. I grabbed him in a head lock, smashed a wine glass and screwed it into his face. I then squirted him with ammonia for good measure.

They all started to run and the police arrived minutes later. The police took one look at us all and told us to get to the hospital. The owners had locked themselves in the wine cellar, so we fucked off before they did a stock check. I needed stitches in my head, Glen had a broken nose and Hughie had a black eye. The opposition couldn't see, walk or smile for quite a while. One of them lost the sight in one eye. And if he's reading this through his squinty eye, I'm not fucking sorry at all.

Daniel Seery, Birmingham

This young lad had turned up in our club with his mate. My mate Tony checked them and found a knife concealed in one of the lads' pockets. He then told them they couldn't come in. One of them was furious and started shouting and poking at Tony, who eventually felt no reason to carry on arguing and launched a sweet right hook onto the young man's jaw, knocking him to the floor. I noticed the other lad pull something out of his pocket, so I ran up to him and gave him a kick into his lower spine area. He dropped to the floor screaming, 'I'm going to fucking kill you, you bastard.' So for good measure I put an axe-kick into the back of his head, which bounced off the floor.

I looked around for what seemed like about two seconds and saw Tony's troublemaker unconscious on the floor. I thought all was going well until I turned around and my troublemaker punched me with a knuckleduster he had hidden in his pocket, splitting the skin open just above my eye. The cut was about an inch long. I hit the floor and he started pounding into the back of my head and across the top of my head with his dusters. Tony came running up and put yet another right hook into my assailant's face, knocking him to the floor. At this point I was very angry at what he had done to me and I started kicking him in his head. Again he was screaming in pain until I kicked him unconscious. I only realised the screaming stopped when I ceased kicking at him. But it didn't stop there.

Being new around the area, I hadn't realised that he was in a very vicious gang who lived nearby. A few weeks went past and we saw the same two arrive at the club again, and coincidentally Tony and I were on duty again. Immediately we refused them entry. One of them swung a punch at Tony, so again we all started fighting. I had Tony's man from last time. I was so pissed off with these two that I thought I'd make it short but sweet, so I was rapidly punching into his face until he dropped to the floor. I started stamping into his face again and I thought I'd won it easy this time, but no. Members of his gang had come in separate groups and before I knew it I had a metal bar smashed into the back of my head. I got knocked onto the floor my head was spinning and I couldn't stop my hands from violently shaking. Another one hit me in my jaw and a massive explosion of blood shot out of my mouth. I thought, *this has to stop or they're going to kill me*. I turned towards the metal bar man and used all the strength I had left in my body to put a punch into his face – and what a beauty it was. It struck him straight on the bridge of his nose and splattered the fucker. I used the momentary stop to kick him in his groin. He went down but as he fell he grabbed hold of my right leg and pulled me down with him.

Luckily our head doorman was coming to check on us. He saw what was happening and came up to my assailant and kicked him in his chest, dropping him. My attention switched from my little fight to Tony's, as he had two on him. My problem was sorted, my head doorman was taking care of the one with the metal bar and the first one was still lying down on the floor. I ran at Tony's man, giving him kicks and put a headbutt into his face. His legs wobbled and then he also hit the floor. Just one more left – but this one was no easy fight, this bloke looked six-foot-odd and about fifteen stone. Immediately after I nutted the first one he came up to me and went to hit me, but this guy being so big and slow immediately put me into advantage. I put two rapid punches into his face and his head span away from me. Now that he had his back to me, I put a kick as hard as I could into his back. He dropped in pain and gasping for breath. Tony hadn't had enough, he went into a mad rage and practically tore this man into pieces. He just wouldn't leave him alone. Andy, the head doorman, and I dragged him away from him. We've not heard anything from this gang since and not one of them dare show their face at our club again.

The queue outside the door is a good place to observe body language, states of inebriation and rowdiness – even among gangs of females

David White, Caerphilly

We were expecting trouble from a rival bouncing firm who said they were coming to the club to take over. We had a few good boys who we could trust in the club, just out for a drink but who would help out if need be. We had phoned them earlier telling them about the trouble we were expecting so they turned up and sat quietly in the corner drinking and watching us on the main door. The night was going tidy with just little scuffles and the odd argument when we threw this young lad out for fighting. He had started a fight with a man who had fallen out with his father a while back. Outside he gave us the same old shit that most do about how we were dead and he's coming back with a team. Seems his father was a bit tasty in his day but we assumed that he wouldn't get involved as his son was a well-known prick and his dad must be sick of him by now.

It was getting late and there was no sign of any rival firm turning up, so we were just about to close the main doors. I was outside on the phone to my girlfriend telling her that everything was all right as there was no trouble after all. As I was on the phone I noticed a minibus back up to the main doors. Some people started to get out and enter the club. One of the last out of the bus was the little prick who we threw out earlier. It suddenly dawned on me that the prick had gone to get his father and his mates to back him up and they had all just entered the club.

I ran back into the club and pushed past the crowd of guys who had just entered. They were all big lads, must have been about ten of them but they had picked the wrong night to come looking for trouble, seeing as we had a number of lads in the club willing to help us. By now the group had realised I had sussed out what they were doing in the club and they tried to get past us into the main hall to drag out the guy the son had been fighting with. The father and his friends got quite aggressive and started threatening us. Push came to shove and I ended up on top of the father, beating his face like a drum. His friends started to lay into the three other doormen and I got a few boots in the face. The gang of lads we had in the club rushed forward thinking it was rival bouncers attacking us and got stuck in. We pushed them back and beat the fuck into them all. There were unconscious men spread out all around the entrance to the club. The few that weren't sleeping were either pinned down or nursing their wounds. I clearly remember a mate of mine who had been in the toilet while the fight was on, walk up and jump on one of the gang's legs. I could hear the guy scream out as his leg snapped by his ankle. Some of us went over to the unconscious guys on the floor and took off their gold chains and rings. I found a wallet, which I hid and later split about £160 with the other doormen.

Seems the guys we fought had a shock when they turned up thinking that they were going to beat up three or four doormen. Word went around that it wasn't a fair fight because we had too many with us but they were happy to fight when they outnumbered us.

Ian Hews, Essex

I was looking after this pub when a team of Welsh rugby players turned up. They were gradually getting pissed and a fight breaks out. I end up with two other bouncers getting me head kicked in. It isn't wise taking on a rugby team, especially if they are pissed and you're only three-handed. The next day it was my little girl's first birthday party. All the in-laws turned up and there's me sitting there with two black eyes and a broken nose. If I'd ever found out where them Welsh fuckers had come from I would have got a JCB and flattened their clubhouse, preferably with them in it.

Steve Wraith, Newcastle

We had rucks with visiting firms. The whole town would be on maximum alert for the North East derbies between Newcastle and Sunderland or to a lesser extent Middlesbrough. We would have the police visit us to have a look around for any notorious faces and they would update us on their whereabouts, but I knew most of the lads so didn't have much bother with them, as there was mutual respect.

One of the worst matchdays I had to work was next to Central Station. The other lad who was supposed to be working, Mick, didn't turn up and left me in the lurch. Newcastle had just lost at home to Sunderland so the atmosphere was evil. In those days the away fans were given a police escort to the station but that didn't bother those intent on causing trouble. The police had for some reason underestimated their numbers and I had a major incident on my hands. The bar was full of Geordies urging the Mackems to have a go and I was one man against the masses. A bottle was thrown towards the bar and the window went. It was like the starting gun to a marathon: the whole place erupted. The Mackems charged the door and the Toon fans charged the oncoming red and whites. Game on.

It made *Braveheart* look tame. I let those go who wanted to and pulled a woman off the ground who had been knocked over in the crowds. She was a little shaken but nothing broken. I managed to bolt the doors, out of breath but all in one piece. The sound of smashing glass was deafening. The aftermath was like a bomb had hit the place. The manager was just pleased that nobody was hurt. Mick chose the right day to be off.

John Scriven, South Wales

I had just gone into work this one Saturday night and there was hardly anyone in the club, just a few regulars there. This police car pulled up and this big huge Canadian policeman got out He was working with local police on some sort of exchange programme. The policeman wanted to know if we have got two boys in the club with bandanas on. He then asks us would we go in the club and escort them out. Both us doormen go in and the two boys are by the bar drinking. We knew these boys and they had never been any trouble to us, so we tell them that they are wanted outside by some policemen. We walk them out with no trouble at all. As soon as we get them outside the big copper pulls this huge, Clint Eastwood-type gun out and starts screaming at the two boys to get up against the wall. We didn't have a fucking clue what was going on. It turns out the boys had been seen on CCTV cameras in the day brandishing guns. We couldn't get over it later when we thought about it. The copper knew they might have had a gun and still sent us in to get them out.

Jason Dicks, Bristol

The trouble in the club was getting worse by the week. There were a couple of dealers working the clubs but we had our eyes on them looking to catch them dealing. Then one night we caught them in the act. One of them tried off loading some stuff to his mate as we cornered them but we grabbed the both of them. One of them then starts screaming at me that I was fucking dead when his boss got hold of me. The 'boss' he was working for was known as one of the biggest dealers in the town. Both he and his brothers had been running the drugs around here for years. They had a big reputation that stopped anyone going near them. I took all the drugs off them for the police to come and collect them. I then gave the boy a slap and told him to fuck off; I didn't need any comeback, especially from those crazy fuckers.

Later I'm called to the front door to be told that my car's just been done over. Someone had put all the windows through and dented it to fuck. The lads on the door then tell me the 'boss' had turned up and wanted to see me but they had told him that I wouldn't come out. I ask the manager, 'Have the police turned up yet?' He informs me, 'I haven't called them as we don't really need the hassle.' My car's smashed up and some mental cases are outside waiting for me, and he doesn't need the hassle. What an arsehole.

The other doorman were shitting themselves and one says to me, 'You should have left them carry on dealing.' I couldn't believe what I was hearing; these were my mates who wanted drugs out of the club. I grabbed my jacket and steamed out of the exit door. I then jumped in a taxi and made a few calls to a couple of my mates to meet me at my house. I knew where this big dealer lived, so we waited across the street from his house for him to come home. It was now the early hours of the morning and he gets out of a taxi with some young slut and starts walking up to his house. I let my mates know that seeing as he was on his own, I would need no help. It would have been different if he'd had a few lads with him.

I run up behind him and call out his name. He turns around, recognises me, sniggers and tells me how I'm a dead man. As I run up I spray pepper spray into his face, which soon drops him to his knees. His girlfriend runs off and locks herself in the house as I start to kick fuck out of his face. His nose and mouth are split wide open and he goes out as I stamp his head into the pavement. We all get away from the scene as fast as we can. I knew I had gone too far and didn't know if the dealer's girlfriend had called the police. I got told the next day that he spent a few days in hospital and his nose was fucked up.

Over the past year I've had to move home, as a breeze block was thrown through my window in the early hours of the morning. My dog was poisoned and my new car smashed up but I still work the doors. I get the odd phone call from different faceless hard men who tell me what damage they are going to inflict on me but for the time being I'm still here.

Cass Pennant, South East London

I once took several bullets in the chest at point blank on a club door down in lowlife city. Which is as true as the witness statements taken at the time and as true as the last bullet they cut out from my back a year after the incident. What's also true is I had fought all my life going forward but that night I went forward on instincts because the fear felt was real enough. To smell the cordite of a smoking gun trained on you tells you I was close enough to not ever want to relive that experience. To put it bluntly, your choices at that level and degree of violence are limited.

Bernard Driscoll, South Wales

We had trouble with a rival firm of bouncers. They had got sent to our nightclub to play hell but had a good team of boys working that night which could handle any situation. These bouncers started playing fuck after a while, chucking empty beer cans at one of our boys. Word got back to us what was happening and we all got prepared to take them on. Now in the club if there were any idiots or if we wanted someone needing doing, we had this boy; he didn't give a fuck that they were doormen, he'd just go across and start trouble. We gave him the nod and he walks straight into these bouncers and puts one on the main fucker. All hell's broken loose and about ten of us have just run straight into them, hitting whatever moves. There was blood everywhere. We were fighting upstairs and fighting downstairs. We did have our work cut out but we managed to do them and get them out of the club. They never came back, so we must have done a good job on them.

Ian Hews, Essex

In the late Seventies, thousands of English builders came to West Germany to earn good money on the building sites. The Germans weren't slow in working out that the builders had bucketfuls of money to spend, especially on the weekends at the local bars or brothels, when they had nothing else better to do. The main local brothels were down a road that had little houses either side, full of working girls. The owner of the brothel had a brilliant idea of putting an English pub half way down the road, with beer half price. He knew that as soon as word got around, every Englishman from miles around would be heading for his pub next to his brothels. He knew that they would have to walk past his girls to get to the pub and if they weren't tempted on the way to the pub they definitely would be when they left. 'Pissed up and well fucked,' as he liked to say.

I got the job as the pub doorman, keeping everyone under control. Everything was going fine, I was having a great time surrounded by beautiful girls and earning a fortune. A couple of months later, I'm in the pub when suddenly there's a lot of shouting outside. I look out of the window and there's an army of about forty women marching towards the pub. I don't know what they were shouting in German but from the look of them I knew we had some sort of trouble on our hands. They stormed the pub and start to lay into a couple of the bar staff. I jump in between them all to calm things down when suddenly I'm getting kicked and punched; in fact I'm getting a good hiding from all these nutty birds.

I don't hit women but on this occasion I had no choice so I chinned one of them. Now, I've got forty women wanting to fight me, who turned out to be forty hookers who were pissed off about losing all their trade to us. Some guys might pay for a hooker slapping them around a bit but I'm not one of them. I put up a good fight but trying to fight forty crazed hookers, I was on a no-win situation and they beat the crap out of me for trying.

Dave Courtney, South London

I was a doorman when racism was at its highest and football violence was at its highest. They were proper wars, real ongoing battles. People would go out purely to go black bashing, Paki bashing and queer bashing. So when you put that little bow tie on you were putting a target on yourself. There might be four of you and 2,000 in the club. If you didn't win fights you were sacked.

Dave McKay, Birkenhead

Every year since my mates and myself were teenagers, we would all go on one big holiday. We still go now even though a few of us are in our mid thirties. Tenerife was always a popular choice and this one year we were there as usual having a few beers and a good laugh together. Okay, some of the things we got up to were a bit naughty but all in good fun. A few of us were strolling up and down the strip, which is known as Veronicas. We were just chatting to people and popping in and out of the various bars. This was about the same time that Ecstasy had hit the scene so everyone around us was buzzing and up for a crack.

My mate and myself spotted a Spanish guy carrying a drunken English lad across the road. I thought maybe he was helping him to a taxi or to his hotel. They both disappeared down some slope next to McDonald's. Next minute the Spanish guy appeared, then the English lad about twenty minutes later. The English lad was shouting that he had been mugged, and had lost everything. Later we spotted two Spicks trying to prise a watch off another drunken lad. We tell them to fuck off and wake the lad up and get him to his hotel. Meanwhile one of the Spanish guys was shouting at us and dragging his finger across his throat. Didn't know what he was saying but the sign language was enough for us. We watched him cross the road to some bouncers that were working nearby, some Spanish and some English. They chatted for a while, then the bouncers flashed laser pens at other bouncers working the clubs around the area. The bouncers were getting the signal that there was trouble and would come to see what was going down. Slowly their numbers were building up, and we could sense the tension in the air.

They marched over to us and some very angry words were exchanged. These turned into punches and kicks from them and the crowd of British lads who had now turned up to support us. The bouncers produced some baseball bats and were swinging wild with them. The response from us was to bombard them with beer bottles and anything we could get our hands on. They backed off into a club and we all sat on the wall watching to see what would happen next. Some British lads working nearby told us that the Spanish druggies and the doormen had a very profitable mugging scam going on in the area. These doormen were helping to roll the drunken British lads even though some of them were also British. We got warned that the police were also in on it and it was a wonder the police hadn't turned up already.

Two cops appear and start chatting to the doormen. Next minute the police came over to our group and start swiping at anyone British. One of our lads, Shawsey, stepped forward and with no hesitation jawed the copper. The doormen rushed to help the fallen copper and I jumped in to back Shawsey up. He gets the copper's baton and we back off, hitting anything that moved too close to us. All the lads that came with me on holiday and some who just joined in for the crack threw everything bar the kitchen sink at the doormen and the police, who were now running for cover. We all did a runner before we got nicked. As we left we could see the doormen using their laser pens to signal for more doormen. I bet every year some poor British lads come unstuck with those doormen. Well, we are all a bit older and wiser now but still there are sixty of us going out next year on a massive stag do. Things should go smoothly but you never know.

Cass Pennant, South East London

We had an axe riot with a 100 Rastas in a nightclub in Peckham. The row had been going on far too long and we'd been fighting for our lives. Now it was stalemate because they couldn't take the club and there was too many of them for us to clear the street. Then a single bus load of Old Bill showed up well late. The club looked like Beirut, with broken glass everywhere and a wild mob of Rastas chanting, 'War!' and, 'Burn them!' They all stayed in the police bus and sent out the oldest copper alive; he looked so old retirement was not an option. He came through the crowd, up to the battered club door and said, 'I can't see a problem here to be called out on, is there a problem then?' We looked at each other through the wreckage and said, 'No problem at all, officers,' and he went back to the younger officers in the van and off they drove.

Anthony Thomas, Merthyr Tydfil

I worked this dive of a club called the Taff Trail. The place was a timebomb just waiting to go off. More and more scumbags were getting into the club each week and we didn't know who they were until it kicked off. Trying to get them out of the club was a nightmare, as the entire club seemed to know each other. Some of the bouncers would pack the job in the first night they started. This one night, big Payney and Terry were working with me and it starts off with me throwing this gypsy guy out for dealing. Away from the club he takes it out on his girlfriend, and like the hard man he was he slaps her around a bit. Terry says to big Payney, 'You know, Ant being a boxer could knock that big gypo out. You couldn't do it. I just don't think you have the power.' This goes on and Terry bets him a pound that he couldn't do it. As luck would have it, the gypsy guy comes up and starts to argue with Payney. The guy is shouting and pointing at Payney, who throws a cracking right hand that smashes the gypo to the ground, lights out. 'Right,' shouts Payney, 'I want my bloody pound.' Terry laughs and gives him his earnings but when Payney looks at his right hand he finds the gypsy's teeth have split his knuckle wide open, so it's off to the hospital for stitches and an injection in his arse.

We are slowly over the course of a few weeks getting the club sorted but still find there are dealers and scumbags finding their way in. It was hard to stop them coming as we didn't live in that area and because the landlord worked on his own through the week days, he was letting guys in who we ban on the weekends. We couldn't just ban them on the weekends in case they caused trouble in the week when we weren't there to help out. Also because we didn't live in the area we never knew what type of people we were letting in. We couldn't ask them on the door if they were tidy, druggie, bully, dealer or scumbag. It would have made our job easier if they answered a questionnaire correctly for us.

I was guaranteed a fight every night that I worked this club, in fact the worst incident I've had on the doors was at the Taff Trail. It began with me throwing some prick out, only to have this short, stocky scumbag offer me outside. He proceeds to push me so we start to fight and I batter him. I'm on top of him and he's crying and begging for mercy. He looked the hard man earlier with all the talk and half an ear missing from a street fight years before, but on the floor he was screaming like a schoolgirl. I get off him just as I'm struck from the side by one of his scumbag mates. Another bouncer, Paul, jumps in and drops the other guy. Now more scumbags are turning up and we keep putting them on their backs. There is a block of flats opposite and loads of the druggies' scum mates came running out towards us. It started easy for us at first with us banging them out but now it was like a scene from *Zulu*. One lad runs at me and I grab him and smash his head through a car window. We make our way back into the club and look out to see bodies lying everywhere. Things calm down a bit but more scumbags are leaving the club to join up with their mates outside. My hand was killing me; seems I'd dislocated my thumb and couldn't make a fist, just what I needed. A few more bouncers gathered at the door, waiting for the scumbags to attack. They were grouped outside, a large mass of druggies holding all types of weapons: knives, bottles, iron bars, chair legs and anything else they could use on us.

I clenched my hand hard and forced my thumb back in the socket. I can't begin to tell you how much that hurt but at least I could make a fist. I turned to my mate Beast and said that my hand was better and ran outside to fight the first five or so that I could get to. Beast and another bouncer ran out and dragged me back in telling me, 'Ant, it's no good mate, there are too many, we'll be killed if we go out there.' Bottles were raining down on us and all the club windows were put through. We all stand in a row by the front door and every so often one of the scumbags tries to rush at us but we hold our own and the scumbags proceed to throw stones and bottles. A big rugby guy rushes towards me; he was big but had a small brain and no idea how to fight. I step forward and knock him back. The only reason he didn't go down was because his mates held him up; he just leant back against them all rocking to and fro with his eyes rolling in his head.

It's not often someone helps the bouncers these days but this small lad of about ten stone decided to give us a hand. He ran straight out from the club into the midst of them all. They put him away in seconds and are all over him, battering him on the floor. I didn't know him but if he was willing to help then I wasn't going to let them kill him. I run in to where I saw him fall and start to lay into them. Well, I held my own for about ten nanoseconds when, from what I gather off onlookers, I'm then smashed on the back of my head by a gin bottle and it's goodnight from me. I'm stabbed in my back and one guy is on me trying to smash my tiny brain to pulp with an iron bar. One scumbag gets what looks like a large plastic chair leg with the end broken off and all jagged, stabs it through my arm and it rips out my bicep muscle. Beast and Paul fight to where I've fallen and manage to drag me indoors. I wake up drenched in blood, a large gaping hole is in my arm and I have to hold the muscle back in. Paul had phoned the police earlier but they didn't get to the club for another fifty minutes, though they only had to drive one mile. The scumbags by then had dispersed, as they knew the police were on their way. A few days in hospital and I'm back on my feet.

Over the past year I have hunted most of the scumbags that I can remember down and battered them. Some have even complained to the police about me. One came to our gym one day looking around wanting to train. A friend tells him that I was in the gym and he leaves straight away. I follow him outside and punch him unconscious and proceed to kick him from one end of the car park to the next. I left him sleeping on the tarmac and went back into the gym. A few weeks later I'm told that he's telling his friends that six others and myself jumped him and beat him with sticks. Of course none of us could put him down as he managed to stand his ground. Yeah, right. And pigs can fly.

Steve Wraith, Newcastle

The Hoppings Fair would visit Newcastle Town Moor for a week in June every year and apart from bringing bad weather it would bring a whole lot of trouble in the form of gypsies. The travellers for me are the worst type you can come across, although Sunderland fans do come a close second. They are always looking for bother with anyone who so much as looks at them. This particular night was no different. It was a Thursday night and a couple of lads were late arriving at the club. There were only three of us on duty. We had let a group of lads in earlier who were on a stag night from Edinburgh. Now have you ever seen a sober Scotsman? Neither have I. The gypsies arrived in dribs and drabs and we were quiet on a Thursday so had no objection to letting them in.

It took all of five minutes before the alarm was ringing. 'Fight in bar one' came the call over the bar staff's radio. Sure enough the Scots and the gypsies had introduced each other and it looked like me and Paul had a riot on our hands. Johnny, the other lad, had to stay on the door, as is standard practice. There was a ruck of about twenty blokes punching and kicking seven bags of shit out of each other, so me and Paul got amongst it as best we could. I pulled the gypos back, sovereign rings and all, while Paul weighed into the kilt-wearing warriors.

Our back-up arrived in the shape of Simon and Vaughan, who had just arrived, and we managed to get them all outside. Blood and snot was still flying as we rag-dolled the lads up the stairs and out onto the street. It was one of the very few occasions where I have had to actually hit anyone at work, a record I'm quite proud of. I like to go into work, earn my money and go home without any bother if I can help it, but this gypsy was from the school of dirty fighting and decided he fancied a bite of my arm. I managed to pull my arm free before he drew blood and caught him with a cracking uppercut. I followed that with a straight left to finish him off.

Jason Payne, Merthyr Tydfil

We get threats on the door all the time. Some you take serious, some you don't. This one guy threatened to crossbow me and said he was off to fetch it. I did the whole shift on the main door and towards the end of the night had forgotten him. I'm in my car just lighting a fag up before I drive home when one of the other bouncers reverses up and warns me he has just spotted the guy who threatened me hanging around. Out of the darkness comes the guy holding this huge boulder above his head. He was going to smash it through the windscreen of my car. With us spotting him first he decides to drop the boulder and fuck off. I'm sure if we hadn't seen him he would have brought that boulder crashing down on the windscreen and bouncing off my head.

Jamie O'Keefe, London

The nearest to a gang war I have seen was at a rock venue I worked called the Borderline in Charing Cross Road. The Hell's Angels and the Outcasts would come in quite a lot and generally gave no trouble. They pretty much policed themselves, as a lot of them were doormen within their scene. I was writing a book about the Outcasts and one of their main guys, Des, was going to take me into the hidden world of bikers to gain some experience of the side that we do not normally see. Having been a Mod myself, I didn't know that much about bikers. Anyway, while the book was being written one of the bikers killed another in this feud that was going on. There were a lot of ugly things going down but I was not party to it. I scrapped the book idea as there was too much shit going, plus I knew people from both groups.

I did have another situation with a load of football thugs coming into the club. They kicked off with us and were outnumbering us five to one and it was getting pretty serious. The bar staff alerted the police, who arrived and told us to keep out of it. The thugs went for the police but got hammered and dragged away in vans. I've got no time for football thugs. Fuck them. If they want to take their issues to a private plot of land and sort their shit out then let them, but to kick off around innocent families, with kids just out to watch a match is not on.

Wayne Price, Mountain Ash

We had these biker types in one night at Ballys bar, full leathers on and they had their women with them. They had all sat down not far from some couples who had gone to sit in the back room where it was quiet. We hear them start to get a bit rowdy and I go to check on them all. This tall one called Lee grabs hold of this guy. Before he can do anything I run over and hit him and launch him across the room. I jump on top of him and start trying to drag him out. With that another one rushes me and brings down a bottle on my head. I turn and throw a punch in reflex, only to find I've knocked his girlfriend out as well. Thing was with all the greasy hair and leathers they all looked the same to me; anyway she shouldn't have smashed me over the head with the bottle. I carry the both of them out and leave them on the pavement for their friends to take home.

A few days later I heard that they were telling everyone what they were going to do to me when they see me next time. I found out where they lived and went around to their house. He opened the door to me and started to argue and stepped towards me. I let him have it and left him lying on the ground outside his house.

Eric Jones, Edinburgh

I had worked various doors in Edinburgh before I got moved to the Eros club. This was one of the biggest clubs in Edinburgh, with an unbelievable 2,151 capacity. I was there for eight months and that was some eight months. I saw some of the worst fighting and yet I also met some of the nicest people. It was at the Eros that I was introduced to the bottle – in fact twice in about three seconds. It was the Friday before Christmas 2000 and the club had been open from noon. It was to be a long fifteen-hour shift. The place was packed out when I notice there's a big kick-off behind the DJ box. There must have been about at least twenty guys going for it. These weren't little guys either but big strong guys who could handle themselves. I've called it in and ran straight in to the heart of the fight. Things were a bit chaotic as I'm splitting fights up left, right and centre. I've got these two by the throat and I'm expecting the stewards to arrive but it's not happening. I can feel some brave fucker landing punches on the back of my head but I stick it out and manage to stay on my feet. The two that I've got hold of fall over each other and we tumble into another fight. I manage to stop myself going completely down on the floor but by this time I'm down on one knee.

This is where someone introduces me to the bottle. It was sort of a dull thud, you know the type, where all the music in the club goes quiet. The bottle never broke and the guy is still behind me. The bastard then smashes it into my face like an uppercut and the bottle breaks. There's blood everywhere from my head and spurting from around my eye and I can't really see what's going on. I go berserk and kick and punch my way to the VIP lounge. Jo the female steward sees the state of me, drops all the tickets and tries to get hold of me. I was raging. I had been out there on my own while the general manager was having drinks in the VIP lounge with friends. Before nearly passing out I kick a few tables and chairs over. The ambulance comes and it's decided that I should go in it with one of the guys who had been fighting. I thought to myself, *magic*. I didn't know if he was the one who cut me open but he was going to get it anyway. Well, they soon changed their minds about putting me in with him. At the hospital I received five stitches to my eye and three staples in my head.

I didn't mind working at the Eros but I had to leave after I was fighting on my night off. I must say I'd still do the same now if the situation arose. A fight breaks out and again there's only one steward in the middle of it all. There was no help in sight for him. I'd had a few drinks and waded in to help. I had my hand around this guy's neck choking him out because he had picked up a bottle. I ended up getting a fag put out on the back of my hand to stop me putting him to sleep. I knew that the owners wouldn't have liked me getting involved so left the club before they sacked me. The only regret I had was letting my good mate Rob, the head doorman, down because he's a right good guy.

Steve Wraith, Newcastle

I was making regular trips to London to see the chaps and had been doing shifts thanks to Dave Courtney at Diamonds club in Hackney and at the Ministry of Sound. Working those venues had given me a taste for club life. I considered moving to London full-time but was told in no uncertain terms by Dave that I should 'stay up north mate and make your mark'. I decided to take his advice. I had been to see the various faces who ran the doors in the North East and made it known that I was looking for club work. I was told that they would be in touch. A couple of months had passed when

I was called by Mike, the manager of Legends nightclub in Newcastle. He said that he had been given my number and that he wanted to offer me a job there. I jumped at the chance and four hours later I was signing on the dotted line with Geoff Capes's (yes, *the* Geoff Capes) security firm.

What Mike had neglected to tell me was that the previous doormen had just been sacked and that the police were keeping a close eye on the club and had compiled a list of criminals and doormen who they wanted barred. It was well known that the doormen had been running the club like something out of the Wild West. Customers were getting beaten to a pulp but the tapes went missing and the club was gaining a reputation as a bit of a drugs den. The police decided to raid the club with over 150 officers, but to their embarrassment caught no dealers and only a handful of people for possession. I had taken on a job and a half here.

Doormen in any town or city are a funny breed. There is a lot of competition in the industry and a lot of pride at stake, and the one thing they hate is outsiders, people from another part of the country being in charge of doors in your area. Capes UK was based in London and relied on outsiders to work problem bars and nightclubs for them. The first couple of days passed without incident but this was the calm before the storm. The ex-doormen weren't happy, despite receiving a substantial settlement, and they were going to make us work for our money. Paul came on board, which give me a lift, because up until that point I was the only Geordie there. Paul and I were now looked on as scabs amongst the door fraternity and were subsequently barred from most bars in the city centre, with the threat of a good kicking if we tried to visit any of these places.

I will admit now that each night was a nerve-wracking experience. I changed my route to and from work, I was careful not to let anyone know my address or telephone number and I even gave a false name to people I talked to in the club. Paranoid maybe, but you cannot be too careful in this game, and although some of the threats lacked any real danger, you have to take each one seriously, because one day someone may just call your bluff. As time went by the threats died down and we had weathered the storm. I'd had a few run-ins with a few faces in that time but as the months passed the lads from other bars started to respect the fact that our Paul, me and the other lads who had now come on board had stood our ground and not bottled. I suggested to our gaffer that he lift the ban on doormen now that the trouble had cooled and that we let doormen in as long as they surrendered their licences to us for the duration of their stay. He agreed and again we made our job that little easier. Our bans were starting to lift one by one in the town and I would soon be able to go for a pint in Newcastle again without looking over my shoulder.

Terry Turbo, North London

The gang culture is scary for the whole country. A lot of it is covered up but there are regular shootings and gang warfare every day. The way we have dealt with it is to let people know in a roundabout sort of way that we will not bow down to them and if they go down that road we will go all the way. We have had protection money threats, the people who want to come in mob-handed and not be searched, the people who thought that they'd test us out.

When I first started going clubbing and decided to become a club promoter, I set up my own security company, made up of mercenaries, ex-Parachute Regiment, ex-SBS, ex-SAS, yardies and some of the scariest head door staff at some of the worst clubs in Peckham, Brixton, Harlesden and Hackney. I had my own army and each one of these guys had twenty nutty mates around with them, guys that don't give a fuck. Over the years there have been many rumours of us being connected to this firm and that firm, but the truth be known we have always been on our own. But we never stopped the rumours, why should we? The more notorious you are, the better. Fear is a great weapon and it's the art of fighting without fighting.

Now there's a very good chance that someone could shoot you if you give them a good hiding or disrespect them by not letting them in. People seem to think it's cool now to wave a gun around and if they shoot someone and get caught they are actually proud of their achievement and think it's cool to go to jail. What the fuck is that about?

The most violent incidents I have been involved in have always been at the large-scale raves, with muggers or firms of geezers who think they are something special. The worst one was at the Sanctuary in Milton Keynes. We had a gang of about twenty black guys from Manchester who didn't want to pay to get in. We made them pay and warned them: 'There's twenty of you, behave your fucking selves or else.' After an hour they started playing up, so we told the in-house security about it and after ten minutes realised they were all shitting themselves, so we dealt with it on our own ten-handed. I walked up to one of them and said, 'Right you cunts, get out.' One of them started all that flailing the arms around shit, accompanied by, 'You don't know who you're dealing with,' for which he got the magic elbow right in his face. Then it really went off.

We managed to get them to the fire exit and then all the tools came out and these guys were left unconscious round the back of the club. We must have been fighting these guys for at least twenty minutes and they were a fucking handful. We were all around the cashbox when we got a call over the radio: 'There's your guys putting guns in their waistbands and putting balaclavas on!' We were obviously worried, as we didn't have any firepower there, and reluctantly locked the front doors and called the police. Luckily for us the police must have been waiting for something to happen and were there in seconds. These guys somehow got rid of their guns but they all got nicked. I wonder how they explained to the police why they were standing outside a rave with balaclavas on? The police said these guys were serious and they put two armed response units outside the rave and had SAS-type coppers either side of the front doors with Heckler and Koch MP5s, in case any of their friends returned. Imagine turning up at a rave at 2 A.M. and seeing that. It's enough to make you paranoid! We had to get an armed police escort all the way home.

I have never been involved in bouncer wars. There's no point killing each other over a silly club contract. Say you earn £200 a week profit from one club; after paying your expenses, that's peanuts. You do have these idiots going around undercutting each other though and putting idiots on the door for £6 or £8 per hour before deductions and normally something serious happens and they run away. Then you get the job back anyway. With us it was quality. You get what you pay for: if you pay peanuts, you get monkeys.

you're havin' a laugh, mate

ALONG WITH THE fight tales that each doorman can tell you in fine detail there are the comical things that can turn a bad night on the door to a pleasurable evening. There's no better recipe for breaking the tension on the door than humour.

Robin Barratt, Manchester

It was my first night on the doors in Manchester city centre. I had quickly learnt the word 'scrote' and I already knew what a knobhead was, and these two black guys approaching my door certainly looked liked both knobheads and scrotes. I looked across at my colleague Steve, who nodded to me knowingly as we instinctively moved closer together to block the entrance. It seems that all scrotes and knobheads are the same the world over. They have a kind of walk that lends itself to severe constipation and they flap their hands and fingers about in various poses that remind me of the mentally retarded in a psychiatric hospital. They also have this vacant look in their eyes, as there is little brain matter in their tiny skulls and even the most basic skills and actions for most scrotes and knobheads are complicated; they understand little and communicating with them is almost impossible.

'Sorry lads, you can't come it,' I said, plainly and simply as they approached the door.

'You 'avin' a laff, in yu?' the taller of the two replied. Now I know I am not the most educated of doormen and had worked the doors for many years in many towns and cities across the UK – it was all

Robin Barratt: 'We're surrounded by over 100 screaming, ugly, shaven-haired football yobs. We were going to die.'

I could really do – but I didn't understand a word he had just said. They were obviously *alien* scrotes and knobheads as well, and I was sure they had just arrived from the planet Zob. They looked as though they had. I looked at my colleague, who shrugged.

'Sorry?' I said to them, confused.

'A laff, you 'avin' a laff?'

I turned again at Steve and asked, 'What is a laff, as I am supposed to be having one soon?'

He smiled and shrugged, Steve was not a man of many words.

'Sorry buddy, don't know what a laff is and I am sure I don't really want one, but you are not coming in tonight.'

'Do you know ooh I am?' the taller scrote replied.

'Do I know Ooiam? No, never heard of him, does he work the doors too?' I asked. There were many Asians in Manchester, a few I knew but I had never heard of Ooiam. Steve laughed.

'Listen lads,' I said, 'I don't know who Ooiam is and I don't want a laff, whatever that is.' I knew they were obviously not of this world, and I simply didn't speak their strange language, so I thought I wouldn't try and communicate with them any longer. I was going to try sign language, or perhaps a few musical notes like *Close Encounters*, but decided to say, '...so just fuck off.'

They must have had the same word on the planet Zob, as they started screaming, waving their hands and shouting in some strange, odd language. Steve looked at me and laughed. 'We are going to have to teach you a little Mancunian,' he said.

Ian Hews, Essex

Many years ago when we had gangs of mods and rockers coming to the clubs, a good friend of mine was working when all these bikers turned up. After a lot of arguing, they were told they weren't coming in. They rode off on their bikes and nothing more was said. A week later two Transits pulled outside the club, a dozen or so bikers jumped out and ran up to the front doors of the club, where a large amount of people were waiting to get in. They were carrying buckets full of piss and shit and proceeded to throw it all over the doormen and the queue of people waiting there, covering everyone from head to foot. Two of my pals got drenched in all the foul sludge. The rockers must have saved it up all week in those buckets, the filthy bastards. It's a shame nobody was around to film it all, that would have been good for *Caught on Camera*.

Anthony Thomas, Merthyr Tydfil

Two large gangs of lads were arguing and my mate Chris and I chucked the local gang outside. The gang from another town were shitting themselves inside the pub; they all looked like big rugby players who could do a bit but they were outnumbered. I decided to have a word with the local gang, as I knew some of them and they were some right tasty boys. They said they were going nowhere till the other gang came out. I had to think fast. Now call me a bastard if you want but this really worked well for Chris and myself. I went up to the rugby players inside and said, 'Look lads, I know it's none of my business but the guys waiting for you outside are a bunch of wankers, there's not a fighter amongst them.' I could see their confidence growing and within seconds they said, 'Let's go and do the bastards.' They shot out of the pub straight into them. We closed the doors behind them so they couldn't get back in, laughing our heads off. Minutes later you could see blue lights everywhere as we watched it from the windows. The police ended up closing the street down again but we didn't give a fuck as we had done our job by getting them out of the pub with no damage to us or the regulars.

Keith Price, Bexleyheath, Kent

My good friend Stilks and myself threw a couple of lads out of a club in West Kingstown for fighting. They sat outside in their car making threatening gestures, so we went out after them. With that they drove their car straight at us. We didn't flinch and they swerved at the very last minute. They turned and went to drive off, so I reached in my pocket and threw my knuckleduster at the car, hoping to make a nice dent in the body work. I couldn't believe what happened next. The duster went straight through the rear windscreen and hit the driver on the back of the neck. He slumped forward across the steering wheel and we just collapsed laughing. Suddenly he got his act together and sped off. He's probably still got my duster but it's like wearing another man's gloves, it will never fit him.

Lee Morris, South Wales

I was working in this pub one night and this guy had been there for ages and wasn't moving. I thought he'd fallen asleep or was pissed. I was going to leave him there for a while and then go and tell him to leave as I thought he was not harming anyone in the corner. Turns out he was dead. He had been drinking earlier and he must have been dead for hours with all nutters drinking around him.

Mickey Jones, London

I have worked with a lot of women on the door, they are the best weapon you have in the nightclub. They know how to hurt a man and how to completely destroy women. They deserve all the respect they get. I remember one night I was attacked by a right whore; she jumped on my back and tried to scratch my eyes out. I had closed my eyes to save me from losing them and I could hear someone starting to bark orders. Next thing I knew this girl had let go of me and went flying backwards. The girl working with me had gone up behind her and wrapped her hand around her ponytail and physically pulled her off. The girl then stood up and the doorwoman whispered in her ear. The whore just turned around and walked straight out with no fuss. Apparently the doorwoman had seen her in the toilets and said to her that if she wanted to keep her customers she should leave now. When I asked the doorwoman how she made the whore leave so easily: 'That's because she's a man who gave head around the corner for £15 a time to unsuspecting guys.'

Steve Wraith, Newcastle

I would say I'm quite tolerant of the pissed general public, and I have always had time for the punter who is ejected from a club on a freezing cold North-East night early on and proceeds to protest with the door staff for the next few hours. Inevitably he or she resorts to, 'My dad/mam will have this place closed down.' What people don't realise is that we hear this sort of thing every night. If anything it keeps us amused and passes the time, and like referees in football we never change our mind. So if you find yourself in that situation, do yourself a favour and go home, you'll either end up in a cell or with a lousy cold – or both.

Humour plays a large part on the door and nine times out of ten you end up taking the rise out of each other. I love a good joke and am lucky that I can laugh at myself. Legends at one stage was renowned for its customers using drugs, and as I spend most of my time there on the front door, I would have to carry out spot searches. I must admit I hated it. Having experimented with drugs myself when I was younger, I felt hypocritical. It wouldn't have been too bad if all we had to do was knock these people back, but no, the police wanted us to, in effect, arrest people. I had to be seen to be doing the job anyway, and this night I had decided to wear my new suit. As I bent down to check the customer's legs for anything he may have concealed, I heard a loud rip … my new pants had given way and a cool draft was evident at the rear. That is the only time in my life that I can say I had my back to the wall. Still it gave everyone a good laugh on the night.

Jamie O'Neil, Wales

This tosser needed chucking out so along with another bouncer I go on to him. He lets us know, 'Keep your hands of me and I'll walk out tidy enough,' so we walked him down these backstairs and out through the door. I thought to myself, *that went smooth*. Before we go back upstairs there's a knock at the door. Now we used to let our mates in this way for free, so I've opened the door. The club had been having work done to it around the back and it looked like a building site. As soon as I've opened the door, the bloke we had just chucked out hits me over the head with a dirty big petrol can. He steps back and starts screaming at me. I'm out on my feet. In a daze I manage to slam the door shut. A big lump like on a *Tom and Jerry* cartoon came up on the side of my head the size of a pool ball.

The tosser is now full of himself and calling me out to fight him, I could see a few people looking at me wondering if had bottled it or not. I opened the door and called the fat fucker on. I hit him straight in the nose with a cracker and he's lying there fucked on this big pile of sand. My soft side then got the better of me and I go over to see if he's okay. As I leant over him, the sneaky fucker grabbed my shirt sleeve. I yanked back, ripping the whole arm of the shirt. He starts laughing and I saw the funny side of it as well. He starts throwing handfuls of sand at me playfully. He then apologises to me. As I'm walking back into the club with no arm on my shirt and covered in sand, some bloke I knew shouts out to me, 'Jamie, you look like Robinson bloody Crusoe.' We all started laughing.

Peter Edwards, Chepstow

One club I worked at had this big TV screen that was connected to a DVD player in the DJ booth. The DJ could play the DVD on the small TV in the booth, then when he was ready flick a switch and the image would appear on the big screen. One night the manager calls me up to the DJ booth and shows me part of a porn film on the small TV. 'Have a look at this Pete, it's fucking mad,' he instructs. I look at the TV. There's these big coloured men having sex with dwarves. I couldn't believe what I was seeing but the DJ and the manager were laughing like mental cases.

There must have been 300 in the club and suddenly a good few of them start shouting and clapping. I look up and right above the stage on the big screen there's a close up of this little dwarf woman giving this guy a blowjob. The manager had flicked the wrong switch. Instead of complaining that it was on the screen, most of the customers complained when we knocked it off. For weeks after we had men and women asking where they could buy a copy or when were we going to show it again.

Lyn Morgan, South Wales

Working in a new club is always a little awkward as you don't really know the customers or the guys you are working with that well. I was covering for another lad and got put with two doormen who were known for their wind-ups. The doorman who had taken the night off had told me about these two girls who play fuck with the doormen, the type who were up for a laugh and didn't give a fuck. The doormen could never do anything with them as they just didn't care.

One of the doormen comes up to me in this foyer and says, 'Can you go and get those two girls off the table in there.' I guessed it must be the two I was told about and I was correct. I went across and start yelling at them to get down. With that they pull their skirts up, tug their thongs to the side and reveal all whilst laughing their heads off. I didn't know what to do next. I turned round to see where the other doormen were and they were doubled up laughing. I then say to the girls, 'Come on get down, you're making me look a right prick by here.' They are still laughing and making no attempt to get down. I thought I'd try something a little different and said, 'Girls, if you get down it will wind the other doormen up, as they can't handle you and can't imagine me doing it either.' Next thing you know they got down and stayed down for the night. The two doormen were puzzled all night as to what I had said to them.

Dave Harper, Reading

One of the funniest things that ever happened to a friend of mine who worked the door at another club, he always sees himself as a ladies man. He would always brag about who he shagged in the toilet, or in the back of his car. One night this tall woman walked in and he made a beeline for her, he kept saying how he pulled this beautiful woman. To his horror and to the other door staff's great delight, it turned out to be a man, the guys never laughed so much. He of course got angry and went to go for her/him but was stopped, he realised that he was foolish and was totally embarrassed by his actions, must say I haven't seen him to this very day.

John Scrivens, South Wales

This one night this kid came to the 'Rock Night' in the club and you could see he was under age. I told him, 'Go and get some ID and you can go in.' An hour later he turns up and gives me this ID Now I could see it wasn't him in the photo. I ask him his surname and he tells me, so I ask him his first name and his date of birth and I could see he'd learned it off by heart. I let him in but as he's walking in I call him back. I ask him, 'What's your middle name then mate?' His face dropped and he says to me, laughing, 'I don't know it.' In the end I just left him in for his cheek.

Marty Dee Donovan, South London

Although it can get a bit nasty you can still find time to have your fun on the door. Once we placed one of those fake plastic dog shits on the floor by the club entrance. The looks on customers' faces as they were queuing up! But because it was a busy queue they didn't say anything so as not to lose their place in line. It would have made Jeremy Beadle so very proud.

Jason Payne, Merthyr Tydfil

We had this manager of a club once, right picky bastard, always on about something, wouldn't leave it rest. I remember he had one of those Jeremy Beadle funny hands and a strange attitude to match it. He came up to us on the door one night and hands us two black bags. 'What are they for?' I ask. 'One's to put chewing gums out of customers' mouths in, the other's for the chewing gums you find in their pockets,' he informs me. He'd had a gut's full of cleaning the club's carpets so this was his way of dealing with it. We felt like right lemons having to get customers to spit their chewing gums into the bag. Thing was we'd have big drug dealers come to the club and had to search them for chewing gums. I wouldn't have done it but he stood on the door with us all night watching to make sure we did it. I can tell you now that idea didn't last long before we kicked it into touch.

Peter Anthony and Phil George, London

Mate of ours was working this really big club. It all kicks off on the dance floor – a massive great fight involving about 200 people; it was a complete riot. This doorman mate of ours was on the balcony and must have thought he was a superhero. He jumped off the balcony aiming to land in the middle of the fight to break it all up. His timing was off, he completely missed all the fighters and landed on the dance floor. He broke his neck, his arm, his shoulder and knocked himself sparko. I think he is the only doorman in history to completely miss a fight of 200 people.

Bernard Driscoll, South Wales

A few of us went over to have a word with these boys who were fucking about in the club. Things turned nasty and one has smashed me across the forehead, splitting me open with a bottle. The other bouncers have gone nuts and are chucking them out left, right and centre. I was dazed for a while and was in shock that I had been bottled. The following night I have gone to work and one of the boys who was bouncing with us has brought one of those building site hats in with the initials BBS on it. I was then known for the night as Bernard Bottle Stopper. You can imagine the shit I had all night. I had my revenge the following week when it was one of the boys' birthdays. He had just turned forty-two so I brought a wheelchair into work for him. You should have seen the look on his face.

Martin Bayfield, Rhyl

Standing in the foyer of the club, I'm looking around and everything is peaceful. Suddenly one of the bouncers came up to me with this guy whose nose is pouring blood. 'Stay here with him,' he tells the guy, and fucks off to the gents. The guy who was bleeding starts to mumble some rubbish that I couldn't understand. Seeing as he was always in trouble and usually started most of it, I open the main doors and proceed to throw him out. He puts up a struggle and holds onto the frame of the door, trying to stay in the club. I bring both hands down on his arms and he quickly lets go in pain. I lock the door and start to walk back into the main part of the club when I'm met by the other bouncer, who's carrying a wad of toilet paper.

'Where's that boy gone?' he inquires.

'He put up a bit of a struggle but I threw him out the main door,' I inform him.

'Why the fuck did you do that? He hadn't done anything wrong, he just had a nose bleed and wanted some toilet paper for it.'

I felt such a dickhead. The following week when the boy came back to the club I couldn't look him in the face.

Mark Thomas, South Wales

It had been a very quiet night. Another doorman and I were walking round the club checking things out and I stuck my head into the chill-out room to see if everything was okay. Over in the corner of the room through all the smoke I can see this girl giving this boy a blowjob. I went back outside and told my mate what was going on in there. He says, 'Watch this now,' ran into the chill-out room shouting 'Geronimo!' and smashes into the couple. The girl jumps in shock and bites the boy's cock. I'm standing there laughing while the boy is screaming in pain. The boy then came out and showed us the bite mark on his old boy. I couldn't stop laughing as the couple then left the club together.

Cass Pennant, South East London

I was once sent a wreath at the gym where I worked, which was a misunderstanding, as I later found out. All because a tasty doorman came along and was told, 'Don't call us, we'll call you.' A wreath is a serious business and you know how it upsets mum! When we found out where it came from we were challenged to go down to this other door and do something about it, so I did. It was some trendy wine bar, more uptown than downtown. I walked right through their door wearing the flowered wreath like a hat on my head. The place was packed. The doorman had run off through the back bar and when I recognised familiar faces I realised this was a local conspiracy. Nobody laughed, nobody dared to laugh and believe me I looked a right cunt with this wreath on my head. We played to the gallery and I walked over to the DJ to give the locals a message. I knew the DJ too and he's all pure, upfront soul music. I asked him, 'Play that record "You Don't Bring Me Flowers".' He didn't have the balls to say, 'That's Neil Diamond, you cunt, no cool soul DJ would have that.' We left him searching for it through his collection. The lads were busting a gut but I was serious. At the time I managed a nightclub in the next town and everyone backing this conspiracy was from my club. It got a whole lot funnier but I wouldn't want to personally humiliate everyone and besides you had to be there to picture it: me with a wreath stuck on my head with the boys marching in and out of every bar along the high street looking for a doorman that had scarpered up the road.

Lee Morris, South Wales

We had just got in to work and the boys had gone next door to get some energy drinks for the night. I've gone into the pub on my own and I can see this boy has got this girl in a headlock, messing about. He then starts getting worse. I go over and warn him to calm down. He starts giving me shit about who I thought I was and what he was going to do to me. I knocked him out. This other bouncer told me to go and hide in the beer garden. About ten minutes later he rung me on my mobile and informed me, 'The guy is still knocked out. What the fuck have you done to him? His ear is on the floor.'

I said, 'Fuck off, you're having me on.'

Turns out the boy had been a bit of a prick in the past and his ear had been bitten off and 'clipped' back on. I thought I'd punched his ear off!

Wayne Price, Mountain Ash

We had to search everyone before they came in. I was searching the guys and Melanie the girls. There must have been some trouble with women upstairs as Melanie had to run up. I carried on searching customers for a while then I ran up to see if everything was under control. I at once notice this suited guy going into the ladies' toilets. I ran up and grabbed him, telling him that he wasn't allowed in the toilets. The guy puts up a bit of a struggle so I try to get him out of there, and because the floor is wet we are both slipping everywhere. After a while I finally get him up to the front door, only to find Melanie laughing her head off. She explains that the guy I was throwing out was in fact a woman and I had just dragged her out of the toilets. I looked at her and realised my mistake. I walked away and couldn't face her even to apologise. Everyone teased me all night over it, even though she did very closely resemble a man.

Ian Hews, Essex

I just can't stand poofs. One night I'm in this club and one of the regulars comes up and said, 'Ian, there's this fat twat in the toilets and he's doing a George Michael.' Now you can't take anyone's word for anything in nightclubs, you have to check these things out yourself. There I am, making myself look a right prick by peeping through the doors into the toilets, trying to catch this poof doing something. Ten minutes later and he still hasn't done anything that I can throw him for, bar watching everyone at the urinals. I decide to throw him out anyway and enter the toilets. Well, one thing leads to another and I end up punching the poof.

Next day I'm at a wedding, a work colleague of my girlfriend's was getting married. The bride came over and was introducing us to her family. 'Come over here and meet my brother,' she said. Yeah, you guessed right, it was the poof I had hit the night before. There he was with two black eyes, he was gay all right and probably spent half his life standing at urinals. He didn't say a word; could have been quite embarrassing if he had.

Anthony Thomas, Merthyr Tydfil

I've met some strange people. One was this pisshead who walks up to a pub I was working at and tries to enter with his dog. The pub was packed so I informed him that he couldn't take his dog in. The guy starts to argue with me that the dog isn't banned and the dog has never caused any trouble in his life. The guy was really serious and was right up for the argument. The other doormen are pissing themselves and I'm finding it hard to keep a straight face. He eventually tells the dog to sit outside and wait for him while he goes into the pub for a drink. He stands by the bar just looking out at his dog and the dog is looking back at him. I felt so sorry for the little dog that I almost let it in. The owner comes back and before he walks off he asks me how long the dog has left on his ban before he can come into the pub. I cracked up laughing and walked off without answering him. I just didn't know what to say.

Phil Bevan, Cheltenham

One of the funniest things I ever saw was when this big fight broke out. We calm the situation down and get a few of the troublemakers out. When I return from the main door I realise there's a crowd forming on the dance floor. Fearing the worst, I run up and push my way through. There on the floor is this lad, sparko, knocked clean out. I reach over and slap his face and he comes around a little. A minute or two later and he's back on his feet and regaining all his senses. I go back to the door where I'm confronted by the lad's girlfriend. She was shouting and screaming about some dirty bastard in the club. I ask her to calm down and start from the beginning.

She tells me, 'My boyfriend gets knocked out by that twat who you threw out. I rush over to see how he is and I can't wake him up. As I'm bent over looking at him some dirty bastard runs up and rips my knickers off and runs away. He nearly cut me in half.'

I'm gobsmacked. She points out the lad who did it and I go over to talk to him. I've seen him before and knew he wasn't really a troublemaker.

'This may sound as a stupid question,' I say, 'but did you rip that tart over there's knickers off?'

By now all his mates are in tears, doubled over. 'Yeah I'm sorry mate, but one of the lads bet me a tenner that I couldn't do it. It was her own fault, bent over like that flashing all her arse off.'

I couldn't throw him out for horseplay so we agreed to forget about it and, being the fair guy I am, I returned the tart's knickers. The least I could do.

Darryl Taskers, South Wales

I was on the door one night eating my fried chicken when a fight breaks out and I get a stool smashed over my head, splitting it wide open. After putting the guy away I was still angry and pissed off, not because I had to go to the hospital but because I'd given my fried chicken and chips to some guy to hold for me and the thieving prick had run off with it.

David White, Caerphilly

I was working on the door of this club with this other bouncer, Kyle. Some bloke comes out pissed and asks do we have a pay phone, so I tell him it's over in the corner. He comes back and says it's not working and that he has to phone his wife straight away or she will play fuck when he gets home. Being the nice bloke that I am, I offer him the use of my mobile phone, which he accepts and thanks me. A few minutes later he's still on the phone, so I say to him, 'All right mate, do you mind if I have the phone back?'

'Can't you see I'm on the fucking phone?' came his reply. He was so pissed he forgot I lent it to him.

The alarm goes off and Kyle and myself rush upstairs to break up a fight. We get the guys who were fighting out and return to the front door. I must have stood there for twenty minutes before I realised the drunk had left with my phone. I never saw him or my phone again. The thieving bastard must have laughed his head off when he woke up in the morning to find my new phone in his pocket.

Craig Paterson, Waltham Abbey, Essex

When I was younger, I used to help out on a building site as a dogsbody. The bricklayer who was working there was also a bouncer. He was a massive bloke and a good boxer. One morning when I arrived on site he was sitting there laughing his head off. I asked him what was so funny. 'Well my missus left me and buggered off with another man,' he said. This didn't seem all that funny to me, so I said, 'So?'

'Well they went on holiday recently and went to a club. Her boyfriend got a bit pissed and starting mouthing off to the bouncers. Anyway they beat the shit out of him and he died.' With that he started laughing hysterically again and said how he wanted to go out there and buy the bouncers a drink. From that day on I always saw the sensitive side of bouncers!

Jeff, Philadelphia, USA

It was the last night one of the most popular nightclubs in the Philadelphia area would be open. It had been purchased weeks before by a well-known restaurant chain and although the owners wanted to keep knowledge of the club's final night a secret, the news soon got out and the club was filled to capacity, and then some. Ordinarily the bouncers were forbidden to consume alcohol during their shift but as this was the last night, every staff member in the club threw caution to the wind and before long, the beer, wine, and shots were flowing. I was tentative at first, for fear that it might dull my senses, but it wasn't too long before my rock-solid willpower (yeah, right) folded like a cheap piece of lawn furniture and I succumbed to the peer pressure of my fellow employees. The night was chaotic, but an enjoyable chaos, at least initially. Topless women were dancing on the bars, beers and drinks were sprayed everywhere, and it appeared as though every patron in the bar were now the best of friends. I too became swept up into the fun as I stood behind the bar handing drinks out left and right, laughing with my friends at the craziness we were witnessing and continuing my assault on my liver via the free alcohol I was consuming.

Well, it wasn't long before paradise was ruined as the sounds and smell of violence pricked the air. Ironically, it was not a patron of the bar that started the fight but a member of the rock band that had been playing in the club. It turns out that the band member had been shot down by a female patron and his ego would not stand for it, so he decided to throw his drink in her face. One of my fellow bouncers happened to witness this and told the band member that he was out of line and the band member took it upon himself to smash a drumstick over the bouncer's head. This was followed by a flurry of punches from the bouncer, which resulted in the remaining band members doing their best to defend their drummer from the onslaught. It wasn't long before everyone was involved and punches, bottles and bodies were flying everywhere.

In my drunken stupor I turned and looked to see the fray and reacted by trying to hop the bar in order to join the brawl. Unfortunately my balance and coordination were somewhat off and instead of hopping over the bar I managed to pitch myself face-first down onto the corner of the heavy oak surface of the bar. My chin slammed into the wood with a loud thud, and I was sprawled out on top of the bar, fast asleep. I awoke a few seconds later and staggered to my feet.

Because I was knocked silly I had thought someone had sucker-punched me and I frantically turned in every direction to try and find the culprit. What I did manage to find was one of the bartenders laughing hysterically and looking right at me. For a second I thought it was he who had hit me and became enraged that he would do such a thing. I guess he saw the expression on my face so he quickly asked if I was okay. He was then joined by another employee who asked the same question. Dumbfounded, I simply asked what had happened and they proceeded to tell me while desperately trying to control their laughter.

By now, the fight had died down, and the bouncers, without me of course, had managed to control the situation as they 'convinced' the band that they should finish early. I was still trying to shake out the cobwebs when one of the bouncers, my closest friend at the club, approached me and said in a kind of accusing way, 'So where were you during all of this?' I felt myself blushing with embarrassment and hung my head, only to have the bartender speak up for me and say, 'Oh, don't worry about Jeff, he was busy teaching that nasty bar surface a lesson with one of the meanest headbutts I've ever seen.' My friend looked at me confused and I simply shook my head and said, 'I knocked myself out. I'll tell you about it later.' He laughed and put his arm around me and said, 'Come on, let's get a drink.' I looked at him out of the corner of my eye and said, 'No thanks, I think I've had enough for the night.'

The next morning I awoke with a pounding headache and had learned the valuable lesson that drinking on the job was a recipe for disaster, yet I took comfort in the fact that the club was now closed and I no longer had to face any patrons who may have witnessed the humiliating event.

Shaun Kelly, Ebbw Vale

Working on the door can be a laugh; when there has been no trouble and it has been a good atmosphere you can enjoy the job. I was working on the door of a pub and these women came in very drunk. Now the boy I was working with was a bit of a character and had said something to one of them on the way out. The next thing I see is these five women ripping my partner's clothes off. He's calling to me to help him as they have practically raped him. I just curled up laughing against the wall. He looked a right old state working the door for the rest of the night.

A professional Welsh door team: (l to r) Chunky, Lee Morris, Milly, Paul Curtis, Daniel, Brendan, Darren Taskers and Shaun

Jamie O'Neil, Wales

This boy I knew used to come to the club to pull women but didn't have much luck. Around the same time these two girls from Aberdare used to come to the club and they were the biggest slags I've ever set my eyes on. Apparently they were ex-pros who just loved it and had yards of cock in their time. They used to brag about this book they had at home where they would photograph their victims before and during having their wicked ways with them. They would walk around the club grabbing everyone by their private parts to size them up and then go for the kill. I walked into the men's toilets once and these two were on their knees giving this Welsh rugby international a blowjob.

Anyway, this boy's there and me and this bouncer Lee are talking to him when one of the girls passes us going to the toilet. Lee says to the boy, 'Go and ask her for a blowjob and she'll take you in the toilets.' Well, he didn't see the exact girl we were talking about; Lee told him, 'The one with the blond dreadlocks.'

I was chatting away to Lee when all of a sudden his face dropped. Walking up the corridor is another girl with blond dreadlocks. Before we can stop the boy, he went and asked her for a blowjob. She starts beating the shit out of him. We ran in to stop her and she demands we chuck him out. We managed to smooth it all over but it was a genuine mistake, even though the boy still thinks we set him up to this very day.

Eric Jones, Edinburgh

Working at Brannagans, I got called to a fight behind the DJ box. Nobody else could see where the fight was so I was left wrestling with these two drunks. Eventually the DJ spots us and calls for some back-up. After some struggling we get these two pissheads carted out of the club. When I came back in I felt something was wrong and couldn't put my finger on what it was. I felt a little colder than usual and then to my horror I found that my trousers had been ripped right across my arse. I'd been walking around the club with my grey boxer shorts on full display to everyone. The worst part was that they were covered in little red devils. I had to stand with my arse against the wall all night. I looked an absolute plum. From that day forth I always wear black boxers, just in case.

Richard Horsley, Hartlepool

These two bodybuilders came in. They were big blokes and they knew it. One of them kept looking at me. I didn't know whether he thought he knew me from somewhere or whether he was just staring because he was cocksure. I hadn't seen either of them before and I hardly ever forget a face. The one who kept staring had overdone it on the old sunbed because he was as brown as fuck. When they finished their drinks and started walking out you should have seen the walk on the pair of them, you'd swear they had a bag of cement under each arm.

As 'Sunbed' walked past he stared at me with this smug look, so I followed them outside. I said loudly, 'Here, Chippendale.' When he turned around I said, 'What's your fucking problem?' In a split second he went for me, he didn't try to punch me though, he went to grab me around the waist. He was trying to use his strength to get me on the floor. As soon as he moved towards me I put a big right uppercut on his chin. His legs went and he soon hit the deck. His mate threw his hands up in the air and screamed, 'I don't want nowt mate'. Sunbed was trying to pull himself together on the floor but didn't know what day it was. I told the other one, 'Just pick your mate up and fuck off.' I left them and went back in the club. When I checked my hand to see if my knuckles were swelling or any bruising was coming up I got a shock: there was false tan all over my knuckles. I still giggle about that to this day.

Anthony Thomas, Merthyr Tydfil

I started work down the Valleys on a Sunday night at a rugby club. People would come from everywhere to start fights. Every week it was getting rougher and rougher, with us either carrying guys out all busted up or having to call an ambulance for them. There was this big lad of about six foot four who for some reason took an instant dislike to me and started giving me shit each time he came to the club, always when he had had a few and felt brave. This one night he turns up sober so I caution him that I'm not taking any more of his crap. He apologises and I let him in, thinking I've sorted it out. A few drinks later and he's at it once more, really pushing his luck. I often work with my mate Paul and over the years we found that working on a three-warning system helps us sort the trouble out. The first warning is where we just talk to the troublemaker, the second warning is where they get read the riot act, and the third warning is usually when it's on top and we have to strike out and eject someone from the club. Some guys of course don't get warnings number one and two and are promoted straight to three. I have a word with the troublemaker so that put him on warning number one. An hour passes and he shouts at me from the bar, 'You're a wanker.' I inform Paul that the troublemaker is now on warning number two. Paul's laughing, as he knows what's coming next.

It's the end of the night and most of the customers have left. The big guy is walking towards me, shouting the odds and letting everyone in earshot know what he's about to do to me. I was already thinking which was the better way to take him out. He was too big to grapple so I thought throw a straight right hand, then smash his ribs with my left, hoping he'd fall to the floor so he could be carried out. He points his finger straight in my face and I at once leave my right hand go, straight between the eyes. I could feel the impact right up my arm to my shoulder. I lean in with my left to smash up his ribs when he slowly starts to rock back and fore, his eyes rolling in his head. Down he comes, crashing to the floor, his head taking most of the fall. I'm stood there looking over him when blood starts to flow from his mouth and nose, making a large puddle on the floor.

He's not moving and I start to worry about what I had done. I call to another bouncer Terry and explain that I thought the big guy might be dead. Now Terry never gives a fuck about anything and starts laughing. Terry walks over to the unconscious guy and shouts down at him, 'I told you not to pick on him didn't I?' Terry turns to me still laughing, 'Yeah, you're right Ant, you've killed him.' I absolutely shit myself; I was thinking about prison and all those tales of gang rapes in the shower, when the guy starts to come around. Terry is great at winding people up and I should have realised.

Terry is a good doorman but just doesn't give a fuck about

anything. One night a fight breaks out on the dance floor myself and another bouncer run up and get right into the heart of the trouble. I turn to see if Terry is helping us and spot him in the corner with his trousers around his ankles with some right old slapper. After the fight is calmed down and some have been ejected I tell Terry what had happened but he of course just laughed and said he hadn't seen anything, the lying fucker.

Terry Turbo, North London

The funniest bloke I ever met was a guy called Gary Gooner. He was the most well-mannered doorman I ever had the pleasure of working with and is one of my most trusted friends. We had this mental thing where we'd both find each other highly amusing and we'd laugh over the most violent and sickest things that we'd done. We were like a couple of birds having a coffee: 'Do you remember the time … etc.' People called him 'the paperboy' as he would always have a rolled up newspaper in his back pocket and out of curiosity I asked him what it was all about. He showed me his newspaper: it was a steel scaffold tube filled with concrete with a newspaper rolled around it.

Every now and again he'd use it. The funniest was when these pikeys [gypsies] came down and were trying to rob people as they were queuing to get in the club. We clocked them and told them to fuck off and one of them said something along the lines of, 'Fuck off you black bastard,' which isn't the sort of thing you'd say to someone as scary-looking as the Gooner. He pulled his newspaper out of his back pocket and said, 'Don't make me use this.' These two dumb pikeys started laughing at him going, 'Oooh, don't hit us with your newspaper, please don't we're really scared.' One of them got the legendary newspaper straight round his chops. I wished I'd had a video camera to have caught the absolute look of 'what the fuck was that?' on his face before he hit the floor. We may have been able to send it to Lisa Riley on *You've Been Framed* and got £250. Oh well, hindsight's a great thing.

Bernard Driscoll, South Wales

It was a Sunday night in the summer in this nightclub. There had been six of us working and we were all on the main door letting people into the club. At the side of the building was two big fire exit doors with steps leading up to them. I had been there about an hour and this local bloke we knew stopped on this horse and asks can he come in for a pint. He did offer to tie it up and leave it with us. Anyway, after a chat he rides off. A couple of minutes later and we could hear all these people shouting and screaming. We ran in expecting a fight and could see this horse by the bar and the bloke sitting there laughing his head off.

We have got him off the horse but the problem we had was getting the bloody horse out. The front steps were too steep so we took him to the exit doors but the stupid horse still wouldn't go down them. One of the doormen then comes up with a suggestion that we pick the horse up and carry it out. Now this horse was a monster of a thing, so after about half an hour of trying to work out what we were going to do, we walked him back through the club and got him to this other exit. We finally got the horse out and the bloke jumped back on him like the Lone Ranger disappearing into the night. I stood there thing to myself, *did that just happen?*

John Oman, Caithness

There's always some cheeky fucker who knows he's banned but keeps coming back up to the door of the club. They just can't get it into their small brains that they are not getting in. These days you can't slap them around because you will lose the job or even get arrested. They know this and will keep causing you grief all shift. This guy Anderson was just like this, we call him 'Angry Anderson' because he is always pissed and up for causing trouble. He is barred from every pub in town but gets drunk in his house then goes to town just to argue with the bouncers. This one night he must have been at the door about ten times calling us out to fight. He asked us what time we were finished because he was going up the road to shag our wives. This pisshead is about five foot six and ten stone soaking wet. We were having a crack winding him up. We shouted things like, 'Any more trouble off you sonny and I'm taking you home for the kids to play with. They broke their last Action Man.' And, 'You were such an ugly baby that your mother put curtains on your pram so you wouldn't scare folk.' Oh, he didn't like it and was getting angrier by the minute.

The boss calls us in for a cup of tea, so I sit down inside with my tea and my snowball cake. Anderson is still outside but he's coming to and fro to the door calling us 'fat fuckers' and all. I get up and tell him to get from the door and I tap him on the head with my hand. I swear to God that I forgot in the heat of the moment that I still had the cake in my hand. There was snowball cake all down the back of his head in his hair. He looked like an ostrich had shit on him. He's so drunk that he doesn't notice it but comes back a wee while later with it all rock solid on his head and he now knows about it. He wants to fight everyone in sight and most of all me.

As this is going on an old boy comes from inside the club and asks me if I would go to his car and get his mobile phone out for him. He's had a good few and you know how the police can be, so off I go for the old boy. Anderson sees me coming out and runs off up the street but all the time he's watching me. I go and get the phone for the old boy and Anderson is standing a distance away smiling. I'm back at the club and Anderson's pissing against a wall and shouting at me to fight him. I wait until he's in mid-flow and run at him, shouting that I've had enough and I'm going to kill him. He runs off with his dick still hanging out and he's pissed himself. He was wringing, must have drunk about ten cans before he came out to play.

A good ten minutes later we hear glass smashing from where the old boy's car was. Sure enough there was Anderson wrecking the car, thinking it was mine. I shout out, 'It don't bother me mate, I've got two more at home.' The car was a nice Rover 620, and Anderson was now on the roof jumping up and down on it. The old boy comes out and sees Anderson on top of the car, which by now is a wreck with all the windows done in. The old boy shouts at Anderson who tells him that it's the bouncer's car and points to me. I have my innocent courtroom face on and pretend that I know nothing. The old boy gives Anderson one and when he's down he sticks the boot in as well. Fair play he was in his fifties and really did Anderson over. Soon the police turn up and arrest Anderson.

From what I gather in court he gets a £500 fine and has to pay £800 for damage to the car. Thing was the prick never got done for stealing my snowball cake or pissing in the street.

Lee Callaghan, South Wales

A girl came running up one night and said there was a guy in the corner with a blade. She points him out and I walk over and immediately recognise him as an old schoolfriend.

'Shane,' I ask him, 'have you got a blade on you?'

'Yes Lee, I have mate.'

Which I thought was quite honest of him and tell him, 'I don't want to embarrass you in front of people, so come with me to the manager's office, where you can hand it over.'

In the office I ask him for the blade and he puts his hands down the front of his jeans and pulls out this huge machete.

'What the fuck do you want that thing for?' I ask.

'Oh it's just my lucky charm, that's all,' he answered. I thought he had a little penknife on him.

Jamie O'Keefe, London

One time at the Borderline we had Liam and Noel pop in. We would let them out back in the office or to just stay backstage to chill, as they get hassled 24/7. Noel went into the office to make some calls and Liam was backstage with us chatting and having a laugh. We were getting the backstage area clear for arrival of a band, so the only one backstage is Liam doing his thing and waiting for Patsy Kensit to arrive. One of the young bar staff arrived for work, so for a laugh we told him that we must have the backstage area clear and nobody should be there. We thought it would be a laugh to see his face when he goes back and asks Liam to leave, then we were going to make out to sack him and involve the newspapers. He was a student who relied on the job to support himself so was keen.

He went backstage, approached Liam and asked him to leave the area. I don't know how but he did not recognise Liam, so that killed our plan. But then he tells Liam to get the fuck out before he throws him out. Liam could have knocked him out but he knew we were having a laugh, so he said to this lad, known as Blue: 'I'm allowed back here as I'm in a band.' Blue replied, 'Yeah, yeah, we're all in a band and I see more bands a week than you could even imagine, so why haven't you played here then?' Liam replied, 'Coz I'm in the fucking biggest rock bank on the planet and I'm having a night off. Go speak to Jamie or Mick and they will tell you who I am, you fucking scally.' Blue came back to us and said, 'There's a guy out back who won't leave, so you better go sort it out.' We replied, 'No prob Blue, we will do that. While we're sorting that out, can you pop backstage to make sure Liam Gallagher is okay as he is meeting Patsy and Noel here later and he is backstage to chill.' Blue developed an instant vacant stare and muttered the words, 'Oh fuck.' Noel then appeared looking for Liam so we got Blue to take him. We got a lot of mileage out of that wind-up.

On another occasion I was taking the band The Beautiful South to the Hippodrome in London. We arrived and within minutes I was spotted by a couple of guys I had kicked out of a club earlier in the week for pickpocketing. They were with about fifty mates and within no time at all it kicked off. So I'm supposed to be looking after the band and end up with the Hippodrome security looking after me. Oh yes, that was one of the classics.

Anthony Thomas, Merthyr Tydfil

We get this punk rock night going once a week and it's bringing in some good money for the club. Most of the lads just wanted to jump around to the music and not cause trouble. I notice this one lad go off to the toilets next to me and not come back for a good while. I enter the toilets to find him smoking his drugs. I tell him he's out of order and take him towards the main door to be chucked out. I walk behind the lad as he quickly puts his fingers down his throat and spews all over the place. My head goes and I drag him down the stairs and, because the door needed two hands to open it, I smash his head against it to daze him and then I throw him out. It's a cold night and I notice two police officers outside so I tell the lad in my posh voice, 'Be gone and never darken these doors again.' As I walk up the stairs I can hear the prick shouting and banging the door. The police wanted a quiet night so they left him alone. I'm still fuming when I notice the bar staff mopping up all the spew. I ask them if they would like me to empty the bucket and take it off them. As he's in mid-rant and still banging the door, my mate Paul opens it and I tip the slop bucket over the punk's head. He stood there with the contents of the bucket all over his head, steaming in the cold air. Cautiously I turn to look at the two coppers who were now doubled up, crying their eyes out laughing.

Steven Curtis, Middlesex

We were on the door with this guy who normally worked other clubs but was making up numbers because our mate was on holiday courtesy of Her Majesty. This new guy was a bullshitter, informing everyone that he was a hard man and a ladies' man. Of course this would have been entertaining if he was a nice bloke but he was such a wanker. We knew we were going to have to put up with him for a while unless something was done about him, so we stuck it out in the hope he would step out of line, being the tosser he was. Maybe he would get kicked out or severely beaten up.

One night a group of girls, all done up to the nines on a hen night, turned up. You know, the normal thing: handcuffs, whips, veil, learner signs, et cetera. Well this tosspot thought he was on a winner with the bride's sister; it was so obvious she wasn't inter-ested but he kept on with the chat. As we let them all into the club he thought he was being clever and pinched her arse. That was a huge mistake. You should have seen the look on her face, like thunder. The night continued with no trouble and my good mate on the door was getting quite friendly with one of the other girls in the hen group and between them they hatched a cunning plan.

Being a hen night they all had cameras but one of them had a Polaroid, which was just perfect for the job in hand. The bride's sister had had a few too many and agreed to lure Mr Tosspot into the girls' toilets on the promise of a blowjob. So there they were in the cubicle, getting all heated, and just when she started to pull his boxers down she asked if her friend could join in. The tosspot thought he'd won the fucking lottery and was well up for it, if you know what I mean. She opened the door to let her friend, who was standing with the camera, reel off a load of Polaroids. Both the girls ran back into the club and joined their mates. I would have loved to have seen the shocked look on his face, but anyway he came back to the door giving it large that he'd just had both girls from the hen party in the bogs.

Meanwhile upstairs in the office the Polaroids were being photocopied and distributed through the club. Turns out this guy had the smallest dick ever; this bloke should have been entitled to a penis extension on the NHS. Pretty soon he caught wind of what was going on and asked to leave early – bad guts from a curry the day before or something. We didn't see him again. We owe those girls a drink.

Jamie O Neil, Wales

Upstairs in this nightclub this bloke is selling drugs and didn't even try to hide it. The manageress called us over and she asked us to take him off to our search room to check him out. We found a bag of speed, all wrapped up and ready to sell. We took the drugs off him and asked him to leave. What happened next I couldn't believe. After he left the club, he goes straight down to the local police station and tells the police he wants to report a theft. He explains that the bouncers had found a bag of powder on him and robbed it off him. The police couldn't believe what they were hearing and charged him with possession of amphetamine. The boy ended up on the front page of the local newspapers.

Martin Bayfield, Rhyl

A bully on the door with you can make your job harder because everyone classes you the same as him. Also you have to back him up when the police turn up: 'Yes officer, the young lad in the ambulance did attack the other doorman first,' I found myself saying on more than one occasion. Now the prick that worked with me knew who he was picking on but on this one occasion he picked on some lad only to have this heavyweight boxer stand up and belittle him in front of the whole club.

He came over to me and said, 'That boxer guy over there wants me to have it out with him. I think he may be a little too big for me. What shall I do?'

'Tell you what, I'll go and sort it out, right now,' and off I walk over to the boxer. The prick stayed on the main door and watched me like a hawk talking to the boxer. He can see the boxer walking away from me and going into the toilets on his own. Back with the prick I tell him it's all sorted and, 'He's waiting for you in the toilets to have a one on one.'

'What!' he panics. 'He'll fucking kill me. Are you stark raving mad?'

'It's okay,' I reassure him. 'You walk in first, then me behind you and we'll beat the fuck out of him between us. If anyone asks I'll tell them you did him on your own and you'll be a hero around here.'

'Fair enough,' he says confidently as we then march over to the toilets. He enters first but I stay outside as the boxer – my cousin John, who wanted work with me on the door – beats the living daylights out of the arsehole. The prick took a first-class hiding and hung up his bow tie for good, which left room for John to join me on the door the following weekend. A good result.

Anthony Thomas, Merthyr Tydfil

This one club I worked at employed this mental disc jockey they called Mad Al. He would start the night off with these stage explosives that looked really wicked. Me and another doorman would watch the front of the stage, keeping the punters well back as he set the explosives off. We had just started another doorman we call Beast and I explained to him about the explosives and asked would he mind the stage with me as they were set off. He was quite eager and we stood side by side, backs to the stage and facing the punters. Every time I saw the explosives go off they always shot straight up in the air and this shell or some sort of cartridge would shoot up as well. This time I hear the loud bang and the shell, still on fire, pops onto Beast's neck. He's jumping around like a headless chicken and screaming. I have to hit it off his neck and jump on it to put it out. Beast is taken to the toilets to put cold water on the burn on his neck. All the time the whole club, myself and the other doormen are crying laughing.

Keith Price, Bexleyheath, Kent

At the comedy club this comedian was struggling against a persistent heckler. Finally the comic snapped and said, 'How much did you fucking pay tonight?'

'Ten pounds, you boring cunt,' came the reply.

With that, the comic pulled out a tenner, gave it to the bloke and told him to fuck off. The heckler just leaned back in his chair and continued his abuse. I made my way to where he's sitting and picked him up by his hair. As I dragged him out he screamed like a little girl, which was greeted by cheering from the audience. Once outside he shouted at me, 'Come on then if you want it.' Well, before I got bored of hitting him, took the £10 from his pocket and threw him into the street. As I returned the £10 to the comic I got a standing ovation from the audience. I couldn't work out why they all started laughing but soon realised that I was still holding one of the heckler's shoes. I did see the funny side of it as well.

Anthony Thomas, Merthyr Tydfil

We were doing a fourteen-hour shift once and were bored out of our minds. The owner of the club comes up with the bright idea of each of us putting £10 into a hat and whoever snogs the oldest woman by the end of the night takes the pot. In total four of us put our money in and after a woman of about sixty gave me a peck on the cheek I felt the cash was as good as mine. There was only about an hour of the shift to do so I was pretty confident when two old women walked in. One must have been about seventy, with a walking stick and no teeth; a right old monster. Paul walks over and asks for his Christmas kiss. He turns his head to get a peck on the cheek when the old biddy goes straight for his mouth, clutching his face in her hands and giving him the old tongue as well. The pair of them was now really going for it when the owner chucks the money at Paul shouting, 'You've won, you've won, now for God's sake stop!' Paul gives the old biddy his thanks and picks up his winnings.

Michael Jones, London

I was working in the local gay bar. It was an unbelievable job. You had to be careful who you spoke to as you didn't know if the sexy young thing you were talking to was hiding anything from you (e.g. their manhood). I had been called in to stop the women fighting the men. This night we set it up so that the new boy met Mindy. Now, Mindy looks like a six foot tall supermodel with huge breasts and long dark hair; very sexy if you didn't know the truth. Mindy's real name was Malcolm and he was a transsexual, always had been since school from what I gather. We asked Mindy to go on to the new lad and proposition him. He did. Mindy went over and spent the night looking lovingly into his eyes. At end of the night he was ready to take Mindy home. The fun started as soon as they got outside and Mindy turned to the boy and grabbed hold of him by his dick. 'She' said, 'Ooh! You have got a big one, but it's not as big as mine.' It was at this point Mindy lifted his skirt and said, 'Like what you see?' With that the boy started throwing up.

Bernard Driscoll, South Wales

This one night there were murders in the club and I wasn't even there. They used to do this 'open the box' thing, where you'd put money in every week and if your number came out you got the chance to open the box. The whole club would go silent when they would announce the number. This night I didn't work and I asked this boy to put my money in. My number came up and it turns out the boy picked the right key for me, winning the jackpot of £2,000. Everyone knew I was running the club and they all thought it was a fix. The place erupted, there was a full riot in there, police were there with dogs to get everyone out. The rest of the bouncers called me some names the next day.

Jamie O'Keefe, London

Me and a mate had to get a collapsed drunk from inside a locked toilet cubicle. As my mate was the slimmer of us two fat bastards, he climbed over the top to try and lift him from behind so I could lean down to unlock the door. All was going to plan until the pressure of my mate lifting him made the drunk spew up. My mate got covered. He didn't drive and had no change of clothes so had to work the whole night till we all went home in the morning. It was hot and steamy in the club and my mate stunk of sick. [Authors' note: Jamie has written many great books over the years and his new book *Teach Yourself To Survive & Stay Alive: How to develop your own personal fighting system* is due for release in December 2003. Further information on Jamie and his publications can be found on his website www.newbreedbooks.co.uk]

Anthony Thomas, Merthyr Tydfil

Wayne, who works the door with me most of the time, has a night off but passes the pub where I'm working to get some food. He stops his car outside just to chat when all of a sudden it has gone off inside the pub, with guys fighting everywhere. The doorman with me gets dropped, so Wayne steps in to help me out, grabbing some prick in a headlock. Suddenly he's hit from behind. His glasses come flying off and his rugby shirt gets ripped off his back as they try to get a grip on him. By now Wayne and I are back to back fighting with pissheads all around us. The place is in an utmost uproar when the DJ decides to play the theme music from the series *The Bill*. Everyone stops fighting and is just looking around, as if expecting the police to turn up. With that we manage to get most of them out before the police really do turn up. This lad runs out and hands Wayne his glasses. 'Fuck me, they're a better fit now the buggers have loosened up a bit,' he shouts out. 'But look at the state of my rugby shirt, it's torn to shreds. I only left the house to get a bag of chips.'

Michael Jones, London

This bloke who used to work with us had a glass eye and every time we had a bit of trouble he would have to take it out and clean it. This one night he decided to spook the young girl we had working with us. He decided to go and get us some drinks, as it was a really quiet Tuesday night. He came back with two pints and vodka with ice and lemonade. He gave her the drink and sat back; as he was drinking he was watching for her reaction. When she looked at him, she said, 'Where's your eye gone?' He put his finger in the orifice and said, 'Fuck me Michael, my eye has fallen out again.' He then made a point of pretending to look for it, the whole time watching the girl for a reaction. It took the girl ten minutes to realise the ice cube in her drink was staring at her. She let out a huge scream and threw the glass across the room. We never saw her again.

Lee Callaghan, South Wales

I got friendly with these two Hell's Angels that would often come to the door and chat with me. The one shows me that he has a handful of Viagra and offers me some. On the spur of the moment I pop three down my neck. A few minutes later and my face and head are bright red. It looked as if my head was going to explode. I laughed it off and stood there on the door with a huge hard on. You should have seen the looks some of the women were giving me as they brushed past to get into the club.

Michael Vaughan, Newcastle

I had been fighting on the doors all week and it was starting to do my head in. Even when I was in my day job I was watching everyone for signs of trouble. I must have had a constant black eye for three months.

I finished my shift and walked over to the nearest taxi rank. Standing on my own waiting for my taxi, I noticed this young lad walk up. My taxi pulls up and before I could say anything the prick jumps in and the cab drives off. I had to wait another twenty minutes alongside this drunk bastard who was staggering everywhere. Car pulls up and as I go to get in, the drunken prick pushes me out of the way and jumps in. I don't know if it was the trouble that I had been involved with at the club or what, but I just saw red. I opened the car door, dragged the drunk out and threw him to the pavement. I was just going to get in the car when the drunk jumps on my back and we start to roll around on the ground. The police turn up just as I'm getting on top of the prick and starting to beat the shit out of him.

I'm held against a shop front by two coppers as another one helps the battered drunk off the floor. I'm not stupid enough to try and fight with the police and just explain to them that the drunk had jumped on my back and I was defending myself. The drunk then tells them, 'I've been out drinking all night and didn't think I'd get a taxi so I phoned my mother to pick me up. As I'm getting in the car that bouncer guy throws me to the ground and beats the fuck out of me.' I look over to what I thought was a taxi and now notice the drunk's mother sitting in the front seat in her bloody dressing gown. I couldn't believe my luck. The coppers arrested me and charged me for GBH. Now I face losing my bouncer licence and a heavy fine. The worst part for me was when I got to the station and the coppers just fell about pissing themselves laughing. Looks like I'll have to start doing more overtime at the factory to get some spare cash in.

Jason Payne, Merthyr Tydfil

I was asked to work this one pub on my own. Now I don't like the idea of that because often you need someone to watch your back or at least you need a reliable witness for when the police come. I was told the place was quiet and there was no need for any back-up. I agreed and worked the pub for a while with no trouble. I got to know the regulars and found out who were okay and who the dick-heads were. There was a gang of about twelve in one night who were messing about with the regulars, making pricks of themselves. I went over and even though I was outnumbered I decided to call their bluff. Loudly I tell them, 'Listen lads, if there's any more trouble we're all going outside and there's only one coming back.'

This one piss-ant shouts back, 'Yes, and that will be us.'

'Shut up, fool. I said one of us, you thick bastard,' I reply.

Well they cool down a bit, but in case it flares up I get a few other doormen to pop down to the pub. Sure enough later on in the night they split into two groups, both start to play fuck at both ends of the pub. We decided to get them all out and it was going well until I tried to push one out the main door and my finger went straight in his eye. One of the other doormen chinned one of the trouble-makers and all hell broke loose.

Outside the other doormen had their backs to the wall fighting the gang. I'm on the other side of the gang smashing the hell out of any that moved. Between the three of us we batter the twelve of them and off they disappear into the night. Next night I'm at the pub when I'm told by the owner that someone had left a bucket by the front door. Inside the bucket was a shitty pair of pants and a note which read, 'Your doormen did this so you can clean them.'

Lee Callaghan, South Wales

We had this one strange guy who'd come to the club in Caerphilly. He was a school teacher, always dressed smartly in his suit and came across as a nice guy. The club had three flights of stairs leading to the exit/entrance. If you tripped at the top you'd have quite a fall before you reached the bottom. This teacher would say goodnight to us as he left, then shout out, 'I'm off lads, I don't want any trouble so I'll throw myself out,' and would then literally throw himself down the three flights of stairs, rolling all the way down, where he'd get up, dust himself down and leave the club. He'd do this every night without fail.

Steve Wraith, Newcastle

I worked at Planet Earth every Wednesday and the promoter had a hard job filling the place. Most of my Wednesdays were spent with Mickey Armstrong and another lad called Anth. The manager, Malcolm, was always up for a laugh, so the atmosphere was fairly relaxed. One day Anth made the fatal mistake of wetting Malcolm with a bottle of water, so the battle lines were drawn! Malcolm and Mickey enlisted me in their revenge attacks on Anth. First up was the standard wetting Anth with a bigger bottle of water when as he least expects it. Simple enough, result: Anth in wet clothes. The following week saw a little more planning. Mickey enticed Anth into a game of pitch and toss with a penny up against the club wall. I went first with a poor attempt. Mickey went second. He retrieved his coin, which was a bit closer to the wall than mine. Next up was Anth and he was really up for the challenge. He'd done it! His coin was nearest to the wall. Only thing was, he hadn't banked on Malcolm throwing an icy bucket of water out of the window. Anth was saturated. By the following week he was paranoid and was doing a new version of the Green Cross Code, looking left, right and straight up. Our plan this week had to be good – and it was.

We asked one of the lasses from reception to pose as a collapsed punter outside the fire exits at the back of the club. We arranged for Anth to be on the front door with a new starter, so when the call for assistance came to the front door Anth would have to go around. It worked like clockwork. Anth went around the back of the club to rescue our damsel in distress and by the time he realised he'd been duped … Spppplashhh! Another bull's eye once again for both Mickey and Malcolm, with Anth in wet clothes and most of us in wet pants. I was crying with laughter. Proof if you need it that doormen aren't the animals that they are made out to be, we are just like the rest of you, we like to have a laugh.

Facing dangerous situations together builds up an incredible sense of camaraderie – but when you are working solo the door can be the loneliest place in the world.